Last Swill
and
Testament

The hilarious, unexpurgated memoirs of

Paul 'Sailor' Vernon

MUSIC MENTOR BOOKS
York, England

Front cover photo © Judy Rolph Ebner. Photographs on 12, 16, 32, 62, 139, 159, 167, 179, 187, 191 and 197 are from the author's collection; photo on page 46 courtesy Xtra Records; photos on pages 93, 99, 119, 134, 142, 144, 161 and 164 courtesy of and © Bill Greensmith; photo on page 206 courtesy of and © Gene Deitch. Illustrations on pages 130, 131 and 132 courtesy of and © Dave Clarke. Magazine covers and illustrations on pages 129, 174, 175, 181 and CD insert on page 208 are from the Music Mentor archive.

British Library Cataloguing-in-Publication Data
A catalogue record for this book is available from the British Library.

ISBN-13: 978-0-9547068-4-5

Published worldwide by Music Mentor Books *(Proprietor: G.R. Groom-White)*
69 Station Road, Upper Poppleton, York YO26 6PZ, North Yorkshire, England.
Telephone: +44 (0)1904 330308 *Email:* music.mentor@lineone.net

Cover by It's Great To Be Rich, York.

Printed and bound in Great Britain by Bonacia Ltd, Peterborough.

For my grandsons Corrie, Ethan and Jack.

So that they may read this,
know where they have come from,
and say: 'What a daft old sod Granddad is!'

A Personal Note from the Publisher

I first got to know Paul 'Sailor' Vernon, as I expect many others did, through the record lists he published in the 1970's and the wacky blues'n'humour magazine they begat, *Sailor's Delight*. Having only recently ceased full-time education, I could never afford to bid for the many rarities on offer and could only sit there drooling over unattainable records by such legends as Tampax Red, Earl Bostic & His Glues, Cecil Gnat, Al Bertammons, and that well-known Spanish duo, Smoke Y Hogg. On the one occasion I did, I received a letter from Mr. Vernon's laywers, Messrs. Shonuff, Badass & Muthafuya, notifying me that I had been successful and threatening dire consequences if I failed to cough up pronto. Happily, the Set Sale and New Records listings were more within my price bracket, and my collection became all the richer for it. Aside from one market stall that flogged US 45 rpm cutouts, there weren't many other options for acquiring genuine American blues records in provincial Bradford.

I only met Paul once, in March 1980, when I decided to hitch down to London for a weekend's record hunting (free travel = more money for records). Ora-Nelle Villas was to be my first stop, after which I would head for Camden Town and Soho. Setting off Friday teatime, I managed to get a lift almost immediately and was dropped off at a roundabout somewhere in north London at around 3:30 am. Far too early, but at least I was there.

It was a frosty night and I was by now in need of a hot drink and a meal. No such luck. After pounding the streets of Mill Hill for several hours in sub-zero temperatures searching for an all-night transport caff (or nearest offer), I eventually discovered a rather genteel establishment which opened its doors at 9:30 am to serve coffee and crossiants. They probably saved my life.

Suitably thawed, I arrived at Paul's around 10:30 am and received a warm welcome and a hot drink. At least one other collector was already there, going through his stock. We chatted about records and about blues, pulled and played numerous examples, and I emerged with a fistful of goodies and a sense of immense satisfaction. The prize catch on that occasion was a pristine copy of Jerry McCain's harmonica blaster, 'Steady' (Rex 1014), which I still cherish to this day. Thanks, Paul.

I continued subscribing to the wonderfully anarchic *Sailor's Delight* and buying what I could afford, but the party ended all too soon. Paul disappeared off to America in the early '80's, put out a couple more record lists from over there, then vanished from the radar.

My interest in blues and associated genres continued of course, and in the ensuing years I became a collector, writer/researcher and most recently a publisher of music books. I was therefore both surprised and delighted to receive a telephone call in the early weeks of 2007 from the legendary Sailor himself, enquiring whether I would be interested in publishing his memoirs. I loved the manuscript as soon as I saw it, and immediately read it end-to-end. Paul has one heck of a story to tell, and he tells it in his own, inimitable way. Blues'n'humour – there's a lot to be said for it. I hope you enjoy the experience as much as I did.

George R. White
York, July 2007

Acknowledgments

In writing this, I gathered a small audience in my head to witness its creation and give me feedback. They have no idea they did it, but I want to thank Bruce Bastin, Alasdair Blaazer, the late Keith Briggs, John Broven, Robert Crumb, Alan Empson, Dana Gillespie, Bill Greensmith, Cilla Huggins, William Least Heat-Moon, Kip Lornell, Pete Moody, Frank Nazareth, Diane Napier, Sylvia Pitcher, Mike and Barbara Rowe, Ken Smith, Frank Weston and Francis and Pamela Wilford-Smith for sitting in my frontal lobes and helping me keep on track. Especially Bill, as he'd been suggesting I do this for years. Bill also generously supplied all the better photographs that appear in this book.

I'd also like to mention that this could have been a much bumpier reading experience were it not for the sharp eye and mind of my wife Judy, who cast her professional editing spell across the manuscript, and who also reminded me of things forgotten and perspectives overlooked.

I want to say thanks to Charlie Gillett for graciously allowing me to reproduce parts of his report on the 1968 *National Blues Convention*.

And thanks are due also to George White, whose decision to publish this in the first place is, I hope, as good a one for him as it is for me.

If I have forgotten anyone, I offer an apology; except to those few who know full well why they aren't in here.

Paul Vernon
Madrid, June 2007

Contents

Contents

Chapter One

1949-64: AMO, AMAS, AMAT

Britain in July 1949, as I entered it – late and screaming, apparently – was a country in shock; the unexpected and very un-British heatwave had caused outbreaks of knotted hankies on heads, burglar-red noses, wickedly exposed limbs punished by agonising sunburn, phew-wotta-scorcher headlines in the morning papers and critical shortages of Warm British Beer. There were other shortages too, controlled by the don't-you-know-there's-a-war-on attitude that grim-featured authoritarians refused to let go of. You couldn't get too much chocolate, butter, cheese or exotic lingerie; this was supposed to be good for you. I mean, it had seen us through the war hadn't it? You've got Marmite, the BBC, Ovaltine and the Royal Family. Isn't that good enough? What more do you want, you ungrateful shower?

What ordinary folk wanted, of course, was to get on with the new life promised them by VE and VJ days. They had had enough of the blackouts, the victory gardens, the petrol shortages and the gas masks – okay, a few hung on to the gas mask habit, but almost four years after Hiroshima and Nagasaki, the shortages continued, and the British were still locked into war mode. There was more, of course, but this, essentially, was the world into which I was born.

My first real memory is of light. An only child living in the converted upstairs rooms of my beloved and war-widowed maternal grandfather's house, with its long, dark passage leading to the unwindowed front door, I gasped with delight one morning when Granddad, preparing to take me out in a pushchair, opened the front door and flooded the hallway with a sudden, bright sunlight. I don't remember what happened after that, I suppose we went out, but I got stoned on light at about age two and have never recovered. I spent considerable chunks of my early childhood in Granddad's back parlour waiting for my folks to return from work, studying the delicate, sparkling patterns created by dust as it drifted through incoming sunbeams. I had the *time*, you see. In a long back garden filled largely with vegetables, I learned how good a newly-excavated carrot, washed under the outside cold tap, could really taste. Over afternoon teas of fresh Hovis and butter taken in front of a coal fire I also learned all my granddad's songs: 'Boiled Beef And Carrots', ' 'Enery The Eighth', 'Any Old Iron', 'My Old Dutch' and others. I

My parents, Edward and Susan, on their wedding day
at Willesden Registry Office in 1947.

really thought they were his. It took me years to realise he was inserting me into the oral tradition of the British music hall songs he had witnessed first-hand as a youth. I'm still a Harry Champion fan.

As we entered the 1950's, the war mentality began to abate a little, with the government constructing a welfare state and plans for the *Festival of Britain* being drawn up. The day's popular music was a mixture of light British fluff-and-nonsense pressed up against a huge wall of terminally cheerful American show tunes. The vast and unforgiving piles of Vera Lynn 78's stood unused, their time passed, their job done, until they were old enough to reap the benefits of nostalgia. Tucked away in odd corners, however, were little collections of more interesting things. Luckily, one of them resided in our house.

We need to step back fifteen years and take a look at the endeavours of Edward Vernon, my father. The son of a solid middle-class couple (his father one of the team who developed Bakelite; his mother a leading light and baker in the local church community who threw out all the Bakelite experiments her husband brought home), Dad was rescued from this environment by music. As a spotty and over-Brilliantined apprentice electrician, he had discovered the guitar. At first, through the tail-end of the Hawaiian craze; then, bursting upon him as fresh and exciting new music, the Quintette du Hot Club de France, featuring the extraordinary two fingers and thumb of Django Reinhardt. In July 1938, the young Edward saw the Quintette perform at the vast and opulent State cinema in the Kilburn High Road. Inspired, not to mention gobsmacked, he bought a cheap guitar and some QHCF 78's and spent close to eighteen months hammering out chords in an attempt to become the British Django. He never made it – no-one ever did – but he had a lot of fun trying, until the cumulative efforts of a certain Mr. Hitler and his chums invited him to spend some time abroad.

Enraged by the death of his merchant seaman older brother Phil in an early bombing raid off Falmouth Harbour, Dad volunteered ahead of call-up. He was to put in five years with the Royal Navy, and was first sent for training at Portsmouth. Still naïve, while on parade at the barracks he was one of two who stepped smartly forward when asked by a Chief Petty Officer if anyone was interested in music.

'Right!' he barked when he'd isolated his pair of mugs, 'I've got a piano for you to shift.'

As signalman on a minesweeper about the size of the average American bathroom, Dad got to see something, at least, of the world. Chronologically, that turned out to be Queenborough Docks, the North Sea in winter (aargh!) and subsequently the Mediterranean, where for four years he ably performed his minesweeping duties amid warm sunlight, blue seas, occasional strafing by both sides, and all the delights that the wartime ports in North Africa, Malta and Italy could offer a young sailor. He came home a different man: the man I knew as my father.

In the meantime, his record collection had braved every device the Luftwaffe could hurl at it, and was still intact and occasionally being expanded by the time I was old enough to realise that these black round things had a purpose. That would have been when I was perhaps five years old. I have a photo (no, you're not seeing it) of me surrounded by close friends I couldn't name now, dressed in a cowboy suit. It was taken in the back garden on my fifth birthday and if I close my eyes I can still smell that suit. What the hell did they use to make it? Cow gum and soylent green? This was 5 July 1954, probably in the late afternoon, and therefore just a few hours before events in a Memphis recording studio would launch the career of E.A. Presley, Esquire. In that sunny back garden in north-west London I can honestly say we had no idea of what was going on over there on Union Avenue:

'I say, Nigel, d'you think this new-fangled "Memphis hillbilly bop" will have any real impact on global culture in the next few years?'

'Hard to tell, old bean. It rather depends on how aggressively it's marketed. In my view it needs a snappy title like, say, "rockabilly". Now stop talking crap and give us a turn with the cowboy suit. The chaps are growing impatient.'

So, at roughly age five, I began to take an independent interest in the records and record player that sat in our front-facing and sunlit upper-floor living room. It was the player itself that first took my attention. A radiogram, with a single-speed automatic record deck and three wavebands filled with crackle, hum, the odd Frenchman and the BBC, it had been purchased from Curry's on the never-never by my newly married parents in 1947, and was about three times the size I was. Unintimidated, I set record upon record on the turntable just to watch them spin, mesmerise myself by staring at the recurring patterns created by the run-off grooves and thrill to the savage speed with which the arm snapped back into place after the record had finished. Listening to the music was a by-product of observing the mechanics, but it sank in nevertheless. What was I listening to? Here's the list:

Quintette du Hot Club de France
Honeysuckle Rose
Sweet Georgia Brown
My Sweet
Night & Day
Stompin' at Decca
Souvenirs
Black and White
Daphne

The Joe Venuti–Ed Lang All Stars
After You've Gone
Beale Street Blues
Farewell Blues
Someday Sweetheart

Ed Lang & Lonnie Johnson
Bullfrog Moan
Handful of Riffs

Les Paul
Deep In The Blues *(I never played the other side. Mary who?)*

Spike Jones & His City Slickers
Cocktails for Two
Chloe

In a shellac nutshell I found the kernel of blues that I didn't know I was looking for. Jack Teagarden's vocal on 'Beale Street Blues' introduced my innocent brain to the twelve-bar framework and lyrics that, even if I didn't understand them, seemed light years from all that '*mairzy-doats and dozy-doats*' nonsense that surfaced with alarming regularity on the BBC's Light Programme:

If Beale Street could talk, if Beale Street could talk,
Married men would have to take their beds and walk.
Except one or two, who never drink booze
And the blind man on the corner who sings his Beale Street Blues.

'Mum, what's a "bedsan walk"? And why do Merry Men have to take them?'

'Ask your father dear, it's his record.'

Les Paul's electric guitar solo was such an homage to T-Bone Walker that when I first heard T-Bone in the 1960's, it seemed strangely familiar: Lonnie Johnson *was* the real thing, of course, and, on another level, Spike Jones' mélange of happy mania and strange noises obsessed me to the point where I knew every sound and exactly when it was coming. And then there was Django. I found myself choosing 'Honeysuckle Rose' and 'Sweet Georgia Brown' more and more, which accounted for their ultimate descent into unplayability. But I had also absorbed elements of the blues before I knew what to call it. Beyond that, not much happened. I could spin tales and tell you I went out hunting up obscure 78's from the age of five, returning with red label Parlophones, Vogues, tri-centre Londons... but I didn't. The music was a small, though integral, part of the life of a suburban English white lad in the 1950's. The foundations had been laid, however. Only later would I recognise that and start building on them.

Beginning about the time I reached six years, my parents became successful small-business people, a real team. They first managed, then owned, a succession of newsagent's stores, supplying the locals with newspapers and magazines – the kind of place where you could also get cigarettes, snuff, pipe and rolling tobacco, chocolates and sweets, soft drinks, frozen Jubblys, luridly-fronted paperback novels, greetings cards, basic stationery, Elastoplast, Aspro, ice cream, a dusty can of emergency peas, a stamp, a pair of nylons, an under-the-counter Durex, the latest local gossip, change for the bus or launderette, and, as seasons came and went, Easter eggs, fireworks and Christmas goodies, all of which I loved. Especially the fireworks; the uninjured fun I had experimenting in the back yard with the loose gunpowder that remained in the shipping crates after they had been unpacked only proves that I had more luck than brains.

My parents' *modus operandi* was to buy an ailing business, build it up, sell it at a profit and move on to the next challenge. We moved often, with the same furniture, always lived above the shop in the frequently vast two-floor apartments, and from this experience I learned that life and work were inseparable. The shop was open seven days a week, 14 hours a day, and no-one thought about clocking on or off, we just did what we had to and rolled work, eating, sleeping, relaxing, entertaining and family time into one huge freewheeling lifestyle, and it became a cornerstone of my outlook. I began work without realising it; by age seven I was pottering about the shop filling up shelves, emptying rubbish, sweeping the floor... it was just what

Me, aged 3, somewhere on the South Coast.

you did. Essentially different from the hard-line Christian work ethic insofar as we hedonistically celebrated our life by spending money, I never remember a day without meat. We always had at least one secondhand car, all the household electrics that Britain could then offer and holidays in unexotic places like Marlow, Clacton and Brighton.

Our shops were always located on suburban main streets, sitting in cluttered rows among butchers, greengrocers, fishmongers, iron- mongers, barbers, off-licences, grocery shops with sub-post offices at the back, stationers, fish-and-chip shops and, often, pubs, each with their own deliciously pungent aroma, most with a window filled with small objects of desire and many nestling behind a shadowing canopy. All the shopkeepers knew each other and a medieval barter system flourished among them. We supplied unsold non-returnable newsprint to the greengrocer and fish-and-chip emporium for wrapping purposes; they supplied us with choice fruit and veg or extra chips and pickled eggs with our freshly-fried plaice. An empty glass confectionery jar delivered to the ironmonger's yielded half a pound of nails and a clutch of sandpaper in return. A pudding-basin haircut for me was discounted because the barber, too, had received a glass jar. The garage mechanic would do small repairs for next to nothing because we kept him supplied with metal soft drink crates for his spare parts. So, I spent the 1950's engrossed in all this and also in attending school, where I vaguely remember the final Empire Day celebrations; reading comics - Biffo, General Jumbo, Lord Snooty, Corky, Desperate Dan and Dennis the Menace; watching the Murphy TV that we had by 1954; collecting Dinky toys; and generally not worrying about the state of the world, or what it really took to put food on the table each night. In short, I grew up feeling safe and loved.

Radio, TV and cinema played a large part in keeping me off the streets. The radio was almost always on, almost always tuned to the BBC, and from this background hum would emerge occasional sounds that interested me enough to stop and take note.

One of those sounds was the *Billy Cotton Band Show*, where cheerfully silly songs like 'Bangers And Mash' ('*Give us a bash at the bangers and mash me muvver uster make*') and 'You Can't Do That There 'ere', alternated with ballads by the superbly tone-deaf Alan Breeze & The Bandits, and a bagful of terrible jokes delivered by Cotton himself, who had the warm, intimate delivery of a favourite uncle doing his party-piece.

Another was the *Goon Show*. At this point I need say no more to Brits of my generation, but for those unfamiliar with them, you should know that the Goons, and their essential creator, Spike Milligan, broke the mould of British comedy and recast it. They were brilliant; iconoclastic, if ever that term belonged to anyone; and, in my view, about a decade ahead of their time. As a tool for deconstructing the stiffness of British society and the class system, they were as important as the Beatles, *Beyond The Fringe* and *That Was The Week That Was*. The Goons pioneered political satire in Britain ('I demand political asylum!' / 'Then try the House of Lords... finest political asylum I know', etc) and inspired us all to become amateur comedians, because they proved you could just get out there and invent stuff on your own. Which, taking those cues, is what the *Monty Python* team did later.

British television in the 1950's was a curious affair. Until 1955 there was one channel broadcast nationwide, and it was the BBC. It offered us an odd mix of home-grown product and American shows brought in to fill the gaps it couldn't plug itself. Thus we kids experienced the odd, gauche pre-war charm of *Muffin The Mule* (for which you can still be arrested under Scottish law) and the hard-bitten contemporary grit of *Highway Patrol*. I spent several weeks saying little but 'ten-four' through cupped hands to anyone who would listen. We sat po-faced through British stodge like *Billy Bunter* and revelled in the *cinéma verité* excitement of *Dragnet*. About half of British TV was of US origin, if you counted the old John Wayne movies, Laurel & Hardy shorts and *Popeye* cartoons.

I always knew I could see the colours on television. I remember remarking to my granddad that I'd just watched *Popeye The Sailor*, and its colours were really different to the ones I was used to. He cocked an eyebrow at me over his solid brown teacup and said: 'Oh? I don't think so. Television isn't in colour.'

'Yes it is,' I replied, in deep surprise.

Confused, I went back and checked. He was right, of course, and the truth burst the bubble of my imagination. Then, in 1955, Britain got a second channel, this time funded not by a mandatory licence fee, but by advertising. Suddenly our screens filled with exciting images of soap powders, drip-dry shirts, cigarettes and baked beans. Entertainment enough, never mind the programmes they were funding, which, of course, continued to be at least fifty percent American. Sitcom lines seemed unreal unless delivered in American accents. My father became convinced that we would become the next US state and, in a way, he was right. For me, the parade of images simply welded British and American culture together into one inseparable pudding (yes, we welded puddings in those days – that's what made British food what it was...).

Cinema in Britain was also at least half-American – and often the best half. The British film industry in the 1950's generally contented itself with cranking out second-feature material to accompany the main Hollywood attraction. Thus, a typical night in a suburban cinema, to which we as a family went every Wednesday, consisted of the latest epic from California, often in colour, and the week's fresh sausage out of the Elstree or Pinewood machines, almost always in monochrome. I came to think of Britain as a pin-sharp black-and-white island, even though I lived it in colour, and America, by contrast, as a lush Technicolor paradise. A typical evening at any of the several cinemas available to us within twenty minutes motoring distance was a lot more than just two films. At the Essoldo, the State, the Gaumont or the Queen's, one endured a lukewarm broth of forthcoming attractions, adverts and shorts before the supporting film had even been taken out of its can. The evening generally opened with the forthcoming attractions, most of which were shouted at you from the screen by a stentorian American voice:

'SEE GLINT STEEL AND WANDA LIMBSKY IN '*A STREETCAR NAMED DERISION*' ! NEVER BEFORE HAS THE SCREEN GROANED SO WICKEDLY WITH OPEN DESIRE ! NEVER BEFORE HAS HOLLYWOOD DARED TO BRING SUCH NAKED EMOTION TO THE BIG SCREEN! NEVER BEFORE HAS A JAR OF PEANUT BUTTER BEEN SO BIZARRELY MISUSED! BROUGHT TO YOU BY HIRAM P. SHOOTER, THE DIRECTOR OF '*SIXGUNS IN THE BOUDOIR*'. SEE IT AT THIS MOOVEE THEEATTETHUR ARGHGURGLE...'

This and similar hors-d'œuvres were tracked unerringly by a series of local adverts for restaurants ('*Following this programme, why not dine at the Sorrydearitsoff Restaurant, 12 Horsemeat Road...*'), car salesrooms ('*The all-new Ford Prefect is waiting for YOU. Test drive it today and see for yourself just what a load of old cobblers a new British car can really be*') and other random goods ('*We here at the Hendon Constabulary look for reliability in our vehicles. What is more, they have to start first time under any circumstances to keep you, the public, safe. That's why we only use batteries supplied to us by Harry Saulton & Sons of Watismoor. Instal one in YOUR car and you will always be reminded of the solid police advice that you'll be charged with a Saulton battery!*')

As if that wasn't enough, we were then served the dreaded Pearl & Dean commercials. How I hated those images of slowly opening heavenly gates, signalling their arrival. Made for nationwide distribution – so you couldn't escape them – P&D plied us with entreaties for soap, fashion, cigarettes, holidays, and just about everything else that was deemed a big enough seller to be filmed in colour. I still remember the extraordinary commercial for South African Airways. Accompanying images of furiously smoking jet-set folk being plied with drink by beehived air hostesses on board a DC-10, the massed white male choir sang in a distinctly Bushveld voice:

> *Lucky yew, en de bloo, when you fly wit Soud Aafrican Aairways.*
> *Doan delay! Buch today! S.A.A.!*

Following this, the hapless audience was assaulted by British Pathé News ('Somebody shoot that bleedin' cockerel!' a voice would yell from the pits as the credits rolled). Monochrome news of little interest paraded in front of us as we wrestled straws into the plastic lids of our Kia-Ora orange drinks, often causing jets of sticky citrus liquid to ejaculate from the straw's top and insinuate themselves over our V-neck pullovers. The rustle of wrapped sweets being debagged could not drown the *sotto* Very British Voice that accompanied assorted scenes of natural disasters in faraway places like India and Wales, Commonwealth sports news and the latest triumphs of British industry (*'Here at Upson Downs, British scientists test the latest fogproof electric self-loading pea-sheller...'*).

THEN, as if that wasn't enough, we were served *Look At Life*. This wet-noodle product of the British film industry was at least in colour, but often so tedious that people took turns in staying awake through it to awaken others when it was over. Running some twenty minutes, but feeling more like ninety, *LAL* offered its thoroughly unreconstructed views on a wide range of topics; often travel, occasionally political and once, if my memory was not fried by too many Delicious Hot Dogs Available From The Foyer, sound advice on what to do if anybody – but especially the Gypsies – attempted to *begin a riot*. The answer was call the authorities, who would, in turn, call out the army who would, in turn, confront the rioters and, if needs be, shoot the ringleader. I am NOT joking! This was illustrated for us by a bunch of raggle-taggle extras-o dressed like people who dress like Gypsies when asked to partake in a duff film, making a great deal of noise about something unexplained on what was clearly a disused airfield. The ringleader, a lanky fellow in a silly hat who had been asked not to shave that morning, was holding a club and exhorting the rest of the fly-blown mob to attack the stalwart khaki lads kneeling 50 yards in front of them with Lee-Enfield rifles pointed steadily back at the herd. The Riot Act was then read by a lieutenant. As it was ignored by the Awfulgyppos, a warning was given that shots would be fired. Again, nothing but theatrical leaping and gesticulating. A shot therefore rang out, felling the ringleader, causing panic and trouser-coughing among the rest of the yellow cads who immediately turned and ran. I REALLY AM not kidding...

Finally, we would get the British Supporting Feature, with Sam Kydd in it somewhere saying 'Yes, guv' in reply to a question and Anton Diffring being shot in the final reel, then FINALLY, FINALLY, the main feature. You got a lot for your 3/6 in those days, but sometimes I could have done with a little less of a bargain.

I absorbed the little rock'n'roll that came my way with the same benign interest I offered all of the above. It was something that crossed the landscape in front of me. I can clearly remember electing to read the *Beano* rather than watch *6.5 Special*. Looking now at a video of the one surviving episode, I think I made the right choice. The first impact rock'n'roll had on me in any real sense was a day at school when the intense interest that my classmates were taking in my newly acquired die-cast battery operated model of an anti-aircraft searchlight was swept away by some nerk who waved a tatty sheet of paper and said: 'I've got all the words to Jailhouse Rock 'ere.' I suddenly knew how it felt to be a Bay City Roller or an O.J. Simpson. Again, I could lie and say that this was the turning point, and that I filled my time henceforth in Herculean efforts to track down every obscure rock'n'roll 45 that the local electrical emporium possessed, but I didn't. I wasn't ready. Too many Dinky toys to collect yet. (Which, by the way, are long gone. Don't pester me with offers of vast sums for the mint-and-boxed Centurion tank.) And so, I loped contentedly towards the 1960's and my early teens, neither of which began until 1962 anyhow.

A quiet interlude, to be accompanied by quiet interlude music of your choice.

In the meantime, without my knowledge, ground was being broken on my behalf and that of hundreds of other cute little tykes who would soon turn into ungrateful monster teenagers. I will call it 'The Blues Cusp', because I am the author and I can do that sort of thing. It was a four-year period, 1959 to 1962, when the audience for the blues essentially altered from a largely African American one to a largely white American and European one. There had, of course, always been both black and white people listening to the blues, and there still are, but this is where the demographics significantly shifted. It's not my job to beat you about the nuts with an ethnomusicological cricket bat, so I will content myself with a simple, rough and probably incomplete chronology of events; you can draw your own conclusions.

1959

Sam Charters publishes his book, *The Country Blues*. Moe Asch issues the companion LP to the Charters opus on the Folkways subsidiary, RBF.

Jacques Demêtre and Marcel Chauvard visit New York, Detroit and Chicago on the first significant Euro-blues tour. Charles Delaunay, Django's first mentor, publishes their findings in his magazine *Jazz Hot* as 'Voyage au pays du Blues'.

Jazz Journal and *Jazz Monthly* cover blues topics and review blues records.

Heritage Records is founded in London by Australian Tony Standish. Throughout the Cusp period, he will issue records by Blind Blake, Ramblin' Thomas, Papa Charlie Jackson, Charlie Patton, Memphis Minnie, Blind Arvella Gray, Lowell Fulson, K.C. Douglas, Little Son Willis, Jaybird Coleman, Snooks Eaglin, Blind James Brewer, Black Ace, Buster Pickens and more; it is the first seriously-dedicated blues record label of the new era, and, by God, IT'S AUSTRALIAN!   Advance, Australia Fair... fair dinkum (whatever that means)... Good on yez, cobblers, strap me wallabee to a tucker bag, and we forgive you (but only just) for Rolf Harris.

Alan Lomax and Shirley Collins go south, discover and record (among others) Fred McDowell, Forest City Joe and Ed & Lonnie Young for the six-volume Atlantic LP set, *Sounds Of The South*.

1960

Jazz Journal publishes the translated version of 'Voyage au Pays du Blues', starting in January.

Paul Oliver publishes his much-delayed book, *Blues Fell This Morning*, actually written in 1958. Had it not fallen foul of a long British printers' strike, it would be seen for what it is: the first serious book about the blues, not the second. Philips Records issues an accompanying LP.

Paul and Valerie Oliver, accompanied much of the way by Count Chris Strachwitz (yes, he really is... but don't tell him I told you), spend the summer in the USA travelling and recording blues artists for what will become both *Conversation With The Blues* and the foundations of Arhoolie Records.

Jazz On Record is published, containing a wealth of information on blues records, largely written by Alexis Korner.

Pianists (specifically, Memphis Slim, Roosevelt Sykes, Little Brother Montgomery and Speckled Red) visit Britain and Europe. Unaccountably, they fail to jam with Mrs. Mills and Russ Conway.

In July, at the *Newport Jazz Festival*, Muddy Waters, John Lee Hooker, Butch Cage & Willie Thomas and Jimmy Rushing appear in front of a largely white audience. The proceedings are filmed by the United States Information Service and Chess Records issue the LP, *Muddy Waters At Newport*, which will gob-smack many a young lad, including a certain M.P. Jagger of Kent.

Work has quietly begun, in a Welsh mining village, on what will become the discography, *Blues & Gospel Records 1902-42*.

Jazz Journal, Jazz Monthly and *Jazz Hot* continue to cover blues topics and review blues records.

In November, Chris Strachwitz launches Arhoolie Records with the first Mance Lipscomb album, recorded that same summer.

21

1961

Jack Dupree and Memphis Slim play in the UK. Unfortunately, they have to use British pianos.

The recordings Alan Lomax made in 1959 are released in the UK to gobsmacked acclaim and taken VERY seriously indeed. Nobody seems to realise that Shirley Collins was there too.

Jazz Journal, Jazz Monthly and *Jazz Hot* continue the good work.

1962

The Origin Jazz Library issues OJL-1, Charlie Patton, generally regarded as the first serious, dedicated heavy-duty Mississippi corblimey headbangers album. But remember, the Aussies got there first with an EP.

Columbia issues the first Robert Johnson album. Origin were going to do it until Columbia said: 'No you don't! That's ours, sod off,' and went off in a minute and a huff to scour their archives. Later that same day, they emerged, went back to the Origin blues mafia and said: 'Er... got any Robert Johnsons you could lend us, then?'

In October, the first *American Folk Blues Festival* tours Europe, setting a pattern for the rest of the decade.

In Sussex two young herberts called Simon Napier and Mike Leadbitter form the 'Blues Appreciation Society'.

Interesting, eh?

———————

End of quiet interlude. Turn that bloody music off.

———————

British pop music in the early 1960's was a dismal bag of old tat. The American counterpart was little better. To quote Jerry Lee Lewis: 'Suddenly everybody was called "Bobby".' As I peeked over the precipice into teenhood, the music industry could only offer me one act that had enough balls to grab mine: the Shadows. Divorced from accompanying Cliff Richard, they had a life of their own, and they produced tight, rocking instrumentals that still sound good today, although I grant there is some measure of nostalgia tangled up in there.

But look at the context. *Before* the Beatles or the Stones, and *after* the very few one-off records by Johnny Kidd, Billy Fury, Vince Everett and Pinky & Perky, the Shadows were the only Brits playing anything like rock'n'roll in what was otherwise a wasteland of cute nonsense mongered by soppy wankers with haircuts way beyond my capacity to emulate. So, being *VERY CAREFUL* not to be seen as a Cliff fan (only girls, nerks and sissies...), I started to buy Shadows 45's about the same time that I began applying Brylcreem in industrial quantities. We're talking reaching 13 in 1962, the perfect age for experimenting with being objectionably snotty, but having to do it on a fractured, post-Elvis teenage bombsite that Elvis himself (or rather the Colonel, damn his eyes) had inspired. Nevertheless, I acquired a black suit, bought a pair of suede winklepicker boots, which our family doctor warned would put me in a wheelchair by age 20, and spent as much time posing in front of the mirror readying myself as I did actually stepping out. 'You can't go out yet, mate, you haven't combed your hair enough,' laughed Dad. Ah, he may have mocked my endeavours, but when the door closed behind me I was, in my head, Jet Harris. Which was more than could be said of Jet, I subsequently learned.

––––––––––––––

Events in October 1962 turned the gas up under the Cold War. The Cuban Missile Crisis was coming to what might be a very nasty head. Russian ships were steaming towards Havana loaded with ICBM's for installation in Cuba, to be pointed directly at the American mainland and Dick Van Dyke. As bloody fools in the White House and the Kremlin attempted to stare each other down, an ultimatum was issued from Washington. Turn the ships around or face the consequences. Marooned in the daily stalag of a private north-west London boys' school, and knowing full well that Britain would cop a gobful of Comradely Nuclear Destruction – not the CND we needed – a group of us lads decided to valiantly meet our fate head on. Not for us the duck-and-cover that we knew would be useless. With the failsafe time locally set for 2:00 pm, five of us went AWOL after lunch and made our way to the school roof via the inspection ladder. We clambered in between the dovetailed sloping roofs, found a clear view of the eastern aspect of the sky that we expected Armageddon to emerge from and settled in to await death and observe it. It was chilly and slightly foggy. Perfect. We had brought McVitie's chocolate biscuits, Tizer and Mars bars to see us into the incinerated hereafter, but, as the distant sound of traffic continued to drift upwards, and no sirens were wailing, we checked the time. 2:10 pm. Nothing. 'It'll take a few minutes to get going,' said Anton Kozmalsky, with the chipper tone of someone awaiting a late kick-off. 2:20 pm. Nothing. I sat quietly regretting all that I would not experience, but also oddly calm. Perhaps frozen.

'Reckon they've turned back?' asked David Margolis.

'No, it's going to happen,' replied Zaffar Iqbal.

'You sure about the time?' I asked.

'Yes,' replied Anton, 'the *Daily Mirror* said two.'

2:35 pm. Still nothing. Sensing now that either the Russians had blinked and lost, and that all the carnage was east of Germany, or that they had backed down – which turned out to be the case – we abandoned our positions and, deflated, clambered back down into the school yard, to be confronted by a severely twitching Dr. McGregor, our fiercely large, hairy and brimstone-laden Geography and Latin master.

'An' jus wha' th' dickens d'ye thank yer doon m'luds?' he seethed, in a tweed-laden brogue thicker than the ones on his feet.

'Waiting for the end of the world, sir,' I answered, missing the final step and falling to the ground heavily, the Tizer bottle and its threepenny deposit rolling from my grasp.

'Ah, wahl, yer in luck luds, for tha' would be in mah awfiss right noo.'

I still blame Khrushchev for that caning. And I still recite what little Latin I have left with a Highland accent.

By early 1963 I had been moved seven times, albeit within a five mile radius centred around Cricklewood, in north-west London. We had now bought our first proper house, a modest semi in Kingsbury with an alarmingly large garden ('You expect me to mow THAT?' I protested), from which my parents oversaw the two shops they – and the bank – now possessed.

At around the same time, the daily beatings that we received at school, which we had been warned would brand us as snitches if we told our families, finally manifested themselves. On a morning following one such attack, the welts on my hands were obvious. I never went back, but my father, armed with outrage and a fierce, if seldom-roused temper, did. What transpired I don't know, but I think he at least got his money back.

Having therefore survived the brief but brutal period in that small private boys' school where corporal punishment and public humiliation were elevated to a high art by dubious unmarried men in tatty sports jackets and stained trousers, I was soon attending a mixed-sex grammar school, happy to be out from under the authority of the leering madmen who had so recently been in charge of my education. In the new environment I passed some free time as score-keeper for the 30-or-more-a-side no-rules basketball and punch-up matches that erupted in the schoolyard, but I still had to absorb Latin. Our new Latin master concocted little rhymes to assist us: '*Amo, Amas, Amat*, I'd like to be a cat. *Amamus, Amatis, Amant*, alas I know I can't.' *Et cetera*. It didn't help.

In Kingsbury, if you listened closely enough, an assortment of early rumblings could be heard. My emerging libido had discovered women, and I wanted to get my hands on at least one to see what they were like, but my luck and charm were about as manifest as the Hunchback of Notre Dame the day before his annual bath. So, I lusted quietly after Mary Tyler Moore, Diana Dors, Sabrina, Sophia Loren, Ava Gardner, Billie Davis, Martha Hyer and just about every other unattainable goddess except possibly Vera Lynn, and resigned myself to a waiting game.

In the meantime, a curious thing called 'rhythm and blues' was beginning to bob up and down on my horizon. I became aware of it in the spring of 1963 when I first heard the Rolling Stones' 'Come On'. I was ignoring the Beatles because they were, in my view, a girls' group, but this sound and the image that accompanied it were different. I bought the 45, joined their fan club. 2/6 brought me a thin membership card (number 56), a poorly-produced photo and a mimeographed one-page newsletter. I never heard from them again (can I have my money back please?) and I then absorbed everything else that was slung at me, including the three EPs. I bought them all from a shoe box of a record shop buried deep inside an old arcade on the High Street in Kingsbury. It was always filled with the scent of bouquets drifting in from the next door florist and was run by a short blob of a man glued to the floor behind his short counter. I don't think he had legs, just a set of wheels fixed to a length of tramline. The records he sold me were packed with more energy than I had ever encountered before. The Stones attacked their material rather than interpreted it. In their young hands Barrett Strong's easy-rolling 'Money' was an all-out downhill run; Berry's 'Bye Bye Johnny' an unexamined leap off a cliff. More than anything, what Mick'n'the lads had in those days was energy and enthusiasm.

Furthermore, I looked to the Stones for cultural direction and obligingly, they gave me one. Very purist in the early days, their message was essentially 'Don't listen to *us*, go listen to Chuck, Bo, Wolf, Muddy...' I took them at their word and dragged my thin wallet back to the record shop, from where I emerged clutching a Pye International 45 called 'Pretty Thing'. Like all good Cockney lads of the era, my inner R&B fan was born within the sound of Bo Diddley; I had never heard anything like it before and found it difficult to believe that something could posses this much power and still be called music. The choppy solo electric guitar introduction, suddenly colliding with that extraordinary Bo Diddley beat, sent *almost* sexual shock-waves down my spine. And that other curious, ethereal wailing... it took me some time to figure out it was a harmonica. If your points of reference for a gob-iron had only ever been Max Geldray and Larry Adler, it was hardly surprising you'd have trouble recognising it. The flip, 'Road Runner', possessed just the kind of swaggering braggadocio I wished I had, and was opened by a guitar that sounded like a land mine being unzipped in an empty bathroom; this extraordinary double-header of a single was the sign at my personal crossroads. If it was all this good, I would take the R&B route. It was, and for leading me there I have the Stones to thank.

In the months that followed, prodded by the surprisingly accurate R&B coverage in the weekly national pop journal, *Record Mirror*, I bought everything I could afford – mostly 45's and EPs, and mostly on Pye International and Stateside. I found not only more Bo Diddley, but also Chuck Berry, John Lee Hooker, Tommy Tucker, and, especially, Howling Wolf. I bought 'Smokestack Lightnin' ' and 'Going Down Slow' as a back-to-back Pye 45 (THANK YOU, whoever at Pye it was who coupled those two for UK release). Cor! I didn't think it could get better than Bo until I heard Wolf. 'Smokestack' was from another world. Literally, as it turned out, for South Side Chicago had little in common with north-west London unless you count bad weather in winter and an unwillingness to get out of bed to face it. That loping rhythm and gnawing guitar! That insistent, pushy drumming! That demonic howl that Wolf produced! And the words, which made both no sense and all the sense in the world.

As if that wasn't enough, the flip-side contained lyrics and guitar licks that curled my toes and all other extremities. '*I have had my fun if I don't get well no more*', delivered in a voice reminiscent of a ton of gravel arriving without warning. YES! That was what I wanted! Women! Cadillacs! Money! More Women! Alcohol! Fried Chicken! Lucozade(?) Yesohyes pleaseyesyesohsendmesomenowargh! And Hubert Sumlin's guitar echoed every blood-spattered word. (I didn't know it was Hubert Sumlin at the time; I just knew I had found someone to replace Hank Marvin.) It also took me a long time to figure out that the spoken passages were by Willie Dixon not Wolf, and even longer to realise that it was an old song. And when you compare the St. Louis Jimmy original to Wolf's electric reworking, you realise just what an innovative bluesman Wolf was. He made a wholly new song out of it, with a wholly contemporary sound and sentiments.

By the autumn of 1963, I had a small collection of 45's and EPs and just a few albums I'd received as birthday and Christmas presents. (You want a list? Okay: *The Blues* (Volumes 1 and 2), *Bo Diddley Rides Again*, *Bo Diddley* (the one with 'Can't Judge A Book' on it), and *More Chuck Berry*, all on Pye.) Then, in November, television offered something that drove the screw a notch deeper. I had read the previous week that a show called *I Hear The Blues* was to be broadcast on ATV. It was the televised version of the second annual *American Folk Blues Festival* that toured Europe. Filled with a strange wonder that bordered on the quietly hysterical I made very sure that I was available to sit in front of the TV that night. Of course I bloody was, the girls at *Spick & Span* had still not replied to any of my postcards. And so, in the company of my parents, I watched as the credits rolled and introduced Memphis Slim, who in turn introduced Matt Murphy playing 'Matt's Guitar Boogie'. This was exactly what I had wanted to hear, even though I wasn't expecting it. My father, too, became immediately enthralled and, when Lonnie Johnson appeared, he recognised him and leaned forward to watch him play an extraordinary guitar solo.

My mother pointedly reported from behind her wall of knitting that Victoria Spivey had spat on TV, and that Sonny Boy Williamson appeared to be eating his harmonica, which to me only added to their lustre. It was, however, Big Joe Williams and his incredible nine-string guitar that made the biggest impression on me. By this time I was familiar with the range of sounds that six and twelve-string acoustic and electric guitars could make, but this was something truly extraordinary. It powered Big Joe's nervous, archaic vocal delivery like a Diesel engine dropped into a Morris Minor.

The country blues had found me, hiding in a front room in suburban London. The next day I visited the local record shop with a list of names. Jack Cohen, the delightful old chap who owned the shop, was able to come up with a Memphis Slim EP on Storyville. Thinking I had bought Big Joe Williams, I eagerly ran home and whipped it expectantly onto the turntable to be confronted with the sound of a piano. My dad said: 'Cor, boogie woogie,' and stopped to listen. I was both disappointed that I had made a mistake, and delighted to have acquired a real blues record.

So, life continued in the mind and body of the spotty oik I was trying hard not to be. I now modelled myself on Sean Connery's Bond, although curiously nobody was able to actually *see* this. Perhaps it was the daft school uniform or the bus pass that obscured the image. I bought more records and continued to lust after unattainable women ranging from Ursula Andress to Alice at the local chip shop. I watched hedgehogs climb into the dog's bowl on the patio outside our kitchen window and sink slowly down as they munched their way through to the bottom, and generally attempted to separate the boy from the man I felt must be due to emerge any time now. But I still had some boyhood imperatives and one of them was fireworks.

November had always held a special meaning for me simply because of Guy Fawkes' Night. We had celebrated it every year throughout my childhood, with not just the fireworks but also the bonfire, the Guy, the cocoa, the hot sausages and baked potatoes consumed in the cold night air, and the camaraderie that pooling resources always brought. Because we often had large back gardens, we hosted November the 5th celebrations many times; it made simple sense for everyone to enjoy everyone else's fireworks, and if a limb was blown off, there was at least plenty of immediate assistance. Fortunately the God of Saltpetre had always smiled upon us. Until 1963.

That huge garden in Kingsbury was on three levels, with a small (nay, piddling) waterfall running from the top patio to a pond on the middle level, which also contained the lawn, flanked by steeply-angled flower beds. Beyond that, the landscape sharply descended to a rough area populated by a dozen random trees and backed by a fence.

Two of my school friends had turned up that night to share, bringing their own black powder inventory. Because we were in the business, we always had the best fireworks. My father didn't stint, since he enjoyed them as much as I did, so we arranged our Roman candles, bangers, jumping crackers, Catherine wheels, air bombs, rockets and large set pieces very carefully, in accordance with Good Firework Practice, in covered boxes, to be extracted one at a time. With one calamitous exception.

The order of the night was to begin slowly with small stuff then build to a grand finish with the big pieces: the largest rockets, the tallest roman candles, the triple air bombs and an extraordinary thing called a 'Wakey-Wakey' (price 5/-), essentially a huge bomb. About an hour into the proceedings, a jumping cracker (a dangerous little squib of a device that leapt around the ground exploding) managed to find its way into the large plastic bag containing all the big stuff. We watched in silent horror as my father desperately attempted to stamp it out by performing a fandango on top of the bag, but we all knew it was a lost cause.

The failsafe point of doom hung in the air for what seemed like the length of an algebra test until, as we knew it must, omni-directional Hades broke loose at ground level. Huge showers of exploding light tore across the ground as enormous rockets slithered over the lawn like mad snakes. Nicholas Antill, closely chased by one, leapt for safety into the shallow pond, launching innocent and startled goldfish into the night. Derek Thorne, potential heir to the Thorne electrical empire if he survived this evening, rolled down the muddy bank to tree city followed by the demonic howl of horizontally launched air bombs. A burning Roman candle, blown free of the bag by an explosion, cartwheeled towards me like a crazed phallic symbol; I remember being fascinated by the patterns it was creating in the dark just before I also remembered to hit the ground. It shot over my head with a noise that I imagined sounded like an incoming 88 mm shell (I was still reading far too many *War Picture Library* magazines) and I bobbed back up again to see it land in a rose bush and begin burning the stems. My father was still struggling to empty the bag. He finally gave up and, shouting 'BUGGER!', ran for it just before the Wakey-Wakey blew up, taking all else with it in a vast explosion that strewed glowing debris across the flower beds, stunned our auditory canals and left us deaf for some moments. All this activity took probably less than 30 seconds, but seemed to last an eon.

We stood there wet and muddy, hearts pounding to be let out, breathing hard, giggling with excitement and relief, our faces blackened and our nostrils overwhelmed by the stiff pungency of spent gunpowder. As a post-apocalyptic smoke drifted across the lawn, I fancied myself the survivor of a battle. Meanwhile in the house, the terrified dog had crapped loosely on the good rug and, panicked, spread it about like Marmite on toast. My mother stepped out onto the top patio. 'Have you QUITE finished?' she demanded, unaware that guest-related carnage had only narrowly been avoided. Miraculously, no-one was hurt, although the adrenalin lasted for hours, as did my mother's detailed views on the events of the night directed at my father's still-ringing ears.

Television was still offering an occasional glimpse of the blues. The teen show, *Ready Steady Go*, which I watched every Friday night (still no life, you see), fed us with a great deal of what passed for R&B in Britain in those days. A 1964 UK definition of 'rhythm and blues' was very different from a 1954 US definition; it could, and did, include:

> The Animals
> Chuck Berry
> Bo Diddley
> Bern Elliott & The Fenmen
> Marvin Gaye
> Buddy Guy
> John Lee Hooker
> Howling Wolf
> The Kinks

Little Walter
The Miracles
Derrick Morgan
Muddy Waters
The Orlons
Wilson Pickett
The Pretty Things
Otis Redding
Jimmy Reed
The Rolling Stones
The Skatalites
The Shirelles
The Supremes
Ike & Tina Turner
Vera & The Lynns *(oh, all right, you spotted that one...)*

And a lot of them appeared on *RSG*. I remember Buddy Guy well, because whoever armed him that night with a loose-slung microphone around the neck had no idea he would be that mobile. Within seconds the mike had bounced round to his back, and slapped between his shoulder blades as he hurled himself around the studio, rendering his vocal chords inaudible. It didn't interfere with the electric guitar though, which was one of the most stunning sounds I'd heard up to that moment. *RSG* also hosted Jesse Fuller, really stretching the term 'R&B' to its limits. 'I'm 65 years old today,' he announced, peeking through a curtain of miniskirts and daft haircuts.

Then, in August 1964, TV served up another goulash archipelago that prodded me further down the road to the blues: *The Blues & Gospel Train*. Videotaped in May 1964, but broadcast in August, B&GT was the televised version of the *Blues & Gospel Caravan* that had been touring Europe, managed by Joe Boyd. When it arrived in Manchester, Granada TV decided to make a programme out of it. The way in which they set about this says a great deal about the British view of the blues at the time. The first thing producer Johnny Hamp and director Phil Casson did was to take over a disused suburban railway station, Chorlton-cum-Hardy, on the outskirts of Manchester, and redecorate it to resemble their view of a Southern whistle stop. Bales of hay, 'Wanted' posters, live chickens and a goat were all pressed into service to authenticate what was about to take place. The next stage was to fill a steam train with artists and audience in Manchester and send it chugging in to what was now called 'Chorltonville'. Thus, the programme began with the arrival of the train, and, as a couple of hundred fans piled off and scuffled for the best seats, they seethed around Muddy Waters standing on the platform singing 'Blow Wind Blow'. Cousin Joe Pleasant followed, accompanied by Willie Smith and Ransom Knowling. (Yes, Ransom Knowling, the Bluebird house bassist! Why didn't anyone interview him?)

As Cousin Joe sang 'Railroad Porter Blues', a sudden and unexpected rainstorm hijacked the proceedings, drenching everyone and everything, but none so much as Joe, caught out in the open with a tatty upright piano clearly purloined from a local pub. Trouper that he was, he continued to sing ('*in the rain and everything*' he interjected into his song). From an overflowing roof gutter, torrents of water poured directly onto the head of Ransom Knowling, who surely must have wondered what the hell he was doing there.

Ceasing as suddenly as it had begun, the rain spared Sister Rosetta Tharpe. She arrived in a horse-and-carriage, laughing, shouting, talking, clapping in the post-storm freshness, to mount the platform, sling her guitar over her shoulder and launch into a blistering and deliriously-received version of 'Didn't It Rain'. (Sister Rosetta was one of the GREAT guitar players. If you ever get the chance to see her performance of 'Down By The Riverside' on *Gospel Time* from 1965, then do, because it will blow you away!)

Muddy followed, singing 'You Can't Lose What You Ain't Never Had', playing exquisite slide guitar that made my eyes water. I had never heard electric bottleneck guitar before that moment and, because I could see it happening, I understood how the sound was made. 'The Hawaiians do much the same thing sitting down,' said Dad, nonchalantly lighting another Passing Cloud.

This was followed by Sonny Terry & Brownie McGhee playing to the audience and the goat, the show ending with a jam session version of 'He's Got The Whole World In His Hands'. You would NEVER have got away with a programme like that in South Side Chicago on a Friday night, but this was Manchester on a wet Tuesday, and Muddy, at least, must have realised that his career path was continuing to alter in bizarre ways.

I taped the proceedings on our newly-acquired secondhand Philips 'Magic Eye' tape recorder, demanding absolute silence throughout the programme ('Whatever you do, *DON'T COUGH*'), as the omnidirectional mike picked up every last little noise. On listening to the playback, however, I realised I had failed to stop the very loud clock that sat next to the television.

That was August. On 24 September we moved again. My parents thought it would be fun to run a pub, so we sold the house and one of the shops, put the other under management, and moved to Hertford, county seat of Hertfordshire, about 25 miles north-east of London, to take up residence in 'The Blue Coat Boy', a 300 year old pub on the main street. This involved my leaving both London and school. I was to attend the Hertford College of Further Education, and I met all this by displaying the complete lack of concern that I hoped would be read as Bond-like cool. Quietly though, at age fifteen and a bit, I was trembling with excitement. The new and the unknown beckoned.

Chapter Two

1964-66: NEW LITTLE OLD BOY

The Patterson's removal van, its side panel proclaiming *'Your Destination Is Only Our Goal'* ('Sorry, that should say *"Our Only Goal"*, ha-ha,' proffered the driver) left Kingsbury in the mid-morning of 24 September, and we followed it in the family Ford Consul with all that my mother considered too precious to be left to the mercies of men who couldn't even paint straight. I sat in the back, jammed between boxes and the dog, reading Cornelius Ryan's *The Longest Day*, singing ribald songs under my breath (*'Oh, the grand old Duke of York, he had ten thousand men / His case comes up in court next week, he won't do that again'*, etc) and also wondering to myself what a spoonful was. Howlin' Wolf sang about it: *'Everybody fights about a spoonful, that spoon-that spoon-that spoonFUL.'* I had no idea, but I bet Len Chess did, and I *KNOW* that the Friday night crowd in a South Side club did too. (You still don't know? It's the rough measure of one ejaculation of semen. Try it sometime when you've got a spare moment.)

We arrived in Hertford around lunchtime. The first order of business was for Dad to keep his appointment at the county court to obtain his licence to serve alcohol. British law at that time did not allow you to acquire this very necessary document until the person from whom you were taking over relinquished theirs. Which meant the same day they left and you replaced them. With all your worldly goods sitting in a quietly chugging removal van, this can be a very hairy moment if the judge decides he doesn't like the cut of your jib, or the rozzers find something to hang on you:

'Mr. Vernon, I find I cannot grant you a licence to serve alcohol, as it appears that the three shilling fine you incurred in March of 1946 for expectorating on the upper deck of a number 16 omnibus in Willesden Green remains unpaid... and furthermore, your jib is badly cut.'

But he got through okay and emerged from the court clutching his licence and beaming.

The removal crew began unloading. Because the old pile we were inheriting was three centuries old, the original builders had foolishly not thought of leaving room for the insertion large pieces of electrical equipment. There was a single, narrow, centre spiral staircase winding from the cellar to the attic. The upper floor back bedroom window had to be taken out and a

Sue & Ted Vernon

" **The Blue Coat Boy** "

TELEPHONE NO.	FORE STREET
HERTFORD 3048	HERTFORD

LUNCHEONS & GRILLS AT ALL TIMES

GOOD WINE LIST

A FULLY LICENSED BENSKINS HOUSE

ladder leaned up from the back yard in order for the bigger items to be swallowed. I watched in awe as our now vintage and huge radiogram ascended that ladder on the shoulder of one of the largest – and flabbiest – men I've ever encountered in my life. Awe turned to horror as, halfway up, the string holding the immense wooden lid broke; the top flew open to the right side of this Jelly Groin Giant, who with a mixture of experience, luck and a torrent of interesting phrases, was just able to keep his balance. I learned several colourful and immensely engaging new words in that moment. It only occurred to me much later that, in the prime moment of danger, I was more concerned about the welfare of the radiogram. My father had only recently replaced the original 78 rpm deck with a new three speed Garrard to upgrade me from the portable Supraphon that I had been using. Clearly, in placing sonic gratification ahead of life and limb, I was already a Record Collector.

That night we held a party at the Blue Coat Boy, to which all our friends and business associates had been invited, as well as the local drinking crew who were to be our customers. Jewish tobacco and confectionary wholesalers from the East End came face to face with the *Old Boys* of Hertford. An *Old Boy* was any adult male, drinking age or above. A *Little Old Boy* was any male child up to but not including drinking age. Dad was the *New Old Boy* and I was therefore a *New Little Old Boy*, an irritating situation I could not resolve until age would allow it. Our other family friends were there too, as were the few relatives we were still on speaking terms with. It was all a great success, as any event fuelled by free beer, hot sausages and ham sandwiches is bound to be.

That was a Thursday. On the following Monday, three weeks late and aware of it, I presented myself at the Hertford College of Further Education. I had heard that the HCFE was different in a number of key ways from any school experience I had so far had. NO uniforms! You could, within reason, wear what you wanted. NO corporal punishment or dreary detention! Yay! The worst that could happen was that you would be asked to leave a class. The average size of that class was to be eight, rather than the 30 I had always accepted as standard. We were to be referred to by the teachers as 'Mr. Vernon', 'Mr. Bernard' and 'Miss Snell'. Smoking was allowed in the canteen, the common room and on the grounds. I obviously needed to begin mastering the James Bond Cigarette Manoeuvre immediately in order to take advantage. This, clearly, was a very different game of soldiers to any I had previously encountered. I was being offered the opportunity to be treated as an adult. It was up to me to show them just how futile that offer could be.

I nervously presented myself to my first class on that dank and misty Monday morning, painfully aware that relationships and secret bonds had all been forged in my absence. I would be the square peg, the fifth wheel, the odd-man-out, the unidentifiable crunchy green thing in the stew. My life would be appallingly lonely. But I would brave it all, not showing my true emotions; the lone wolf against all odds, keeping my own counsel. I would lose myself in the work. Nose to the grindstone, shoulder to the wheel, instep to the coal scuttle, knee to the tea kettle and groin to the barrel. I had my records to console me. I stiffened my upper lip as best I could (it's VERY uncomfortable) and fixed a steely glare... then someone stepped up and said: 'Hi, I'm Ian.' Ian Eddington and I became furiously fast friends. Within the week we had visited each other's homes, attempting to cook chips in his and nearly burning the house down. We nevertheless devoured the carbonized results.

I began smoking. It was a deliberate choice based on the necessity of being part of the world I'd been thrust into. I was offered a Woodbine during my first lunch break and took it because to say 'No thanks' would have meant the turning away of every head on my new planet. For a tobacconist's son to have had no previous smoking experience might seem odd, but I grew up with the stuff and, like the chocolate-factory worker who never eats the product, I was simply too familiar with the feel and smell of cigarettes. So, on that first Monday lunchtime I took the offered weed, had it lit for me and then puffed away furiously, both not inhaling and being noticed for it. Embarrassed, and hearing the jeering mantra 'You can't inhale, you can't inhale' echo in my ears, I bought a packet of five Woodbines and a penny match book and repaired to the woods at the bottom of the college grounds to practise my nascent art.

I took the cigarette, put it in my mouth, lit up and drew on it. The paper on the unfiltered Woodbine stuck to my lips, so that when I came to extract the cigarette, it took two small pieces of fragile lip flesh with it, top and bottom. I winced with pain at the same nanosecond that the first cloud of nicotine smoke hit my throat and then rolled down into my lungs. My eyes bulged. My breathing seemed to desert me. A sudden panic set in, exacerbated by the pain in my now bleeding lips. An ominous rumbling began somewhere in my chest. I remembered finally that I also needed to exhale. As I did so, my first smoker's cough was born, travelling from deep inside my shell-shocked lungs ('How could you DO this to us?' they screamed), back up the pipes to my throat where, like a fat rat in a narrow drainpipe, it got stuck, causing me to retch. Reflexively, I drew breath again so that the smoke bounced back into my lungs ('You BASTARD,' they howled, 'we're *never* breathing for you again') and then, once more, like the vaporous ghost of a demonic yo-yo, the smoke hurtled back up and I managed to expel it along with bits of saliva, lunch and possibly, I feared, inner tissue.

Hopelessly dizzy, I fell off the log I was sitting on and lay gasping on the wet bracken. The cigarette had somehow fallen onto my flies and was quietly burrowing its way towards my crotch like a hungry leech. I leapt up to extract it and grabbed the wrong end, burning my fingers. I shouted 'FUCK!' in final exasperation and hurled the still smoking weed to the ground, tromping it into the bracken. As I sat back down to recover, a voice behind me said: 'First cigarette, then?' It was Bernard Bentley, a year older than me and very sure of it.

'You won't tell anyone, will you?' I requested hopefully, still licking my burnt lips and digits.

'Not if you give me the other four Woodbines I won't. You're no bloody good at this game anyway.'

I agreed. However, I also persisted, and in the coming weeks got used to a habit that would last for another thirty years. Which just goes to prove what a silly sod I could be, but then a lot of us were in those days.

Notwithstanding that stupidity, life was going to be good. I was settling in well, making more friends than I could ever remember having had before, and exploring a new and conveniently compact town, including its delightfully dotty pre-war tea rooms, its eerie canal and its two record shops. Sensing that the move would mean a quantum leap in my journey toward adulthood, my father struck a deal with me. If I would put in some serious time working in the pub, evenings and weekends, with two nights a week off, he would pay me five guineas a week, one of which I was to return to my mother for housekeeping expenses. He would also throw in a packet of decent cigarettes on a Friday, my choice, from stock. In 1964 this was a fortune to a fifteen year old lad with no further expenses and, opting for Benson & Hedge's King Size, I immediately agreed. This would fund the record collection I seriously wanted to build.

One of the first things I did was ask our local newsagent to get *Jazz Journal* and *Jazz Monthly* for me every month. I could afford them now. I absorbed everything that their blues doyens offered me in print, not so much reading Paul Oliver, George Melly, Gina Wright and Derrick Stewart-Baxter as inhaling them. I also retrieved *Jazz On Record* from the college library and read everything Alexis Korner had to say, which, for the time, was a great deal. He knew a lot more than many people and he knew it a lot earlier, even if his writing style was a shade baroque. From these sources I learned more about the history that lay behind what I was used to calling 'R&B', and it was clearly the blues that I needed to look into more thoroughly. The local library held a copy of Paul Oliver's *Blues Fell This Morning*, hard going for a young lad, but filled with extraordinary graphic images from Hogarthian pre-war record adverts that truly spoke to me of another world, one of which I knew little, but that nevertheless fascinated me. I also found myself frequently reading the appendixed list of records quoted in the text, and from that encounter realised that I had a natural affinity with this thing called discography. Astonishingly, the College library yielded a further surprise; a copy of Sam Charters' *The Country Blues*, which read like a racy novel. I hoovered it up in one long night, then re-read it time and again. In later years, I roundly criticized it as being fatally flawed and ego-ridden, which of course is true, but I have also come to see it as the key offered to many of us for a door that would lead to a lifetime of involvement.

Our Maths master at college was a splendidly eccentric fellow called Herbert Caunter. Short, ginger-haired-and-tempered, limber, acerbic and opinionated, I remember describing him to an unimpressed aunt as 'A sandy little cove – the sort you find at Bournemouth beach, ha-ha', an old joke I'd stolen from a safely obscure Victorian issue of *Punch*. Over a two-year period he battled against appalling odds, attempting to instil in us the idea, at least, of applied mathematics. As a group, we loathed his lessons, but grew to respect the hard core of his sarcasm, a fearsome weapon he always applied with total success. Questioning Mark Wilson about his trousers and the gap between their turn-ups and the uppers of his sandals, Caunter asked casually, while removing his pipe from the corner under his moustache in which it lived: 'Are those actually long shorts or merely short longs?'

At times it was possible to pull him into group conversation and allow him to present us with the benefit of his opinions. Anything was preferable to a bout of freestyle wrestling with the eternal triangle of Maths. He would sit at his desk, legs crossed, head nodding, with his arms folded across the old green woollen waistcoat he invariably wore. In a pre-side stream awareness society he would stoke his pipe and announce: 'Ladies and gentlemen, you may smoke if you wish.' He revelled, as we did, in the abrupt change of atmosphere, and for a few minutes while we organised our makeshift ashtrays, he would stare through the window and watch the exhaled smoke and the vestiges of his planned mathematics lesson drift away. We sought his views on a wide variety of topics from long hair on men to how he thought Harold Wilson was handling the Rhodesian question. Of hairy lads he had said: 'If a person has thought about WHY he wants to wear long hair, and then pursues the resultant path, I can only applaud him. If, however, the yob down at the butcher's has grown his simply because he has seen another yob on the goggle box screeching tunelessly and earning more money than his stilted intellect has any concept of appreciating, I would earnestly consider purchasing my Friday leg of lamb elsewhere.' He concluded by remarking, as he scratched the stubble above his ears: 'You will notice that, as it is winter, I am wearing mine long.' We laughed sycophantically, hoping that applause would spur him on to further pronouncements and the rigours of constructing fuel consumption figures for a flight across the Andes would fade blissfully from view.

It was shortly after such a session that we encountered a side of Caunter that indelibly coloured our perspective if him. Released from the exercises one winter day, we exploded into the snow to spill our tightly packed energy in classic form – the collective small boy in us had organised a major snow brawl within minutes. Caunter, having stayed back warmly inside to gather himself and re-light his pipe, strolled, naïvely at peace, gazing into an open book and deep in thought, through the corridor, out of the door leading to the yard and straight into a huge fluffy custard pie of snow I had just heaved ineptly at Clive Turnbull.

A wedge of wet ice lodged neatly behind his spectacles, while the crystalline glob that had hit the lenses slid gently off them and sank slowly into the fibres of his flannel shirt. Miniature jewels of ice danced the conga through his twitching moustache. Every facial orifice was blocked with snow. His pipe sagged in his astonished jaw, then snapped back to attention and fizzled out wetly.

We all stood stock-still and a quiet horror lay across us as we awaited the feared reaction.

'WHO THREW THAT?' he shouted from inside his new and uncalled-for ice helmet.

'Uh – afraid it was me, sir. Sorry.' I felt like a man facing a firing squad and imagined the imminence of hot lead tearing through my adolescent breast. Caunter flourished a home-made handkerchief – the kind you boiled on a weekend – wiped his face with it, shook himself like a Labrador emerging from a winter river and stared directly into my eyes. Oh-God, here-it-comes. My heart is pounding on its own door. The lump in my throat is arguing for seniority.

'Jolly good shot, Mr. Vernon,' he remarked casually, as though he were not wearing a mask of dripping snow and ice, and stepped back inside, closing the door with a faint smile.

Every month, the inside back page of *Jazz Journal* listed jazz and blues records offered by Dave Carey of the Swing Shop in Streatham, south-west London. Having disposable income and an appetite for something I had yet to really taste, I phoned him up and asked for 'the best pre-war blues LP you have'. A truly gauche request from a spotty oik that Dave met with the courteous, helpful, honest and dead-on-the-money-advice that he offered everyone.

Cannily, he asked me what I knew. I told him I had some R&B, liked Big Joe Williams and had just read Sam Charters' book, *The Country Blues*. 'Do you want the record that goes with it?' he enquired. *DO I?* I knew about it from the appendix in the book, of course, but I imagined that, in 1964, a 1959 American album on an impossibly obscure label would be about as unattainable to me as a night of passion with Honor Blackman. It cost me half a week's money, but I said yes, sent him the postal order and quivered through an expectant week until its arrival.

Like your first kiss or your first car, you remember that initial encounter with your premier pre-war blues album in extraordinary detail. (I'm NOT alone in this am I? Please? Someone?). I marvelled at the presentation: a sturdy cardboard sleeve with an inner divider, one pocket for the record, the other for the booklet. This was serious stuff! I devoured the photos of Gus Cannon, Leroy Carr and Blind Lemon, presented in archaic oval frames, as though discovered hanging on the wall of a forgotten, long-lost archive and transported, unaltered, to the album cover. The sturdy vinyl and appealing cream label filled my senses with a fragrant expectancy. The booklet read like a private letter from Sam to me.

I lowered the disc onto the player to be immediately ambushed by an extraordinary panorama of sounds I could never have imagined. The surreal speed of Gus Cannon's vocal delivery; the distant, dry and ethereal sound of Blind Lemon; the contrasting intimate warmth of Leroy Carr's singing; the unbelievable power and sheer manic dedication of Blind Willie Johnson; the terror that Robert Johnson communicated in what I still think is his most committed performance, 'Preaching Blues'; the Saturday-night barrelhouse sense of fun that lay behind Tommy McClennan's 'I'm A Guitar King'; the sheer *swing* of Willie McTell's 'Statesboro Blues'. I had no idea that the blues could be this varied, this exciting, this enticing, THIS BLOODY GOOD! It's the pre-war blues for this lad, me buckos.

In the meantime, my life fell into a pattern. I attended college during the week, Ian Eddington and I hanging out at Hertford's Midtown Café afterwards, talking about everything. I would come home, eat something, glance at my homework and at 5:30 assume my position behind the bar. Yes, I was an underage barman, I admit it; but I was a big lad and the drinking laws in Hertford at that time were... um... relaxed. The early-evening crowd was a breed apart, mostly businessmen looking for a short period of relaxation after a hard day at the orifice, and mostly the same businessmen, so that they knew each other well and we quickly came to know them.

John Portious and Old Jock were two of the pre-dinner regulars. Like many folks in Hertford, they had their eccentric ways and, when it came to beer, both men clung fiercely to beverages that were judged exotically subversive by the Great Unwashed. Old Jock, in line with his self-styled image of no-nonsense spartanist pragmatism drank 'the only REAL beer left', Worthington's India Pale Ale. Anyone who, like me, has had the deeply unpleasant experience of pouring one for the first time will warmly agree that bomb disposal rapidly becomes a viable alternative to bartending.

When dispensing this volatile beverage, one has first to take into account:

1. The weather in the previous two days.

2. The length of time the selected bottle has been sitting in its present position.

3. The distance between the bottle's present position and the nearest opener.

4. The light factor.

5. Vibration levels inside a 20 foot radius within the previous two hours.

6. The reading on your own personal Zen-O-Meter.

Having strategically assessed the situation, one moves firmly but cautiously towards the unopened Worthington with a dry and, above all, steady hand. The dark glass bottle is carefully and silently brought towards the front of the bar. At this moment any drinkers worth their salt will quietly stop whatever they may be doing to amuse themselves and simply watch and wait. Blokes love explosions – it's in our genes – especially if a fifteen year old spotty herbert might be the likely recipient of a beer bath.

Gently, with a respect for precision bordering upon the discographical, one eases the cap off the way one is supposed to squeeze the trigger of a gun. An almost silent grunt of acknowledgment ripples through the bar. The first crisis is over.

The trick now is to hold the bottle up to the light, watch the ringlets of excess gas escape from the neck and check the bottom of the bottle to ensure that none of the sediment has been disturbed. This is no time to get sedimental. If the little beach of particles underneath this rare nectar lies quiet you are, at least so far, a good barman.

The moment of truth, however, is staring straight down your nose at you. With a steady hand, you pour at eye level. This must be done with the bottle neck at a sufficient distance from the angled glass so that a rich head, ideally a quarter-inch thick, is achieved when the pouring is completed. One must constantly monitor the sediment and cease the smooth, seamless pouring the second any particle reaches the mouth of the bottle. At this point, the glass should be level, and the bottle drawn quickly and quietly away.

Holding the finished product up to a stream of light (ostensibly to check for purity, but in reality of course, to bask in the triumph of completing such a dangerous and skilful task), the Meisterwerk is presented to the customer. Light applause may be expected to break out at this point. You can look your client straight in the eye and say casually, as though no miraculous feat had been performed: 'That'll be 2/3 to you, squire.'

My first ignorant attempt at this caused explosions of gas, beer and derision, followed by a suggestion that I might be more profitably employed as landfill for the new by-pass. Deeply stung, I devoted immediate attention to Gaining The Knack and Polishing The Art, so that by high summer – potentially the most dangerous time for a Worthington – I was, at least in my view, a master craftsman.

The latest example of my work had just arrived in front of Old Jock at the same time John Portious strolled through the door. John was a man who used Brylcreem not just on his hair but his entire head. When he wore a camel-hair coat, as he often did, he resembled a vast mobile advert for chip fat.

A huge man with appetites that frequently outmatched him, he had been ordered by an exasperated doctor to cut down on alcohol, nicotine, work, stress, fatty foods and all the sundry unsavouries necessary to a debauched nature. John had thought long and deep about this and in consequence switched to the least-caloried spirit he could find – gin – followed by a special alcohol-and-sugar-free German lager. This allowed him to routinely order a 'Gin & Teutonic', so that sycophants hoping to catch some of the money he loved to throw about would have to work for it by laughing. Old Jock, always his own man, remained unimpressed.

In one of those perfect moments when you are convinced that God must be a seven year old boy and that there is indeed synchronicity in the universe, the four components of disaster – John, Old Jock, the Worthington and a mysterious brown paper bag that Jock had placed on the bar – all marshalled themselves into the correct positions around the bar-flap at the far end of the counter. Quickly honouring the standard topics of weather, sport and politics, John enquired (for he was a nosey old bugger at heart) as to the content of bag.

'Plumber's mate.'
'Eh?'
'Y'know, a sink plunger.'
'Oh.'
'Aye.'
'Mind if I have a butcher's?'
'What? No, course not.'

It was akin to watching a spoiled child opening a present. Audible was the greedy smack of lips. Nothing in the world excites in quite the same way as a Brown Paper Bag Containing Something Unknown. The content becomes an immediate object of desire. A simple rubber cup with a wooden handle attached is seized upon like the Holy Grail.

Within seconds, the spoiled child had succeeded in planting the instrument firmly on top of the bar. I saw Jock move quietly away but didn't catch on. Neither did John.

'Cor, good innit? Works well. Lotta suction power there.'

Now I saw it myself, and, like Jock, secretly hoped that John hadn't. Of course, he hadn't. With a mere flick of the wrist, John planned to pull the little sucker straight off the bar-top and demonstrate his testosterone to the assembled hordes.

Needless to say, he had completely ignored the fact that it was upon the *hinged* bar-flap that he had planted the seed of his own destruction. Energy and physics laws being immutable, as John pulled the instrument upward he brought the bar-flap with it; his glass vacated its position and the beer parted company with the glass. The former tumbled chest high across the room and crashed amidst the dominoes, scattering them like teeth in a fist fight. The latter insinuated itself over George Brown's cap, newspaper, open tobacco tin and dignity. Ignoring the nervous sweat erupting through his greasy scalp, John mustered what dignity was left to him and ordered drinks all round before suddenly remembering a pressing appointment. I had never seen Old Jock laugh before, nor would I see it again.

I continued to buy records on the phone from Dave Carey ('Ah, you've read *Blues Fell This Morning* have you? There's an LP... would you...?') By the middle of 1965, I had amassed a considerable collection of pre-war country blues LPs, perhaps 25, including the precious American Columbia pressing of the Robert Johnson album. All of them recommended by Dave and every one a winner, as far as I was concerned.

Dave's philosophy was to get to know his customers, remember what they liked, and then recommend just the right album. Often, he would have the honesty to say: 'No, you don't want that, it's really not very good. However, I happen to have...' It was brilliant, created a trust on the part of the punters who felt like they belonged to a very exclusive club and, years later, when I came to be in the same position, his was the philosophy I attempted to emulate. It's the same spirit that drove the much-missed Red Lick Records and that you'll still find alive and well now at Roots & Rhythm (Google them).

Dave took half of my money every week for two years, and I never regretted half-a-crown of it. He sold me my first Origin LP – truly a revelation, for the Origin Jazz Library offered the deepest of country blues from the rarest of pre-war 78's by the most singularly obscure artists I'd never heard of.

In 1965, the names Dave was reading to me on the phone rang no bells whatever. 'Okay, this one's got William Moore, Garfield Akers, Tommy Johnson, Henry Sims, Jaybird Coleman...' They were all ciphers to me, but Dave said the album was great and that was good enough, even at 45/6 plus postage.

A week later OJL-8, *Country Blues Encores* arrived. *Stone moi...* I knew right away this was Deep Stuff, and it became one of the three albums you would have to have pried from my cold dead fingers before I gave it up. The black, hard-cardboard sleeve with the paper slick pasted over the front spoke to me of '*Special pressing for inner-sanctum users only. Do not expose to daylight, Vera Lynn fans or random plebs.*' The vintage photos of Ishman Bracey, Big Bill and Jaybird Coleman stared back at me as intently as I stared at them. If I concentrated long enough, I could see them breathing. I really must cut down on smoking the wine gums. All this before we even got to the music.

The music? Ishman Bracey's 'Saturday Blues' had such deliriously complex and subtle rhythms that I simply couldn't help but dance to it. (In private, of course. I do have *some* dignity.) Henry Sims' extraordinarily sweet-and-sour fiddle, the first blues violin I'd ever heard, came as a complete shock to someone who'd grown up listening to Stephane Grappelli. And I am still certain now, as I was then, that he sings:

> *I'm going to Farrell, fuck an' have my fun* (x3)
> *Gon' get me a girl and... fuck and have my fun.*

Fourteen years later I visited Farrell, Mississippi. There was, literally, nothing left except a signpost. Perhaps the one he had his fun under? I took a photograph just in case. I've since lost it.

Jaybird Coleman's 'Man Trouble Blues', accompanied only by his own harmonica, broke out my goose bumps. The sheer power of his voice as he sang *'I'm sooooo worried, don't know what to do'* left me wondering what his experiences could possibly have been to bring such intensity to the microphone. Certainly very different from mine, that's for damn sure.

Tommy Johnson's 'Cool Drink Of Water' offered me an encounter with that falsetto I'd heard Howling Wolf use, although it took my thick brain a while to see the connection. Big Bill's 'House Rent Stomp' got me dancing again. (Was this the same Big Bill I'd heard on Folkways and Storyville? Surely not.) And, however wonderful an example of classic Delta blues Rube Lacy's 'Mississippi Jailhouse Groan' was, it simply could not outshine the sheer romantic majesty of its own title. It told my already overheated imagination everything it wanted to hear in just three words.

The following week I was back on the phone to Dave: 'What else have you got on Origin?'

'Ah, that went down well, did it? Okay, here's one called *The Mississippi Blues.*' Another forty-five bob well spent.

I was still listening to other stuff (the Stones, the Kinks, the Animals, the Pretty Things, the Beach Boys, the Who), I just wasn't buying it. Radio, TV and the record player in the college common room regularly offered me the day's pop music – it was not easy to escape it – and I also became familiar with every passing phase of the 1960's British cultural experience. Indeed, I was occasionally seen as part of it by some of the older generation. Hertford is an ancient town, with narrow streets that wind around in a delightfully unplanned way. Walking one afternoon from College to the Midtown Café, I became absorbed in observing a flurry of Vespas. Several anoraked mods were making a great deal of noise and fuss about getting from Point A to Point B, mostly to display the chrome that adorned the fronts of their vehicles. Clearly intimidated by this undisciplined swaggering and over-indulged thuggery, an old couple crossed the street to put safe distance between themselves and the End of Civilization. In doing so, they landed just a few feet from me, standing innocently in my pea green collarless needlecord jacket, bright yellow open shirt, deep red leather belt, blue jeans and brown suede Cuban-heel boots. I thought I looked cool. I probably resembled the colour scheme of a week-old fruit salad. 'Aaagh! There's another of them!' gasped the husband, pointing at me and putting his arm protectively round his wife. 'No I'm not,' I protested, but to no avail whatever. They fixed me with a how-dare-you-threaten-us-when-we-fought-in-two-wars-and-lost-three-limbs-for-your-kind-pity-we-won-the-Germans-would-know-how-to-take-care-of-the-likes-of-you-get-a-haircut-you-over-financed-layabout-nancy-boy look, and then scurried away. I was left as helplessly outraged as they believed they were.

In May 1965, the inside front cover of *Jazz Journal* featured a full-page advert for an LP called *Conversation With The Blues* on a major label, Decca. This, clearly, was a Very Big Deal. I could never remember anyone shelling out for a whole page in either jazz magazine for a blues record before. It told of the release of field recordings made by Paul Oliver in 1960, issued as a serious documentary with an accompanying booklet; it would present the meaning and function of the blues in a sound-portrait of words and music. I knew intuitively that this would become a major milestone in my personal journey into the music and that I had to have it. I picked up the phone and called Dave Carey.

When it arrived, I opened the package with religious care to be greeted by the stunning colour photo of Butch Cage and Willie Thomas on the front cover. I had NEVER seen a blues photo in colour before. It seemed almost three-dimensional, and I turned the album at angles to ascertain if I could peek beyond the parameters of the frame and see what else was going on. (Those wine gums have gotta stop...) The LP-sized glossy booklet slid fluidly out of the sleeve to greet me. It contained a complete transcript of every word on the album, sung and spoken, and would come to assume an almost Talmud-like importance to me. The deep red label glowed, its pleasure to be in my possession obvious.

I read Paul Oliver's essay on the back sleeve before listening. It seemed appropriate somehow to prime myself for this experience. Lowering the needle into the groove I heard Boogie Woogie Red say *'Well, I'll tell you about the blues...'*

The portrait I had led myself to expect was more fulfilling than I could have possibly imagined. I listened not just to the words and music, but to the ambient noises that are an integral part of any field recording. The raucous background din that accompanied Boogie Woogie Red's rolling piano, the clink of glasses behind Little Brother Montgomery, the clear silence behind J.B. Lenoir, the giggling and good-time-crowd snickering of the crowd around Butch Cage & Willie Thomas, meant us much to me as the music and the message. The cool detachment in Arvella Gray's explanation of his blindness, or Lightnin' Hopkins' tales of the chain gang, or Lil' Son Jackson's gentle timbre as he told of sharecropping, spoke so directly to me that I fancied that I could understand their pain. I couldn't, of course. I was merely made aware of it. The music offered a rich assortment of styles from Texas and Louisiana, Chicago, Detroit and Memphis, painting the portrait it promised with a delicious accuracy. Performances by Roosevelt Sykes, Little Brother Montgomery and especially the deep blue waters of Otis Spann also prodded me toward an interest in piano blues. *Conversation With The Blues* thus became the second album you would have to employ a crowbar to part me from.

A little later I got the accompanying book, filled with extraordinary photos, every one of which I just wanted to step into and be a part of. I looked at them so frequently, sometimes under a magnifying glass, that I memorised every detail in my minds' eye. Whenever I played the album, which was very often, I could just close my eyes and *be there*, feel the sweaty heat of a Delta or Chicago summer, experience the dryness of Texas, the heavy bustle of Detroit's Hastings Street, or the rollicking, good-natured warmth of a Cage & Thomas performance, and then wake up to the aroma of steady rain and a nice pot of fresh tea in a small English market town. I was beginning to live in more than one world.

One of those worlds was the pub, of course, and one of the pub's major activities was darts. Our team played home and away on alternate Tuesday nights, and because the Hertford and District Art Appreciation & Reproduction Société Egalitarian also gathered every Tuesday night and unfailingly repaired to our saloon bar after their weekly attempts at producing a Home Counties Dadaist movement, Tuesday evenings were often deeply interesting when the team was playing a home match. In the public bar, the very serious business of darts, in the 'Half-Crown End', the equally absorbing matter of Art and its relationship to life.

While the Morris brothers, Lou, Gerry, Little Tommy, Old George and the visiting team battled for league points, ego strokes and the top of the beer queue, members of HADAARSE loudly and earnestly discussed Monet, Van Gogh, Dali and Klee. By 10:00 pm the noise was at motorway level – and this from people who spent large chunks of their other time telling errant offspring to 'turn that noise down'. Of course, the two groups never mixed. They probably didn't despise each other, but peer group pressure ensured that they said they did. And so, as Lou or Gerry elbowed and shouldered their way to the beer pumps, they would glance across to a back room filled with 'jumped-up ponces wot talks aht the back o' their wescets'. Lou uttered this mantra as he approached the bar every other Tuesday, without fail. Lou was a member of the 'Dunno Much About Art But I Know Crap When I See It' school. He thought René Magritte was a French detective.

This was fair enough, seeing that Roger the pre-Raphaelite regarded the noble game of darts as a legacy of the Cro-Magnon experience. 'It's just an excuse to chuck a few spears at a target, dear lad,' he'd been overheard lisping to his portable audience one evening. No love lost either side, then.

There was, however, one fateful winter's night when the troops left the trenches to face each other. On a bitter January evening, some ten minutes before they were due to arrive, the away team called from what sounded like the bleakest phone box in all creation to inform us that 'the bleedin' van 'as bleedin' broken down and we're bleedin' stuck out 'ere freezing our bleedin' bollocks off – there's no chance we'll make it, no chance...' The voice faded like a final message from Captain Scott. Disaster stared every Man Jack in the face. What now? Turn it in for the night? Play each other? Watch *Panorama*?

Gerry, never one to cave in when the only option was going home, suggested a frankly outrageous alternative. 'Ask that lot in there if they want a game,' he said, dead-pan. Lou spilled his beer. For some reason old Septimus Teals took out his teeth and looked at them as if checking a weapon. Little Tommy Malone, in genuine class-driven angst, grimaced and clutched his Guinness like a mother would a daughter when the Navy comes to town. But the Morris brothers, young, fit and muscle-bound to the eyebrows leapt upon the idea like campaigning politicians let loose on a fleet of babies. Hitching his trousers and running a comb through his hair, Paul Morris bravely announced that he'd 'go an' 'ave a word'. He disappeared, taking the long route out and round the street rather than via the lavatory. I guess he needed time to compose himself.

While the public bar buzzed with taut excitement, I slid round the curtain of the saloon bar to witness his arrival. English class-sense being what it was, I knew why he'd combed his hair. He'd pushed back the forelock in case he inadvertently tugged at it while putting forward his proposal. For the art crowd, his sudden appearance in their midst meant trouble at t'mill. Why else would this burly pleb present himself? Roger, natural leader that he was, met Paul on behalf of the group There was a quiet exchange of murmurs, then Roger turned and loudly explained the situation to his peers. The visiting team's charabanc had bogged down in the wilds. No-one to play against. Shame to waste the food. Would we care to... Food? Yes. Hot sausages, jacket potatoes and butter, ham rolls. Integral part of the ceremony. Food versus sherry? No contest. Trumps class every time. Within minutes every single living soul had packed themselves into the public bar. Had the old place been a ship, it would surely have turned turtle.

Teams and pecking orders were worked out over the first plateful of sausages. 501 points per game, best of three games or, if the third was to be a tie-breaker, best of five. 'It'll never get that far,' chortled an old prole voice from behind a brown ale. 'This lot wouldn't know a dart if they sat on it.'

Scrawny old Mackeson Ada flipped the coin; Roger called it and won. Gallantly, he offered the home team first shot. 'Ho, I say, 'ow hawfully naice of yew, old bean,' sneered an unshaven Lou, and stepped forward with his trusty arrows, their peacock feather flights bristling with malice. Double top, treble 19 and bullseye. The crowd roared and spilled its beer as he mockingly minced and grinned to the board to recover his darts. Derrick the score-keeper, stupid in every respect save his one God-bestowed gift of idiot savant ability, immediately chalked up the scoreboard with the new total. Now, of course, it was Roger's turn. Except that, with Cromwellian tactics, Roger had chosen Marjorie The Librarian to open for the Art Team. The silence that greeted her appearance at the chalk line was derisory in its completeness. Marjorie was short, grey-haired, left-handed, flat-shoed, adorned with pebble glasses, thick woolly tights and a mobile squint of Tango-esque intensity. She had, until now, been perceived only as the purveyor of tatty romances and greasy-spined detective novels on behalf of the Borough Council. As far as the home team was concerned, Ray Charles stood a better chance of scoring than Marjorie.

By the time the third dart had landed The Boys knew that they might be in trouble. From a throwing position resembling Quasimodo learning to waltz, Marjorie had landed her trinity of flying alloy in triple twenty. It was, of course, a massacre. It didn't have to go to five games, the Art Team had won the first two, but The Boys, howling with injured pride, demanded Best of Five. Marjorie trampled them. Bullseyes and triple-tops landed with sickening regularity. Old George was so unnerved he had to get someone else to roll a cigarette for him.

The final, awful moment of truth arrived, Marjorie stood in front of the board with 71 left. The anxiety was almost visible and hung in the air with the exhaled smoke. Double twenty, eleven and double ten ensured not only a new reputation for Marjorie but for The Boys as well. In the explosion of inflating and deflating egos that followed, Marjorie was hoisted upon arty shoulders and carried in jubilation to the wickedly icy streets, more drunk with success than cider. I saw in that moment that the soul of every English art lover might very well harbour a Sports Hooligan.

'Fink I'll join the library tomorrow,' said Gerry.

Pirate radio had successfully attacked and boarded Britain's stodgy airwaves in 1964, slinging mucky handfuls of current pop at the mainland from ships in the North Sea. Radio Caroline and others gave us the week's releases and the Top 20 which, if essentially unadventurous in format, was at least a bright change from the unstably-glued mix that the Beeb served up on the Light Pogrom, as well as being deliciously illegal. We had a large portable radio in the bar and I often tuned it into Caroline because it went down okay with the punters and I enjoyed it well enough myself. Then, in the spring of 1965, someone told me about Radio 390. It was different, they said; it broadcast not from a ship, but from a disused oil platform. It didn't have a Top 20 format but instead played 'light music' during the day. 'Sounds dreadful,' I replied. 'Ah, but at seven o'clock each night there's a bloke called Mike Raven...'

Mike Raven doing the business, 1966.

Announcing himself as 'The Oldest Living Teenager In Captivity', Mike Raven was indeed different. Every weeknight he took the airwaves by the throat and throttled them with the most extraordinary mix of new and old soul, R&B, rock'n'roll and post-war blues. Through him I became familiar with the latest sounds by James Brown, Joe Tex, Etta James, Wilson Pickett, Aretha Franklin and Otis Redding. More though; he played records by Phil Upchurch, the Soul Sisters, Ike & Tina, Buster Brown and Buddy Guy. In a measured, resonant voice that my mother called 'dark brown', he would dispense detail about each record, what label it was on, what was on the flip. That was Monday to Friday. On Saturday nights he dragged his old inner rocker out and assailed us with original and often desperately obscure 1950's rock. On Sunday nights, however, he played The Blues.

Mike Raven spun an exotic web with every blues record he could lay his hands on. He laid siege to my senses with Muddy, Wolf, Little Walter, Sonny Boy and Elmore; deeper and more obscure he got with Lightnin Slim, Slim Harpo, Freddy King, J.B. Lenoir and Homesick James. Further back he reached, to Tommy McClennan, Memphis Minnie, Washboard Sam and Big Boy Crudup. Further yet to Blind Lemon, Ma Rainey, Charlie Patton and Gus Cannon. He took my ear, inserted a funnel and poured music in through it. I learned more from his Sunday night shows than anything I had yet encountered. He took the time to explain and illustrate the difference

46

between the two Sonny Boy Williamsons; he played the occasional gospel record, ranging from Pearly Brown to the Dixie Hummingbirds. And he gave outrageous free plugs to the cause of The Blues. He exhorted us to subscribe to *Blues Unlimited*, which I immediately did, slightly embarrassed to discover I didn't know about it before.

He acquired and then played several tracks from that rarest of all jewels, a limited edition collectors' album. It was on the Post War Blues label, carried the heroic catalogue number '-1', was called simply *Chicago*, and cost a small fortune. But he had just slammed me up against the living room's green flock wallpaper with a prime selection, Johnny Young's 'Money Taking Woman'. The rest, he said, were at least that good. My postal order was in the mail the next morning. There were only 99 copies available... I had to be quick, or my life would be ruined. Would I be left out in the cold, pointed at and mocked by the 99 lucky Masonic-like inner sanctum members who got there ahead of me? Would I ever smile again? How much is a decent sackcloth and fresh ashes these days?

It arrived, and, with its perfect vision of the first post-war transitional period, immediately became the final element of the vinyl trinity I would gladly stand in front of a firing squad clutching rather than surrender. Mike Raven also, a little later, announced that he had acquired the latest epic release from Post War Blues, an EP called *Hobos And Drifters*. He played 'My Babe' by One String Sam, an itinerant singer recorded in the back room of a Detroit record shop, accompanying himself on a home-made one-string bottleneck guitar. It was the most excitingly archaic sound I'd ever heard, and I was writing the order as he announced: 'For 19/6 you can get this EP from Mike Rowe, 8 Brandram Road...'

Mike Rowe went on to produce a further four LPs on Post War Blues, a label which, while modest in output, defined the essence of what we then termed 'downhome blues' and remains the classic capsule view of the prime post-war blues era. I would emerge from our living room at about 8:00 pm each Sunday night clutching a pad full of desperately scrawled notes and wearing the face of one who had just been slapped silly with a fresh haddock. Thanks, Mike; and thanks, Mike.

My first girlfriend erupted in front of me at a college dance on a spring evening of my sixteenth year; I had gone to offer support to the local rhythm and blues band, a scruffy aggregation of Stones-clone oiks who specialised in 37-minute versions of Chess tunes and called themselves the R-B-Q, an acronym for 'Rhythm and Blues Quintet'. Her name was Sue and she was, frankly, a very odd duck. Apparently glued into an oversize black plastic coat that she wore no matter what the temperature, she looked older than she was and acted like her planet was in for service and she was just borrowing ours for the duration. She rode a moped and commuted ten miles to and from college every day. Since I had no visible means of transport and hers was a single-seater, this limited our relationship to the confines of Hertford. We had our first date in the creaky old tea rooms that were already an anachronism by 1965. 'Our little nook, I will call it,' she said, unnervingly, of the bright, high-ceilinged old glasshouse as the 87 year old waitress tottered off in search of her spare set of teeth, leaving the table groaning with gallons of tea and several pounds of leaden cake. We didn't last long as a couple, perhaps a month; but I had had a girlfriend, even if all my friends declared her odder than a pink rugby ball in a tennis match.

Bereft of a working speedometer, lights or windshield, untaxed and rusting in worrying quantities, our College scooter was both a useful mode of transport and a dangerous statement of our collective rebellion. Found abandoned in the street, it had been dragged back from its fate and tinkered with unmercifully until it at last relented and kicked back into a coughing, rattling life. It was a standard Vespa – the kind mods rode – but stripped to a level that would have made a Spartan feel uncomfortable. It immediately became common property and was probably the single greatest contribution to unreported traffic violations the town had ever experienced. Even if anyone had been rash enough to want to tax and insure it, we could never have afforded the fees. Roger Blanton remarked that he found it taxing enough just riding pillion and saw no reason to pay for the privilege, a sentiment whose bandwagon we all readily climbed on. At least half those who regularly piloted this social menace had no licence to do so. The other half held provisional licences with vintages of sometimes six months or more. Since the machine was almost never seen without a pillion passenger, this second group of operators was perhaps even more guilty than the first. None of us set out to actually *break* the law, we just never thought about the law at all. With the arrogant logic of youth we simply saw the college scooter as an interesting and exciting way of solving a few problems. For the next several months this astonishingly robust machine carted students, equipment, books, food, fags, records and other necessities about the town. We clamped a rubber-belled claxon on the handlebars to announce our arrival, singularly unnecessary since the death-rattle of the two-stroke engine could be heard streets away.

The Vespa survived the occasional spin-out with a hardy grace. Having recently read the life story of Jack 'Legs' Diamond, the gangster who believed he couldn't be killed, I became convinced that his spiritual hand guided and protected our precious machine. I deeply admired its ability to withstand the bewildering variety of abuses it received and it became my totem for survival in a hostile world. Twit thoughts of this nature were apparently common in people my age, so I didn't worry too much about it. Inevitably, fate's patience was goaded once too often. Rounding the corner of a hill, Ian Eddington sliced across the wrong side of the road and found himself suddenly practicing the Palais Glide across the roof of a Hillman Minx. His ungainly return to the tarmac snapped his left leg in two places. He was hospitalised for weeks. We visited him bearing gifts of shrivelled grapes, a lone sock and a pogo stick. The police cleared away the remains of our precious Vespa and, strangely, nobody ever heard another word about either the accident or the fate of our beloved two stroke. Perhaps the rozzers were relieved that the town had survived the tyranny of its brief two-stroke life.

As the pillion passenger in that accident, I got away with no more than a few bum bruises when I fell off the back. However, the experience convinced me that four wheels were better than two and so, on the day of my sixteenth birthday, I presented myself at County Hall with a fresh ten-bob note to acquire my provisional driving licence. Thirty minutes later, little red cloth book in hand, I emerged glowing with pride and expectancy. I was about to be a driver!

My father, a courageous man, had promised to give me lessons. In those days you could still do that, you didn't have to squander money at a driving school; it was better saved for the body repair shop and the Aspirin. So, that afternoon he and I climbed into the Ford Consul and drove out to a quiet back road. He pulled up and we both got out to change positions.

'Now,' he remarked with the tone of one who knew the afternoon could be stressful, 'before you even put the key in the ignition, you must learn Rule One.'

'Which is?' I enquired, expecting to be enlightened by some deep life-altering secret revealed only now from Father to Son in the sanctity of the family vehicle; one which I would, in time, need to pass on to my own precious but as yet unconceived offsprog.

'*EVERYBODY* else on the road is a complete bleedin' idiot, and likely to do something fucking daft at any minute. Got that? Now, adjust your mirror.'

We set off. Or rather, we didn't, as I stalled the engine immediately. The Consul had a three-speed gear box with the lever mounted on the steering column. You really only needed first gear to get rolling in, then you could drop it into second and stay there at any speed from 10 to about 35 mph before slipping into top. If you knew what you were doing, that is, which clearly I didn't.

'You need to get your feet to the point of balance between accelerator and clutch, that's when you start to...' *THUD CLONK DONG DAFT ONOMATAPOETIC WORD OF YOUR CHOICE* '...move. Ah... Let's try that again shall we?'

Eventually I got it, and had the car moving at a buttock-clenching speed of 30 mph. 'Right,' said Dad, lighting one cigarette just before the other had finished, 'now we'll go on the dual carriageway.' I remember the butterflies in my stomach suddenly turning very nasty and arguing with each other about who was going to die first. Sweat broke out like a prison riot. I pulled onto the A41 with white knuckles, red face and slightly brown Y-fronts. Then I began to enjoy it, and in the weeks that followed even improved. But I wouldn't take my test for another year or more. Too much other stuff got in the way.

The big thing looming on my horizon was the 1965 *American Folk Blues Festival*. Painfully aware that I had already missed three of them, I was determined to see this one and so, on a week in September, sent my money, for once, not to Dave Carey ('What the hell are we going to do for food this week?' I could hear Mrs. Carey wailing), but to the Fairfield Halls in Croydon. I had, in fact, organised a charabanc outing at college, drumming up enough interest and money to buy six tickets and hire a minibus with driver. That's how keen I was to get there. I also had a hidden agenda; one of the people I had talked into going was the beautiful Gemma, who wandered through my dreams on a regular basis creating absolute bloody havoc with my hormonal system.

The journey to Croydon was uneventful unless you were riding inside my head. I was as intoxicated by the coming event as I was by Gemma's legs to my left. The driver called out landmarks as we progressed: 'Seven Sisters Road.' I looked out the window but saw only legs and blues singers. The Fairfield Halls were impressive. Relatively new, they gleamed and blinked at us in the clear night air as we rounded them in search of the car park. They spoke not only of hope for the future, of a new enlightenment that would obviate the need for war, of music, dance, literature, of all human artistic endeavour, but also of hot dogs at 1/9 a throw and ice creams at half-a-crown. Art was clearly an expensive pursuit. I spent my money on a programme instead, adorned with pin-sharp monochrome photos and features on the blues singers I was about to see and hear. It was large, glossy and extraordinarily exciting. So were Gemma's legs. I was about to experience my first live blues; not in a noisy, smoke-filled juke joint, jostled on a beer-slickened floor by drunks, straining to hear the music above the boisterous mo-fo yelling, but in the quiet, reverent comfort of a cool English auditorium, seated on a red plush fold-down seat, surrounded by quiet, reverent, comfortable people who would go home, like I would, to a house full of solid furniture and good china. Except, of course, for the few bohemian types who chose to freeze in an empty garret and consume only lentils because they had elected to lead an Alternative Lifestyle.

First on stage that night, and therefore the first blues singer I ever saw live, was J.B. Lenoir. He sat on a centre-stage chair, pulled his acoustic guitar across his lap and, in the complete silence that he was about to break, smiled into the darkness he was facing. Then, with head bowed over guitar, he began to sing:

> *I never will go back to Alabama, that is not the place for me,*
> *You know they killed my sister and my brother,*
> *And the whole world let them peoples down there go free.*

and

> *My brother was taken up from my mother*
> *   and the police officer shot him down.*

The song was 'Alabama Blues', and it was deeply socio-political. We, the audience, in the spirit of the times, were enthralled by this. I witnessed his performance in the deepest, most vivid colours I could ever remember, the spotlight clarifying every detail. I could see light bounce off his face and the body of his guitar, the machine-head of which threw glittering silver starbursts at me. The sound that reached my ears was an ecstatically received mix of hard, stinging guitar notes and soft, mellow vocal tones delivering a message that, in the grip of sympathetic Civil Rights observation, we found intoxicatingly righteous. That it was not the blues you would have heard him play in Chicago; that it was the blues he had fashioned, in collaboration with bassist-songwriter-entrepreneur Willie Dixon, to bring to Europe, were facts most of us were simply too enthralled and naïve to know. Like Big Bill a generation before him, he was tailoring his art to a new audience, one that Willie Dixon already knew well.

I sat in the dark and absorbed it all. The ebullient Roosevelt Sykes, whose '44 Blues' I had already encountered aurally; the enormously likeable Doctor Ross, whose incredible rhythmic cohesion as a one-man band completely outclassed that twit in the Charing Cross Road who played to the queuing theatre audiences; Big Mama Thornton and Walter Horton (he was scared witless of her – and with good reason) duetting on harmonica.

And Fred McDowell, who came on stage with a broad smile, announced that he was glad to be here and that he did not play 'no rock and roll', then immediately proved himself wrong. He was, without doubt, the most propulsive, rhythmic, driving guitarist I'd ever heard. His electrifying 'Shake 'em On Down' was performed with the skill of a man completely comfortable driving downhill at speed with the brakes gone. Inside of a week I would be clutching his first Arhoolie album ('Thank the Lord, he's back!' – Mrs. Carey). The show was closed by Buddy Guy, who pulled a stunt that I had never seen before. So amped-up was his guitar that he could play phrases by simply fretting; for several bars of a solo he didn't use his right hand at all. Another small milestone of amazement for this lad.

It was all very, very overwhelming and also very, very welcome. I had connected with the blues in a new and real sense and it was more than I could have hoped for. This, I knew now, would be a lifetime's journey. J.B. Lenoir and Fred McDowell bounced through my head all the way home. In the dark comfort of the minibus's back seat Gemma and I shared a warm, timid kiss. But the legs were strictly off limits. The minibus driver, a 50-something Hertford Old Boy, had joined us in the auditorium, accepting the offer of the free ticket caused by a last minute no-show. It was warmer than sitting in the vehicle for three hours. As I climbed out of the van around midnight I asked him what he thought of the evening. Through a cloud of exhaled Old Holborn smoke, he simply said: 'I prefer Max Jaffa meself.'

The immediate effect of this near-religious experience in Croydon was my decision to widen my record-buying habits. I had bought largely pre-war blues in the previous year, with which I had no problem, but I felt I should take a wider view. I was still missing a lot of essential post-war blues, as well as a great deal of contemporary stuff. I therefore divided the blues chronology into three overlapping time zones and drew up plans to buy one album from each zone on a rota basis. Clearly, I needed a decent enema. What I got instead was Snooks Eaglin.

He arrived without warning in a mysterious package addressed to me from Sarasota, Florida. It had been sent by my aunt, a 1946 war bride from my mother's side, in response to a mention of my new enthusiasms in a letter from my mother. My aunt had, astonishingly, gone to a record shop somewhere in the area, explained that her callow little nephew back in England was listening to the blues in between extended bouts of bowler-hatted tea drinking at fog-bound royal cricket matches, and someone had had enough savvy to lay the Snooks Eaglin Folkways album on her. I couldn't have been more surprised if you'd told me that Burt Lancaster was a transvestite. (He was, as it turned out, but I digress.) The album captivated me. Recorded in a flat, stark, almost claustrophobic ambience, Snooks' clear tone and resonant guitar painted for me pictures of the life of the blind street singer that the notes suggested he was.

I imagined him living in heroically grinding poverty, a will-o'-the-wisp character who would appear, disappear and reappear without pattern, drawing deeper and deeper insights from his experiences and embroidering the soul of his eclectic songbook with the barbed thread of them. He surely carried a knife in his sock, drank moonshine, absorbed bullets without wincing, spat blood into his coffee for added taste and was searched for, *sans* success, by the police, heavily-armed husbands and God herself. He avoided them all with his devil-endowed ESP, and this rare snapshot evidence of his existence was nothing short of miraculous. All complete bollocks, of course. By the time I heard him, he had already had a career as an R&B singer on Imperial, and was the author of Little Richard's 'Lucille', but I didn't know that, and it helped keep my fevered imagination off the streets.

Kick-started by this event, I began the attempt to build a 'serious, balanced collection' as I explained to my peers. 'Seriously fuckin' unbalanced if you ask me,' retorted Roger Blanton. He illustrated this by placing two cigarettes in his mouth, clutching an LP to his breast and lying on the floor. 'This is how you'll die, Vernon', he said. For some years I believed him, but it didn't stop me.

I wrote an execrable article on the history of the blues for the college magazine – one which I mention now only after checking that no archive copies have survived. It told of the heroic endeavours of the oppressed blues singer who could only now emerge into the daylight, after years of struggle, because his European fans recognised and supported a truth that White America had a vested interest in closeting away from the world. Something along those lines. My excuse for this arrant nonsense? I was sixteen-and-a-half and still a virgin. Nobody, however, challenged it. The bland leading the blind.

Lunchtime trade in the pub was fairly predictable. The claustrophobic back bar, transformed to the best of our ability into a somewhat claustrophobic dining area, was full of the usual suspects. Old Hannanswaffer, as we called him, the gardening and cinema critic of the local paper, was busy flirting with the Misses Smithers, a pair of genteel 60-something spinster sisters who drove twenty miles in an ageing Morris Minor each day to take lunch and peer at the world from behind the safety of steak and kidney pudding. Police Sergeant Harrison was making a serious study of the consumption of my mother's home-made soup, producing a revolting chorus of sloppy noises that ensured him a table to himself. In the public bar, Septimus Teals had taken his God-bestowed fireside armchair for the duration, and was indulging in the twin habits I had come to accept if not love; rolling his loose false teeth around in saliva after each swill, and then dunking his hand rolled cigarette in the trough of beer that remained between gums and inner lips. Bernie the bus driver, fish-eyed and Brilliantined, was staring intently through the golden sea of India Pale Ale I'd drawn for him and mumbling the usual obscenities about what he'd do to any sixteen year old virgin who was lucky enough to cross the path of his throbbing and clearly underused organ. It was a normal Wednesday lunchtime.

In a town like Hertford visitors were obvious. Accepted so long as their wallet didn't outstay its welcome by becoming empty, they were nevertheless objects of curiosity and a strange, benign animosity that manifested itself in off-hand comments between partisan locals. This particular Wednesday's lamb to local slaughter was a travelling salesman with a company car and, so far as the Old Boys were concerned, way too much money for his own good and possessed of – or by - a moral corruptness that they could only guess at and then embroider at length following his departure.

Devil-may-care roadmen of this stature enjoy displaying titbits of their high-and-wide lifestyles in ways that are at once childishly unsubtle and gallingly attractive. This mid-week specimen was not about to let his team down. He ordered a Dewar's with a Barley Wine chaser. This combination of classic Scotch and small strong ale was known locally as the 'wee yellow man with a small heavy', largely due to Old Jock's influence. The brewery had informed us, in terms of great clarity, that it would be unwise to serve more than three Barley Wines to one person at any one sitting, as the alcoholic content was disarmingly powerful. Roadmen, however, brush such advice to one side, convinced of their ability to handle anything that comes their way in greater quantities than the mere sedentary peasants with whom they are forced to rub shoulders.

In the course of the next hour this kipper-tied man of the world took his three small heavies, lined his stomach with a chicken sandwich and ostentatiously dipped his 1/9 Castella cigar into the beer the way he would dunk a Cuban into a vintage brandy at the company dinner. Eyes traced him from every angle. Darts and dominoes fell short of their mark as the players watched discreetly from behind the safety of numbers they knew they were a part of.

At five to two Kipper Tie ordered his fourth Barley Wine. I knew that as a callow youth I could hardly refuse him, for to do so would be to invite the angry ridicule that I had painfully learned lay close to the surface of such people. I gave in to the situation by calling my father from the saloon bar, explaining the situation as I saw it, and asking him to take over. The argument that ensued covered such basic topics as parenthood and its specific origins as applied to my father, the size of the testicles of every man in the bar save the offended, the age of the meat in the long consumed sandwich and the general condition of the bathroom facilities. (What facilities? It was a *wall!*)

'I'll tell you something else, too, you bloody old fart,' he seethed, rising up from his stool, 'you can poke your empties up your bum and shit in 'em!' He strode manfully towards the inner door. Pausing for a moment, he gripped the handle and turned his head, twisting his lips to add zest to his final remark: 'I'm known – KNOWN, mark you – in my trade as a man who can hold his drink in any situation. Good day to you, peasants!'

The door swung open under his powerful grip, bringing with it the cold November air. The naked temperature attacked his senses immediately. His initial gentle swaying seemed to suggest an impromptu impersonation of the Eiffel Tower in a high wind. Raising a hand in attempted further admonition, I saw his glazed eye drawn inexorably towards the tip of his finger. The moment hung in the air as if it expected to be absorbed into local folklore and then, as we knew it must, the finale arrived. Like a building demolished by an explosive expert, he collapsed from the ground up. Ankles, calves, knees and hips gave way, drawing him to a gravitational conclusion that both he and we knew to be inescapable. Silently and swiftly his line of vision plummeted. I could see clearly he was attempting to tell us something but those final remarks remained unsaid as his head hit the floor. We checked him for blood, scooped him up, loaded him into his car and closed the door. At 5:30 that evening, when we reopened, he was still sleeping soundly in the car park.

Christmas 1965 contained a wonderful surprise. My major gift turned out to be a first edition copy of Godrich & Dixon's *Blues & Gospel Records 1902-42*, the standard pre-war blues and gospel discography. I had lusted after it for months, to be told it was out of print. My father had gone to the extraordinary lengths of visiting the printer, Steve Lane, and buying almost the last, slightly damaged, copy directly from him. Suddenly, I was the bibliophile confronted with Caxton's first edition. I couldn't believe it. I threw myself into exploration, to be exposed not only to more information about what little I already knew, but also to the vast amounts that I didn't. I stared at names that meant both nothing and everything to me. Who was

Black Spider Dumpling? Freezone? Big Road Webster Taylor? Henry Spaulding? Jim Thompkins? Tommy Cooper? (I knew the answer to *that* one!)

I continued buying, listening, reading, turning the pages of *Blues & Gospel Records* and thinking overblown thoughts. I also began scribbling letters to people. I wrote to Derrick Stewart-Baxter with a dozen or more daft-sod questions that never garnered a reply. I don't blame him in the slightest, I must have come across as a complete nutter. I approached Simon Napier at *Blues Unlimited* with offers to review LPs for him. He replied by postcard saying: *'Thanks, I'll put you in the book.'* I think he was being kind. I never received anything.

I also wrote to Bill Givens at Origin, enthusing generally about his record label and how much pleasure it had given me and asking what his future plans might include. To my astonishment he replied, thanking me for investing in his brainchildren, exhorting me to continue and telling me about the new releases. He also included a catalogue. Spurred by this event, I called Dave Carey with a simple question it had never occurred to me to ask before: 'Got any catalogues?' They arrived the following week, a dozen or more of them, for labels like Piedmont, 77, Vulcan, Delmark, Takoma, and, most precious of all, Arhoolie. I spent hours poring over these enticing documents, absorbing every detail. I kept them in a special folder so that they would remain unsullied by life's dust bunnies. I vowed to add to them as frequently as possible. Already armed with *BGR* as a weapon, the budding discographer that resided deep inside me starting knocking hard to be let out. He lived right next door to the budding anal retentive and they exchanged sympathetic views often.

It never occurred to me that Easter Sunday 1966 was the 50th anniversary of the Irish uprising, but it had occurred to Bernard O'Shea. Bernard viewed the world through dung-coloured spectacles, this having at least as much to do with his own specific private demons, rather than just the downtroddenness he felt living as an Irishman in England. The general consensus, one shared even by Brothers Of The Old Sod Tommy Malone and John Dempsey, was that the O'Shea view of any topic was likely to be at least negative, probably also reactionary, and often just plain bitter.

That Easter Sunday night the bar filled up for what everyone expected to be a night of family entertainment: Drinking, Dominoes and Darts – or 'the old 3-D effect' as Jerry put it. Bernard sat sullenly at the bar, peering out from behind the prejudice that cloaked him like a coat of matted hair, and swilling light and bitter in between muttering increasingly dark epithets to himself. My father spotted the potential for havoc as early as 8:00 pm, when the invariably tightfisted Bernard dropped three half-crowns into the charity whisky bottle that sat on the counter.

'There could be trouble tonight,' Dad warned me from the corner of his mouth.

'Why?' I asked.

'Bernard just put 7/6 in the bottle. Conscience money.'

His fears proved correct. At about 10:00 pm, in a sudden and calculated move, Bernard picked up a full beer glass and hurled the contents at Paul Morris. Little Tommy's anguished cry, 'Hey! That's MY bloody Guinness,' arrived at almost the same second Paul Morris felt its impact on his duck-tailed hair style. For a few seconds everything in the bar – movement, chatter, music and drinking – ceased. Paul stood frozen, a dart poised ready to throw at the board, his eyes open wide in amazement, his two large and dangerous brothers equally startled if less damp and sticky. The air hung heavy with the imminence of retribution; then, as we knew it must, simultaneous reaction exploded throughout the bar.

Without waiting for detailed explanation, the Morris brothers launched their counter-attack, not only on Bernard but also upon the unfortunate Tommy Malone and John Dempsey. All reason had vanished. Old battle lines, long drawn and slowly seeping with pustulent prejudice, suddenly burst like boils. Someone – I never knew who – shouted: 'The fight's on!'

A barstool rolled across the domino table, scattering the worn black ivory like an explosion in an upright piano. Dad grabbed the phone and called the police. I ducked down behind the bar and moved, guerilla-like, I imagined, under the bar-flap for protection. It took only a few seconds to realise that, while this was safer than standing bolt upright, I was nevertheless unacceptably missing the biggest fight I'd ever encountered. Peering back up again, I felt the down draft from an empty Mackeson bottle as it sailed past my neck and fell behind the bar spinning across the lino. Now off the phone and moving fast, my father called me sharply: 'Outside, quick, through the side door!' I tried to reach it, but a couple of overweight inebriates barred my way as they ineptly wrestled one another into a chair and from there to the floor, where they lay sideways, locked in one another's limbs, screaming 'FUCKYOUYOU'REAFUCKIN'FUCKYOUFUCKIN'FUCKYOU FUCKIN'ENGLISHPIGAHFUCKYERSELFYOUFUCKIN'FUCK!!!' at a distance close enough to exchange saliva. I turned and looked down past the bar to a seething mass of frantically battling bodies. Irish skulls were meeting English fists; genitals from Hertfordshire were being introduced to knees from Cork.

Most worrying of all, the fearsome Morris Wives were up and moving, armed with Size 5 Freeman Hardy & Willis stilettos in their manicured hands. 'I'LL TEACH YOU TO 'IT MY BLEEDIN' OLD MAN!' screamed Linda Morris, as a three-inch heel landed in a Celtic hairline with the gut-churning squidge that I knew meant real blood. The fracas spilled out into the porchway and from there to the street. A young and probably innocent Irishman arrived on the pavement through the left window, bringing shards of glass and wood with him. As he lay on his back an unreasoning mind brought an unfeeling boot down on his throat. His eyes bulged with pain and shock, the noise he made was a blend of scream, obscenity and cough. His head bounced on the cement and he passed into oblivion.

Meanwhile Bernard had been pinned against the old iron drainpipe that ran down the front of the building. Paul Morris had a massive hand on his victim's shoulder and with his free fist was aiming for Bernard's head. Somehow Bernard managed to twist his head and dodge the blow. Now woefully off-course but moving too fast to stop, Paul's clenched fist hit the pipe, cracking it open. 'OOWWWWSHIIIIITTT!' he screamed, plunging the fist between his knees for comfort. Released, Bernard vanished into the night. The police arrived too late to do anything but take notes and climb back into their Land Rover. Later, I swept up the debris into a surprisingly large pile and found, upon inspection, that it contained not only glass, beer, fag ends and ash but also two metal combs, several clumps of hair and a set of false teeth. They sat on the counter in a jar for a week, but nobody claimed them

---

Other music still drifted past me. Bob Dylan was a college favourite, the common-room record player often contentedly chewing away at his first and second albums. While I admired his dedication and noted his distinct lack of any threat to the advancement of harmonica playing, I pointed out to those who would listen that he was clearly influenced by the blues, and I could demonstrate this effectively by playing some originals that he had copied. 'Who wants to hear Dylan when I can play you Bukka White?' I would ask. I became famous for my ability to clear the common room faster than anyone except Sulphur Monty the Silent Farter.

A large, bespectacled youth with the body of a wrestler, Monty acquired his long soubriquet through the singular habit of chewing sulphur tablets and, having digested them, quietly letting one go in the canteen or common room, or at the back of the class. People vacated territory when they saw him coming. 'It gives you plenty of elbow room,' he remarked.

Monty also played the role of a degenerate vicar during College rag week, spending all his time in a grubby suit and yellowed dog collar with an unlit cigarette hanging from the corner of his mouth and a copy of *True Confessions* rolled into his jacket pocket. We all adopted a persona for that week; Mark Truman spent the seven days in a mini dress, tights, boots, wig and sunglasses, and had to be talked back out of them on the final day. I dressed up as a decrepit old man, with bowler hat, long coat, walking cane and moustache, tottering about the town demanding charity donations in a Henry Crun voice. We all partook in the Saturday afternoon parade through the high street, airing our alter egos. Some of the stiffer members of the community objected to all this tomfoolery, but we pointed out that it was in aid of cancer research.

'I hope you bloody well *get* it, then,' snorted one outraged old fool.

Bus inspectors, like foremen and senior clerks, stand awkwardly between the working masses and the management. Consequently they are hated by the former and viewed with suspicion by the latter. They earn enough money to sit in the saloon bar but cannot talk to the people who surround them. Many turn to workaholism for comfort. Such a man was Bert. Despised by bus driver Bernie and his colleagues for being a 'jumped up Nazi arselicker' – and that, on a good day – he sat alone among a small lumber yard of pencils making notations on carefully preserved timetables.

Bert's life also ran according to a timetable at least as strict as the ones he was paid to oversee. I amused myself imagining him sitting on the loo in the morning, stopwatch in hand. I envisioned him spending his day off mapping out the coming week on a wall chart, details from which would be carefully copied into a waterproof notebook and then cross-referenced to a desk diary for posterity.

Every working day, at midday precisely, just as the last noon pip emerged from the Light Programme time signal, Bert would appear at the door in his shapeless raincoat and matching smile; sitting in his chosen and unvarying seat he would exercise his eyebrow communication skills by feverishly waggling them as the signal of his arrival.

'India Pale Ale, Bert?' I'd enquire, pouring one as I spoke.

'Oh, I think so,' he'd reply, as though ordering a rare wine. 'And could I see the menu please?' he would add, handing me the correct amount for both the drink and the meal. Bert knew that being first regularly meant both very fast service and the freshest meal of the day. He liked chicken and, whichever way we offered it, he would 'plump for poultry, ha-ha'. What a twerp. Watching Bert eat could be a distressing experience for the unprepared. Loud, juicy gulps orchestrated by the squelch of open mouthed mastication ensured him a wide reputation if few close personal friends.

On a bitterly cold lunchtime Bert arrived to play his part in the daily theatre. Plumping for poultry, as we knew he would, he got his dinner within two minutes of ordering. We had it ready dished up and sitting in the oven for him. I set it before him and moved swiftly back behind the bar to put a safe distance between my appetite and his ability to ruin it. I was re-tuning the radio when tragedy suddenly arrived. A loud, dull and disturbingly short gloop of a noise, akin to a knot of cold porridge landing in an empty bath, caught my attention. I turned to follow it and found the trail littered with increasingly frantic messages that Something In The Dining Room Was Amiss. Sitting – but only just – at Table 2 was a saucer-eyed bus inspector clearly demonstrating the habits of the domestic goldfish. The constricted 'O' of his mouth bubbled noiselessly. Semaphore arms spelled out alarmingly confused signals for help. The Adam's apple ran up and down the throat in a glissando of pain. Bert had swallowed a chicken bone.

'Are you all right?' I lamely enquired.

'Augh, eck yk grp phrt.' Wet chicken dribbled from the corner of his mouth.

'Okay, don't panic, that's my job. What do you need?'

He waved in the general direction of his back like a man with a broken arm. At that time I would have said, if asked, that Heimlich Manoeuvre was a Panzer Tank commander and so, taking Bert at his unspoken word, smacked him heavily on the back between his shoulders. Half a wet Brussels sprout rolled over his teeth, out and down the inside of his coat. His leg jerked involuntarily and caught the table leg, spilling his beer. India Pale Ale from the toppled glass floated gently in his mashed potato and bubbled lightly in the gravy. Bert swallowed hard, sweat beads married themselves to the Brylcreem slick that hovered above his hairline. In a sudden and surprising move, a cough that had travelled from his inner defence mechanisms arrived at his mouth, carrying the errant bone in its wake. A sound similar to a dropped pin being detected heralded its arrival on the lino. Napkins of solace were offered.

'My fault entirely,' he gasped gratefully, catching his first post-bone breath. 'Not looking what I was doing, see?'

He had soup the next day.

———————————

In the late summer of 1966, my parents received a disturbing phone call from their accountant. Our shop in London, under management since we had been in Hertford, was losing money fast. He suspected that the manager was siphoning funds, since the takings were good and the overheads were all accounted for. He further suspected that as much as two thousand pounds was missing, a calamitously vast sum for the time. We had to do something fast or re-enactments of the *Titanic* were going to occur. In short, we needed to abandon our career as publicans, fire the shop manager and move back to London to rescue the business. I would have to leave college and come into the family business right away if we were going to survive. I never gave it a second thought. We left Hertford on 24 September 1966, two years to the day from our arrival. I saw in this tidy coincidence a clear message that a new, glittering and pre-ordained chapter of life was about to begin. I was three months past my seventeenth birthday and riding heroically back to the old homeland to rescue the family fortune and honour. What a twerp! I was also bringing over 150 records with me.

Chapter Three

1966-68: FORTUNATE YOUNG SOD

To cut a long and bloody story short, we got back to London, confronted the guilty manager, advised him to sod off while he was still ambulatory, moved back into the flat above the shop and set about rescuing the situation. Running a business that opens for 90 hours a week requires a rota system, of which I immediately became a part. I was now working full time, including alternating the early morning duties with Dad. Newsagents are perhaps at their busiest in the very early morning. Up at 5:00 am therefore, I would quickly brew up, ablute, dress and tumble down the stairs clutching my half-gallon tea mug. The task immediately at hand was to heave into the shop the hundredweight or so of newspapers and magazines that had been delivered by the wholesaler's van around 4:00 am. They sat in the closed doorway in great bundles, tied with rough string, and often fell inwards as I unlocked the door. I would then prepare large quantities of newsprint for home delivery by a small army of yawning teenage boys. They earned about 35/- a week, and there was always a waiting list of hopefuls ready to take the place of any poor soul who might drop dead one morning halfway through his duties.

This hell-for-leather process included serving the few who picked their way through the pre-dawn mayhem. Those early birds, mostly regulars, knew the score and `kept their requests to a predictable minimum. 'Mornin' guv, *Daily Mirror*, 'alf ounce o' Boars Head, packet of Throaties,' growled old Dan, a night watchman, weaving home from his duties protecting the Handley Page factory from midnight wide boys. It was assembled before he had finished speaking; he had the same request every morning. '*Daily Telegraph* and twenty Players,' snapped a military voice from inside the folded crevices of a matching face. 'Pay you tonight.' We knew he would, because he always did. Soon after 6:30 am, with the papers all distributed, the foot traffic picked up as the long procession of workaday folk began their daily grind. Machine oil-scented factory workers, manically cheerful bus crews changing shifts, talkative cab drivers with new jokes, small children on emergency errands from harried kitchens, bright young shop and office girls in tightly chattering groups that left a trail of blended perfume, worn down cleaning ladies, tautly-wired middle managers with bristling moustaches and

My dad outside the power base of the family empire –
the Cricklewood Lane shop – c. 1967.

attitudes, harassed mothers trailing demanding children; they all passed
through the shop every morning for the same things: The *Daily Mail* and
twenty Embassy Filters. Two Mars Bars. A tin of Wilson's Snuff and the
Daily Sketch.

There was a trust that the community placed in itself, and we, as
shopkeepers, were an integral part of that system. We could be relied upon to
always be there, always supply what people expected of us at the expected
price and, in turn, they could be trusted with short-term, often unbooked,
credit if they needed it. Not so much because they didn't have the money, but
simply because they didn't have the time. 'Pay you later', called on the run
towards a bus, or a screaming child, or a double parked car meant an hour, or
that afternoon, not a month. It was a cash business, credit cards simply did
not exist, a cheque was a rarity accepted only by prior arrangement for
amounts above a fiver, and the people who had their papers delivered paid
their bills weekly. There were a few abuses of these simple rules, but nothing
like enough to undermine the system. Our comrades-in-arms, the other
traders who flanked and faced us, did much the same thing. The Hoffs,
1930's Jewish refugees, who lived and worked next door in their crowded and
cosy little drapery and sewing shop; Stella, the strong and striking middle age
single mum who owned the café-greengrocers-and-boarding house empire
two doors down; Pinky John the butcher, named for the finger he lost to a
meat cleaver; Tony Papandreou, the Greek grocer and his family, all held
much the same philosophy. It simply made sense for the times.

The ethnic mix in Cricklewood at that time was roughly divided into
four quarters. There were the old Cricklewood types: English working class,

non-practising C of E, been here for years, done the Depression and the Blitz, survived it all. Life goes on. Know this place like the back o' me hand. What's on telly tonight?

Then there was a group of upper middle class types, mostly – but not exclusively – Jewish, who lived in the 'better' houses that curled in broad, calm loops behind the main street leading towards the sports grounds. He went off to business, she looked after the house. This was our post-10:00 am clientele for top-shelf cigarettes, glossy fashion magazines and the hand-made chocolates in the glass case that my mother took such pride in displaying. We called them 'Mrs. Weisfeldt' and 'Mrs. Rappaport', not 'Ethel' or 'Flo' as we did others. Ethel, permanently head-scarfed and war-weary from her cleaning job would rummage in her ancient hand bag looking for the right change for ten Woodbines while muttering mantras like 'Such is life without a wife' that I guess made sense to her.

The Irish were all Southern and Catholic. They came and went every day like all others, but every Sunday morning, on the hour from 8 to 12, they filled the church that sat only three hundred yards from our door. As each mass ended, they poured out through the church doors and directly into our shop. We knew exactly when each wave was due and positioned ourselves in readiness. It was too fast a pace to use the mechanical cash register, so we cleared a space on the counter, tossed thirty shillings worth of loose change down as a float and two of us, often Father and Son, would work directly from the money pile, making fast mental calculations, as people picked up and waved Sunday papers, magazines, sweets and soft drinks at us while requesting their choice of cigarettes from the several hundred brands stacked like battle-ready troops behind us. We were patronised not just because we were local but also because we stocked Irish cigarettes – Carroll's No.1 and Sweet Afton – and because we carried Irish newspapers and magazines. In the pre-decimal days when a Sunday newspaper cost 6d and a decent packet of cigarettes was 3/6, we could often take over £40 in a five-minute flurry of activity.

Then there were the newer immigrants. This was a broadly Caribbean community, the bulk of whom had arrived in the late 1940's and, especially, the early 1950's, in response to a somewhat underhanded British government campaign to work in the Mother Country for at least five times the salary they were used to earning on the islands. What the government failed to explain fully was that it also cost at least five times as much to *live* in the Mother Country. You also got rained on a lot more. Nevertheless, the first wave of Jamaicans who populated the two up, two down houses that stretched along the opposite side of the street from us were a good crowd – open, friendly and talkative. They were nurses, garage mechanics, drivers, house cleaners, bus crews and railway workers. They were also very good customers – a point made by my father when, having stopped an irate racist in mid-rant one morning and told him to bugger off, turned to the staff and said: 'The only colour that matters in this shop is the colour of your money.'

He also implicitly made the point to me that working for yourself meant not having to suffer fools, a philosophy I carried with me into later years.

There were smatterings of other folk; a few Indians and Pakistanis, a small clutch of Greeks, some Nigerians, Chinese restaurateurs, the odd Australian and Canadian, a huddle of Ugandan Asians displaced by the eccentricities of Idi Amin, and a clutch of white South Africans who had left Jo'burg because of the apartheid that they fundamentally abhorred.

I thrived in this soup of activity. There was never a moment so dull that it passed slowly. If I had taken the early shift, I would then go upstairs around 9:00 am when the staff arrived – the 'Day Ladies' they called themselves – and demolish a vast fried breakfast in front of the *Daily Herald*, rest for an hour, wash up and go back down to tackle the rest of the day. I now drew £18 a week from the business, and within a few weeks of our return had opened my own bank account, passed my driving test and was buying the Ford Consul from my folks on very favourable weekly terms (Dad had upgraded to a secondhand Rover). We had rescued the situation created by our errant manager and were celebrating it in the usual way. I considered myself to be one very fortunate young sod.

Being a newsagent meant more than just dealing with the morning papers. From midday until 5:00 pm every day except Sunday, the *Evening News* and *Evening Standard*, London's two essential *post-meridiem* news digests, arrived in three editions. They turned up in a dramatic process that involved grown men, young lads, John Bull and the redoubtable Bedford Dormobile.

But first, appearing in a leisurely fashion around 10:30 am was the driver-salesman assigned to the route we happened to be on. This, for us, was Ernie, a hefty rolly-pollster with an aging mohair suit and a fresh joke every single day. He must have told the same gag forty times as he weaved his way around north-west London, but then it was bagged forever and replaced. Where he got them from I never knew. Perhaps a joke-a-day jobber in a Camden Town café wrote and sold them to the cabbies, busmen and other van drivers?

His mid-morning arrival was therefore both pleasure and business. He told his joke: 'So this geezer goes to the khazi for a quiet pony...' Then, the joke told, a laugh and the previous day's returns collected, he worked out what had been sold and we paid him cash for the difference. It was a simple ritual.

During the afternoon, however, the pace altered radically. There was stiff competition between the two journals, and it was a matter of pride to beat the other fellow and be *'First with the News'*, as the logo on the side of Ernie's yellow van proudly announced.

Both papers used the Dormobile, a squat, wobbly tin-box workhorse with an always-open corrugated up-and-over back gate and sliding front doors latched open. No seat belts, naturally – these were REAL men. Inside, as well as the papers stacked in turned batches of 26 (a 'quire') were generally one or two teenage lads, school leavers in their first jobs. As one worked in the back making up quantities, the other would crouch ready for rapid delivery.

If you stood outside the shop at the appointed time – and Ernie was as regular as a Bavarian clock – you could see the van come flying up the road, weaving around slow-moving Ford Anglias and pensioners attempting to cross the street for a packet of tea, then watch as a wiry and nimble young lad hit the ground running with the papers under his arm, pounding across the pavement and into the shop to dump his load on the counter, shouting 'News up, guv!', scamper out again and leap back into the still-moving van that had, in the meantime, executed a 360 degree turn, often in front of an enraged bus driver.

If, as sometimes happened, the rival journals were running neck and neck, then the eager lads would turn the run from the van into a real competitive sprint, shouting their arrival within seconds of each other, while the drivers exchanged genial Cockney rhyming unpleasantries from their cockpit seats. On Saturday nights, when both papers published an Extra Late edition to include football results, the crew would listen to the van's radio and log any late results by rubber stamping 'Arsenal 2, Leyton 3' in the blank stop-press column with their on-board John Bull printing kit.

I once accepted a very hairy ride from Ernie when he spotted me at a bus stop about two miles from home. 'Hop in!' he shouted, not stopping. Being used to jumping on and off Routemaster bus platforms, I reflexively leapt into the back to find the lads counting papers and ticking things off of a clipboard-mounted sheet while rocking and swaying to the rhythm of the airy journey. As the guest of honour, I was handed my own shop's delivery and invited to take a running jump. I did. Clattering loudly through the open front door, I was going so fast I couldn't stop until I reached the back of the shop, marginally avoiding a collision with the greetings card rack. While the startled staff ducked, Dad looked up briefly from his counting and quietly said: 'I see the cavalry's arrived, then.' It took lot to rattle my Dad.

In October of 1966, barely a month after our return, the fourth annual *American Folk Blues Festival* arrived in London. Somewhat distracted by recent events, I bought a ticket only at the last minute and took myself off to the Royal Albert Hall for a second dose of live blues. The huge, echoing vat that is the RAH had just undergone a sonic metamorphosis. Hanging directly above the stage was a cluster of inverted white semi-domes, suspended from the ceiling to catch and reflect the sound as it rose from the performance. They looked to me like intrusive alien spacecraft monitoring the endeavours of a study-worthy species. I freely shared this opinion with the chap seated next to me. 'Why don't UFO?' he replied.

Even with baffles hanging over the stage, the RAH was about as far removed from an ideal blues venue as I was in my bedroom. Nevertheless, we sat in gulping awe as Otis Rush, Sleepy John Estes and Yank Rachell, Big Joe Turner, Junior Wells, Sippie Wallace, Roosevelt Sykes, Little Brother Montgomery and Robert Pete Williams performed for us in this Victorian theatre-in-the-round. The new sonic experiment didn't work too well, and the sound was all but lost. But I loved it all anyway.

My hero that night was Robert Pete Williams. I'd had his classic album, *Those Prison Blues*, recorded in the Angola penitentiary, since my Hertford days, and listened to it often, especially the achingly poignant 'Pardon Denied Again', with the added acid twist of liberated birds singing freestyle counterpoint to his gloomy tale of incarceration. I knew the Leadbellyesque saga of his imprisonment for murder, his discovery by folklorist Harry Oster, the subsequent stir that this caused in folkloric circles, of Robert Pete's eventual release on probation and his new life as a professional musician. Now here he was at the Albert Hall, externally light years from his experiences in Louisiana, but internally still a guarded, nervous man, pouring himself directly into his free form singing and guitar playing. Robert Pete Williams' music is not easy to listen to, even if you are familiar with the deepest of rural blues; it demands your complete attention, and to give it anything less is to miss it all. Seeing him live, even at the distance that the Albert Hall put between us, was for me to connect perhaps more directly with the spirit of deep blues than anything I had encountered up to that moment.

I also saw that night something that had escaped me the year before. The audience that I was a part of cut right across the English class system like a rusty cutlass through a stale British Railways sandwich. In front of me was a short, mid-life tub of a man in a pin stripe suit, as enthusiastic as the young mod to my left, the twenty-something besandalled folkies to my right and the hairy anarchist behind me. There were women there too, and I regarded this as an excellent harbinger of my future sex life, which had STILL not begun... Seventeen years and four months in this world, and not a wick yet dipped.

Blues Unlimited arrived one month carrying an advert for the new John Lee Hooker limited edition LP available by mail on a label called Advent. The address was 143 Cricklewood Lane. I lived at 172! I marched over there that evening, rang the bell of his family's comfortably large house and asked to speak to Dave Sax. His younger brother called up the stairs and, following a brief inspection of colours at the door to establish eligibility, I was invited in. Dave's back bedroom barely had room for the bed. Records were stacked everywhere. I saw huge rows of shoe-boxed 45's piled on every useable surface. A cupboard filled with LPs hung open behind the door. As I inched towards an offered chair and sat facing Dave, I looked around the room and, not seeing what I hoped I would, asked if he actually had any original blues 78's. 'Oh, yes,' he replied, opening the double doors of another cupboard, revealing two long rows of brown-sleeved shellac. I was struck dumb with trembling awe. Then I asked if I could see one, as I had never been in the company of a Real American Blues 78 before. He fished in and handed me a Muddy Waters Chess. My hands shook. He replaced it with a John Lee Hooker Sensation. A small, fragile bubble appeared at the entrance to my left nostril. He had many other Hooker originals, knew more about John Lee than almost anyone and was the compiler of the original Hooker discography. He cracked open two bottles of Brown Ale, handed me one and said: 'So, what do you want to hear?' Perfect; I was in Aladdin's Cave, and it was licensed.

I sat and listened to people I'd never heard before – John Brim, Hot Shot Love, Blue Smitty, Baby Boy Warren and Eddie Hope – on labels I had never seen; Howlin' Wolf, John Lee Hooker and Little Walter songs I'd never encountered; Baby Face Leroy on Parkway, with a sticker on the label that read '*Joe's Record Shop, Chicago*'. It was the beginning of a long friendship and regular sessions at the Sax household. That evening, something else occurred; Dave offered me the chance to dig through his pile of spare 78's. I emerged from his house with an empty wallet but in a state of delirium, three blues 78's clutched to my breast. Two were by John Lee Hooker and the third was by the dreaded Smokey Hogg; but it WAS his one classic, 'Penitentiary Blues'. Why couldn't he have made a single duff record and 567 good ones, instead of the other way round?

In the middle of a winter's night in early 1967, I was awakened by the sounds of distant panic. I imagined at first that a fist fight had erupted in the greasy mews that lay behind us, but the noise persisted and involved more and more voices. I glanced at the clock; it was 3:00 am. Drawn by curiosity, I got up and went to the window from where I could see a fractured red glow and dark shadows jogging frantically in every direction inside it. Whatever was happening was more to the front of the building than the back, though. I went to the front window, opened it and stuck my head out to be immediately threatened by a roaring stew of noise and light. Stella's empire was utterly and horribly on fire. The heat struck my face like a new brick. Up on the second floor, just yards from me, there was a young lodger – I recognised him – clinging to the wide old window ledge, hunched over, twitching and ducking in attempts to evade the crimson bush of flame bursting from his burning room. It overtook him. With a howl that sent me cold despite the flames, he fell to the ground, where his howling stopped. I still remember the frightening suddenness of the moment his pain ceased. His name was Pat, he was a 25 year old construction worker from Kerry and now he was dead on a cold London pavement. Horrified and disbelieving, I ran down to the shop below. My parents had got there just ahead of me and were on the street with looks of horror and helplessness on their faces.

Dreadful sounds of shouting, gurgling, splitting and crackling poured from the building. Showers of sparks erupted inside and tumbled out of windows. The fire brigade arrived, spewing their equipment across the street, setting hoses against the painful flames, hacking their way in to the café below. Steam and smoke rose into the cold night from the now-ruined frontage. Broken glass crunched underfoot. There was an oddly warm and terrifying odour that I couldn't and didn't want to identify. We learned that, in addition to Pat, Stella's mother and two sons were also dead. In a truly British gesture, my mother and a few neighbours brewed vast quantities of tea for the firemen and each others' families. The whole neighbourhood was out. We all stood in the cold at 4:30 am, subdued, shocked into muteness, sharing mugs of tannic acid, wandering in and out of each others' houses and shops. 'Kristallnacht' murmured Mrs. Hoff, largely to herself.

The fire had begun in the café kitchen, possibly a paraffin heater, we heard; it had spread through the largely wooden interior and up the stairs at alarmingly unstoppable speed, and there had been no warning for the sleeping victims. A policeman approached us. Did we know the deceased? Yes. Would we be prepared to identify the bodies? Yes. With dawn still unbroken, Dad and I followed a police car to the local mortuary to look at the stilled life that we had known only the day before as neighbours. 'You all right son?' Dad asked as we were about to enter. I nodded, but I didn't know; I had never seen death before this night. David was eight; Peter was eleven. Old Maisie probably in her seventies. None of them would ever be any older.

As 1967 progressed and we drew far enough away from the January tragedy to get on with life, I found myself more and more hungry for original blues 78's. They wandered through my dream-time enticingly displaying their wicked labels to me, shimmying their shellac in my face, giggling coquettishly and running off round corners to play peek-a-boo. Some of them, mostly on Sun and Chess, also wore stockings and high heels. I had to do something about this before the threatened blindness overtook me!

My initial source of salvation was *Blues Unlimited*, and I began by responding to all the adverts for record auction lists. In due course they arrived: closely-typed and mimeographed pages from Kerry Kudlacek in Oklahoma City, Peter Brown in Streatham, Bruce Bastin in Sussex, Mike Rowe in Lewisham, Fred L. Davis in Memphis, Chris Strachwitz in Berkeley... Dave Carey was going to have to go on iron rations, I had fresh cod to batter. These precious documents listed artists, titles, labels, catalogue numbers, and a code for the condition of each item, ranging from unplayed to unplayable. There was a closing date for offers received, and you made bids on the items you wanted without knowledge of what others might be offering. Then you waited, with sweaty palms and stomach cramps, for the answer and the invoice. This much I understood so far.

I made my offers on best quality Basildon Bond blue notepaper with matching envelopes, in the hope that this would impress the guardians of the objects I so deeply desired. I don't think it made a ha'porth of difference. The key was to offer the highest price. I made the mistake of assuming that I would have the crap beaten out of me by long-standing collectors who knew exactly what to buy and precisely how much to offer. So, I went ahead and bid on several dozen items in the six lists that arrived and therefore closed almost simultaneously, in the hope that I might get, oh, 5% of what I wanted. To my delight – and the horror of my quietly snoozing bank balance – I started to receive invoice after invoice. It was a stretch, but I gave up movie-going for a month, paid up all round and sat waiting for packages to arrive from exotic locations like Oklahoma, California, Tennessee and south London. I had the boxes from across the river inside of a week, but surface mail from the USA took at least a month to arrive, longer from California. Eventually they came, delivered one by one to me at mid-morning from a red post office van. During this time of expectancy, my excitement would rise around 10:00 am each morning. Would this be a day when a brown cardboard box covered with bright, unusual stamps would arrive?

'Twenty Rothman's and the *Radio Times*, please.'

Or would I again be cruelly disappointed by the vagaries of the International Mail System, a tangled and obfuscatory operation whose job was principally to ensure angst and torture in budding record collectors?

'Ahem. TWENTY ROTHMAN'S AND THE *RADIO TIMES* PLEASE!'

'What? Oh, sorry...'

Like your premier country blues LP, or your initial encounter with Mrs. Palm and her five lovely daughters, your first box of blues 78's... I really am NOT alone here, am I?

I stared fixedly at these exotic survivors of not just another world, but of one already passed. I couldn't get there myself, even if I had had a plane ticket and a packed suitcase, because it was simply gone, locked into another era. But the records had travelled to *me*. Caught by circumstance in time warp-proof cardboard boxes, they had finally found their resting place: a 1930's double-door cupboard in the upstairs room of a London flat. THIS was where they belonged! Welcome home, lads.

Who were these initial custodians of my new emotional responses and shellac-shocked bank statement? Here, for the dedicated collector, is the list. More balanced readers may either by-pass this indulgence directly or have a quiet cup of Bovril until it's over:

Lewis Black – Columbia
Blind Blake – two Paramounts
(one had a chunk out of it but... it was still a Paramount)
Gabriel Brown – two on Joe Davis and one on Gennett
Clifton Chenier – Specialty
Arthur Crudup – RCA-Victor and Ace
Big Boy Teddy Edwards – Bluebird
(it was with this record that I fell in love with the Bluebird label's
buff-coloured design – collectors know full well what I mean)
Stick Horse Hammond – Gotham

John Lee Hooker – a Gotham, two Moderns and a Sensation
Wright Holmes – Gotham
Country Holmes – King
(I thought it was Wright Holmes. It wasn't.
I broke it across my knee in a snit.)
Big Boy Knox – Bluebird
(badly damaged, which only made it all the more precious)
J.B. Lenoir – JOB
(with a Joe's Record Shop sticker on it! Who the hell was this 'Joe'?)
Little Junior's Blue Flames – Sun
Pete McKinley – Gotham
Memphis Minnie – OKeh
Memphis Eddie – Globe
(I expected a downhome blues and got big band R&B.
I detested it because it wasn't what I imagined)
Snooky Pryor – Parrot
Jimmy Rogers – Chess
(His first, 'Ludella'. I spent weeks startling people by shouting Jimmy's
call to the guitar, 'Knock me some racket', in unguarded moments)
Doctor Ross – both the Suns and the DIR
Johnny Shines – JOB
(the common one...)
Frank Stokes – Victor
(VERY worn)
Jack Surrell – Sensation
(You've never heard of it, right? It's a boogie piano solo.)
Baby Boy Warren – Drummond, Gotham
Junior Wells – States

The week the final box from that initial batch arrived, I turned eighteen. An almost COMPLETE wally... but only *almost*; after all, nobody's perfect.

I had Wednesdays off. People trailed in on a Tuesday night and said 'blimeyguvitsnotevenwednesdayyet' and I would reply, brightly enough to generate a throttling: 'But to me, it's the weekend!' I almost always hopped on the graphite-scented Northern Line tube train up to the West End of London, where much that I cared about – well appointed cinemas, vast bookshops, snug cafés and Dobell's – were centred around Soho, Leicester Square and the Charing Cross Road. Dobell's was one of several specialist jazz record shops in London at that time, but it was the favourite among blues collectors for the simple reason that the Blues & Folk department was a separate shop, next door to the main jazz outlet. It carried an extraordinary stock of imports, secondhand bargains and rarities, played host every lunchtime to a small group of fanatically dedicated blues collectors, and was presided over by its truculently affable manager, Ray Bolden.

Ray liked a drink. Or two. If you caught him at the right moment, just after a lunch of more fluids than solids, then you could get some startling bargains: 'Let's see, two at forty-five bob, one at twenty-nine-and-six, one at a pound... er... okay, give us a fiver.' Not a collector himself, in fact quite the opposite, he generally tolerated the daily gathering of Dave Sax, Terry Marshall, Clifford Martin, and others, augmented by occasional appearances of provincials – anyone outside WC1 and 2 as far as he was concerned – with an amused, indulgent attitude. Clifford Martin, at that time a horn rim-bespectacled waif with a knitted tea cosy hairdo and a short white tent of a raincoat, was obsessed by obscure blues 45's.

'Oh, my arm hurts,' he said one day, flexing it and wincing as if the pain were unbearable.

'Why's that?' I asked.

'Well, I've just been putting *so many* 45's on the turntable these last few... oohhhh... argh... days.'

Terry Marshall was an original teddy boy who never lost the faith and had managed to survive by widening not his time frame but his view of it. Now into everything from Elvis to Bull Moose Jackson to Little Walter to Hank Williams, he could flip through LP browser bins two at a time, knowing precisely what he was looking at. He rarely bought anything. He already had most of it.

Ray occasionally lost his temper with all this ('FUCK OFF THE LOT OF YOU, YOU'RE ALL STUPID CUNTS, GO ON, BUGGER OFF! LOOK, I'M NOT FUCKIN' KIDDING, OUT, ALL OF YOU!') But the next time round he had completely changed his view: ' 'allo mate, all right then? Cor, I wasn't half fuckin' *drunk* yesterday... fell asleep goin' home, woke up in the railway yard... one in the mornin'. Geezer in a cap says to me: "You drunk mate?" I says: "Can't you see I'm kippin'? Fuck off!" Lessee, two at twenty-five bob and one at thirty... er... as it's you... cash, right? That'll be...'

Often hanging out waiting for him in and around both the blues and the jazz shops, chatting to friends, customers and – quite regularly – Ben Webster, were Ray's two inseparable drinking partners, Big Henry and Indian Arthur. Henry was a nightclub bouncer, jazz fan and daytime layabout who lived and breathed only in the West End of London. He seemed to have no life elsewhere. Called Big Henry for the simple reason that he was nearly always at least twice the size of anyone within a hundred yards of him, he was an affable, laid-back guy during the day. However, I once made the mistake of dissing him while his was on duty at the door of his club, and received a swift, heavy knee job that my balls still remember.

Indian Arthur was a very different fishkettle. An architect by profession, but a drinker by vocation, he once landed a job in Holland and was given a royal send-off by all and sundry on the night prior to his new life. So thoroughly did he celebrate that he was still drunk the next afternoon when the boat landed in Holland and the Dutch authorities – the *Dutch*, mind you – refused to let him in. 'Hi lads, I'm back,' he announced the next night at the pub. 'Hello Arthur,' they all replied, with no surprise whatever.

One evening at the Eagle, an old Victorian pub that sat behind the Charing Cross Road, Arthur executed his usual party trick of falling down. It was a startling performance. One second he was vertical, the next horizontal. A pudgy man, he landed with a soft thwomp and lay there quietly gurgling. A woman who had witnessed this realised that he and Ray were a team, and also being a Professor Of The Bleeding Obvious, stepped up and said to Ray:

'Excuse me, but your friend has fallen down.'

'That,' replied Ray from inside his beer glass, 'is because he's fuckin' Arthur.'

Ray also introduced me to the delights of 'The Cottage', a drinking club just behind the other side of Charing Cross Road. George Melly had written about it in *Owning Up*, a book I loved, and I was as pleased to be there for that reason as any other. Still a haven for jazz musicians, old music hall performers and faded queens with long afternoons to fill, I went not regularly, but often enough to get a feel for the place. I bought as much at Dobell's as I could afford, given that I was now committed to buying 78's, and spent most of my Wednesday pre-cinema attendance time in there just hanging around, chatting, rummaging, smoking, listening and reading sleevenotes. It was a club, and Ray was the president whether he accepted that or not. I think he did. He sold a lot of records to a lot of people in his career simply by putting up with them and he was a genuine unsung hero of the 1960's London scene.

Although the final *Goon Show* had been broadcast in January 1960, earlier episodes were often repeated on the BBC and I listened to as many as I could. I had also continued to follow Spike Milligan's solo career. I read and re-read all his books, and followed his often-reported moves in the newspapers. Every once in a while someone would allow him on television and he treated the medium as a wonderful, wild experiment. Nearly always broadcast live, they were often so funny that the studio staff behind the cameras could clearly be heard laughing helplessly. Milligan himself would frequently break up, turning to the camera to say things like: 'You see, this is what we think television should really be like.' And I agreed wholeheartedly. It was anarchic, sometimes surreal, always full of surprise and, because there were times when Milligan had only a vague sense of where things might be heading, filled with the ever-present possibility of genius simply exploding in front of you. Had it not been live, it would have lost its edge, but knowing full well that this was a real-time experiment, both Milligan, his cohorts and his faithful audience – however many of us that might have been – shared the delightful danger of exploring the unknown.

The videotapes, if they ever existed, are probably now lost, but my humble contribution to the restoration of this wedge of eccentric televised genius is to reconstruct 'The Poet'. I call it that, but they didn't. It was simply an untitled segment of one show. A young and very serious poet was introduced; he was going to recite his latest work, a diatribe against the Vietnam war. Verse after angry verse was articulated, and in between each was a recurring stanza:

> *So, stick my legs in plaster,*
> *Wrap my head in bandage,*
> *Tell me LIES about Vietnam.*

It was all very serious and, given Milligan's own well-known radical politics, came as no surprise. We expected it to simply segue from a serious moment to another wacky Milliganesque scenario. However... as the poet continued, the single-camera shot got tighter and tighter. What had begun as a full-length figure standing on a studio floor was now just a talking head. And that head was reaching the climax of the poem as, for the last time, he recited the disdainful and venomous hook:

> *So, stick my legs in plaster,*
> *Wrap my head in bandage,*
> *Tell me LIES about Vietnam.*

The split second he had uttered the final word, a giant custard pie hit him full in the face. Off camera, Milligan, in his best Cockney voice, shouted: 'The Viet Cong strike again, mate!' There was never anyone quite like Spike.

I went to see Dave Sax regularly. It was almost always his place rather than mine because he had far more records. On any given night his room was filled to bursting-point with other collectors. It was here that I first met Ray Topping, who was creating the artwork for Dave's Advent releases. Their very hush-hush Jimmy Rogers album was just out. Secret because it was all Chess material, Dave had allocated it a non-sequential catalogue number in the hopes that he could deny all knowledge if suddenly confronted by Scotland Yard's crack Bootleg LP Squad: 'Mr. Sax, my name is Cole-Bunker, Inspector Arthur Cole-Bunker, and I 'ave reason to believe that yew hare the mastermind be'ind not only the recent Jimmy Rogers crimes but also the Big Boy Spires EP caper. I 'ave a warrant for your harrest, an affidavit for the confiscation of your stock and a small tobacco-stained moustache under my nose. It's no use protesting, as I 'ave 'ere the concrete evidence against yew. I always do. That's why I'm known as "The Concrete Cole-Bunker" in the Yard. Yew 'ave the right to remain seated while we knock six bells out of yew. All right Johnson, book 'im then!'

Others who squeezed into the inner sanctum included John Holt, a partner in Advent, president of the Texas Blues Appreciation Society of North London and publisher of a booklet containing the first proper discography of

Lightnin' Hopkins. And the slightly older Bill Rattray, a gaunt, bony, smiling man with a worn suit and a shock of grey hair that had not been remodelled since his teddy boy days. He collected principally old hillbilly music and was the first guy I knew with albums on the County label, the old-time equivalent to Origin.

Lightnin' Slim once sang: *'If it wasn't for bad luck, poor Lightnin' wouldn't have no luck at all.'* The same could easily have applied to Bill Rattray. Originally from Coventry, Bill was the fellow who scrimped and saved to buy himself a teddy boy outfit and finally got it the week it went out of fashion. Leaving university and moving to London in the early 1960's, he became a scientific research assistant and lived in a long series of squalid rooms all round London with his burgeoning LP collection. His luck included everything from walking between two parked cars and having his ankles discover the tow-rope, felling him directly into a large pile of fresh canine turd, to his basement flat suddenly flooding at suppertime with ankle-deep raw sewage when a backed-up main drain chose his toilet to escape out of. He would tumble into sunken baths filled with soaking underwear; spit out half a yellowed thumbnail lurking in his pork pie ('I thought that last bite was a bit crunchy'); realise that his wallet had slipped through the hole in his back pocket; fall asleep on the couch to wake up covered in cat vomit. And yet he continued smiling through it all. We became friends, he visited me every Tuesday night to listen to music, and my mother took him under her wing, regularly feeding him vast quantities of shepherd's pie, steak and kidney pudding, spaghetti bolognese, apple pie and bread-and-butter pudding. 'He just looks so *hungry*,' she would say. It was, he told me years later, the only decent meal of his week. The reason? He was a founder member of the Vinyl Before Nutrition Club. Almost all his money went on records.

The summer of 1967 was the apex of Flower Power in London. It helped that the weather was good. Hippies bloomed overnight, often next door. In London, it was more of a fashion statement than the social movement California was nurturing; nevertheless, it was serious enough to outrage the middle class and draw the fire of the gutter press that Britain was, and still is, so good at supporting. As a newsagent, I flicked through every paper every day and knew full well what warped reportage, salacious faux-morality and abuse of power they were capable of. However, the hippies were often too blissed out to be any real danger to anyone except, perhaps, themselves.

On a high summer night Bill Rattray and I double-dated two 'exotic dancers' – members of a travelling Jamaican dance troupe – and took them to a late-night film show in a rescued-from-bingo cinema somewhere in Notting Hill that was now run by hippies. The bill was to include not just an eclectic selection of celluloid (W.C. Fields, Bunuel and Dali's *Un Chien Andelu*, Betty Boop, Big Bill Broonzy, George Pal's *Puppetoons*, Will Hay, Tex Avery and experimental German colour footage from the 1920's), but also a 'happening' live on stage.

The air was filled with the fresh romance of exotic exhalations. Boy meets spliff; boy loses spliff, boy gets spliff back again. What's a nice joint like you doing in a girl like this? The lights dimmed and the buzz of voices died away as two silly buggers and a guitar appeared on stage. They began to perform a tuneless song that I started to forget as I was hearing it, something to do with flowers being our friends. Abruptly they ceased and without warning or explanation, the guitarist began playing a choppy, stop-time rhythm as the singer started to chant '*Peace, love, understanding, peace, love, understanding...*' while gyrating his hips in what he probably hoped looked cool, but came across to me, at least, as a man in urgent need of a toilet.

Without warning, he undid his trousers and let them drop to his ankles, revealing his complete lack of underwear. A gasp erupted to my right as my date, a girl called Sonya, put her hand to her mouth in disbelief. Meanwhile back on stage the rhythm and the gyrating were continuing at a fair clip, causing the newly-freed member to bounce between our hero's inner thighs like an enraged ferret trapped in a ditch. People began clapping along, not so much to the rhythm of the guitar as to that of the flailing organ. Eventually the music stopped and the thigh-walloper came out of his trance to realise that he was standing in front of several hundred people with his trousers round his ankles. 'Er... thanks, man,' he mumbled, shuffling awkwardly off to the left, still debagged. I never saw Sonya again. She made very sure of that.

As autumn approached, I began to look for early signs of the annual *American Folk Blues Festival*. Sometime in September I got the news that we were to be offered Koko Taylor, Hound Dog Taylor, Little Walter, Sonny Terry & Brownie McGhee and, astonishingly, Skip James, Bukka White and Son House.

Son House! I was electrified. I had followed his career in a discographical chronology. His first recordings, from 1930, had all surfaced on Origin; I found them, as everyone else did, to be the deepest and most committed of all Delta blues. Then I bought a Folkways album that offered me part of his 1940's Library of Congress session. Mike Raven had dropped examples of the rediscovery sessions for Columbia on me from that platform in the North Sea, causing an immediate parting between my wallet and forty-five bob for the imported pressing. I loved it all. Son sent shivers up into places that I couldn't reach myself. Now I was going to see him!

The venue was the Hammersmith Odeon, a huge cinema in west London. It was far from ideal; Son was on and off stage almost before he could warm up, as was everyone else. While I was still astonished that this huge array of talent was standing in front of me at all, my budding critical faculties began to murmur about the need for a more sympathetic treatment of the music, smaller venues, longer sets, better sound. I had no idea that my fantasies would, to some degree, soon come true.

Pasted to the walls of the listening booths at Dobell's was always a helter-skelter collection of handwritten requests and announcements:

Blues harmonica lessons given, 10/- an hour. Bring your own gob-iron, please.

DESPERATELY WANTED First Lightnin' Hopkins Crown LP. Will pay £3 if mint.

Martin guitar for sale, or will trade for small house-broken dog and a hundredweight of decent anthracite.

And also, for a long time, a list of obscure 78's and 45's wanted by someone called Bill Greensmith. I was hanging out, as usual, one winter Wednesday lunchtime when a squarely solid guy in a thick blue coat entered and started talking to Ray, who clearly knew him well. After a moment or two he stepped from the counter to the listening booth, grabbed the detailed wants list and tore it off, screwing it up while announcing, with a laugh I would come to know very well: 'That was about as much fuckin' use as a broken arm.' I approached him and, with the deductive powers that have made me a legendary discographer, asked: 'Are you Bill Greensmith?' He was, and we arranged for him to come over to Cricklewood and listen to what I had amassed.

George Melly had compared 1950's British jazz collectors to early Christians, always eager to meet, talk, exchange views and share with each other their part of the support network. It was the same with 1960's blues collectors. You became instant friends purely on the grounds that you shared a common passion that few others, often including immediate family, could fathom. In the case of Bill and myself, that friendship is over forty years old and still running. More of him later.

I was fortunate in that one member of my immediate family, my father, was more than sympathetic to my cause. Always a general music fan, and especially a jazz guitar buff, he still played guitar and continued his interest in Django Reinhardt, replacing his worn 78's with vinyl reissues. I began buying him LPs as birthday and Christmas presents, as much as anything because I wanted to continue enjoying Django too. He pointed out to me that I had been listening to the blues all my life, simply because he had. Often thick as two short planks glued together, I had not realised that before. He regularly put his head round the door to hear what I was absorbing and offer his opinion. He enjoyed a guitar well-played by anyone, and came to recognise Muddy, Fred McDowell, Blind Blake, Big Bill and others at fifty yards or more. 'Draw the line at One String Sam, though,' he said one day as the strains of 'Need a Hundred Dollars' drifted down the hall. He was an intelligent, open listener and a great support – the opposite of a Manchester friend's father, who, when confronted with the news that he was going to be subjected to yet another dose of shave-and-a-haircut rhythms by the author of 'Pretty Thing' whinged: 'Oh no, yer not playin' tha' Joe Bidley feller again are yer?'

I bought most of the Django vinyl not from Dobell's, but from a small independent record shop nestled behind the Kilburn & Brondesbury tube station that sat at the gateway to the Kilburn High Road, just four traffic lights from home. It took about twenty minutes to get there, and it was always worth every second. It was called, simply, 'Foxley's' and was run by the thin-haired, wiry and very pleasant Ralph Foxley. A professional musician between the wars, he had been called up, survived his experience in the Royal Signal Corps and set up business immediately after demob.

My mother began to buy her records from him in the late 1940's, and I had dim memories of accompanying her into the shop as a child. Now, however, I discovered it for myself and every visit was an education. The shop sat in an extraordinary shaft of natural light that squeezed its way down into the choked urban mash that was lower Kilburn. From Foxley's window you could look up and actually see a clear sky, the light from which was magnified by a pair of huge arched front windows, in which the LP browser bins sat on spindly wooden legs. As you came through the door the aroma of massed sun-warm British Celanese coated LP covers greeted your olfactory senses. It's a smell you never forget. (Er... I'm not alone here again, am I?)

The long, narrow interior was divided into two sections, Popular and Classical, separated by a bamboo wall and a doorway covered by a beaded curtain. From his position behind the lengthy hip-level counter, Ralph Foxley could see and service his entire operation. Behind him were racks of stock, 45's, EPs and albums arranged alphanumerically. Each record was housed in a brown card sleeve with sales and ordering information handwritten on it. This was the standard and very effective stock control method used in the pre-digital era, but most of it was also in Ralph's head, as was much else. I had always thought of him as principally a jazz and symphonic man until he surprised me one morning, as I walked in, by nodding his head vigorously to Lowell Fulson's 'Talking Woman Blues'. Extracting the cigarette that had accompanied this above-shoulders blues groove, he said to me, simply as one fan to another: 'What a *GOOD* little record!'

From that moment, I began to understand just what an extraordinary breadth of knowledge he possessed, about music in general, the music business and the retail trade. As I was a younger brother-retailer, he would share with me his views on how a record shop should operate, how stock control and display should be handled, where to look for bargains, who the good and not-so-good wholesalers were, how to handle a naked record to keep it mint. I listened to every quietly delivered word like a student in the presence of Einstein. Or even Two Steins. This, I told myself, was who and what I wanted to be.

More than just a good record man, though, Ralph Foxley had tales to tell, and perhaps the most fascinating was this one. In about 1953, responding to numerous local requests from recently-arrived Jamaicans, he privately pressed fifty copies of an Amos Milburn Aladdin 45 he happened to have. It sold out in one morning. Realising the potential, he contacted a friend who worked the passenger lines sailing from Southampton and arranged to have him buy a regular selection of new R&B records in New York. These would then be copied and cut onto metal acetate singles, which he sold across the counter. News quickly spread, and Saturdays at Foxley's became famous inside the Jamaican community. He presided over what was, to all intents and purposes, a regularly-scheduled record party. People came from all across London and further – Birmingham, Manchester and Bristol – to talk, listen and buy. It served as a meeting place for fans and musicians alike. So, that nice Mr. Foxley turned out to be a proto-bootlegger. Well, well... good for him.

By the spring of 1968 I was the proud owner of a considerable number of blues records and all the books that I was aware of. I was also a subscriber to every magazine I could find: in addition to *Blues Unlimited, Jazz Journal* and *Jazz Monthly*, I absorbed *Blues World, Vintage Jazz Mart, Record Research*, the Swiss *Jazz-Rhythm-and-Blues* (which nobody ever remembers), and the even less-remembered New Zealand magazine, *Blues News*. I was also a total berk, as another photo you aren't seeing would prove; it shows me posing, arms crossed, smirking with self-satisfaction, in front of my assembled collection.

It was about this time that I began writing – first for Bob Groom's *Blues World*. Out of the blue I offered him a series called 'Pre War Country Blues Obscurities', in which I egotistically proposed to describe pre-war Blues 78's in my possession that were currently unavailable on LP. To my astonishment he accepted and I fired off badly-written assessments of arcane performances by the likes of Whistlin' Rufus, Teddy Edwards and Spark Plug Smith. I got to know Trevor Benwell, editor of *Vintage Jazz Mart*, who lived only a couple of miles from me, and began a column for him also. And for the New Zealanders I wrote articles on pre-war Memphis Blues, Johnny Shines and Magic Sam. All of it was, essentially, crap. But my ego was deliriously happy.

Bill Greensmith and I saw each other regularly, either in Cricklewood or over at his family's neat little flat in Wimbledon. Bill's room, like many rooms belonging to emerging blues collectors, was built around his records, books and record player. There was room for a bed, but if more records had arrived, the bed would probably have gone. Even by this time Bill had a considerable collection, and probably the best clutch of B.B. King records in Britain. He also had a record player that I envied; it had been built for school use, and was a Garrard SP25, the play-anything-in-any-condition three-speed record deck that could track unerringly from one to five grammes (more, if you loaded threepenny bits onto the head). It was housed in a sturdy wooden box with built-in controls and loudspeaker, and was perfect for playing blues records on. Bill's mum, like mine, kept us fed with tea, sandwiches and cakes and his dad, an insurance representative with a lugubrious demeanour and a wicked sense of humour, would sometimes put his head round the door. I was in their living room one evening when Mrs G. put the nightly dinner in front of Mr. G. It was veal, and it appeared to be on special offer, for this was its second appearance that week.

'Ah, the Vera Lynn special,' said Mr. G.

'What?' replied Mrs G.

'Veal Meat Again.'

We also often went round and saw Frank Nazareth in his large and comfortable ground floor converted apartment. It had a big picture window overlooking a neglected front garden leading to a busy street, and was always playing host to local music fans, friends, layabouts and musicians sitting about on the big, scruffy sofas that lined the walls. There was always tea in the pot, a cosy open fire in winter and lots of good records; it was a very friendly, mellow place to be. I met Frank's sister June there one Sunday, and we dated once or twice in the following weeks. Her parents, unlike her or Frank, were still very traditionally Indian, and invited me over for an elaborate and wonderful meal in their flat. But June and I ceased going out and she apparently never dated again for the longest time, moving to the Potteries and starting a new and celibate life. 'See what you've done?' remarked Frank. 'She goes out with you and it's so bleedin' traumatic that its "Finito Benito" from now on. You've completely altered my sister's life! Fancy a cuppa?'

I had been striking up extended correspondence with American collectors, including Fred L. Davis in Memphis, who always replied on wafer-thin blue air-letter forms, cramming every available millimetre with type. Fred offered me a deal: for $30 he would send me thirty mint original 45's and 78's on the legendary Sun label. I took him up on this and in due course the box arrived. It contained an extraordinary mix: R&B and blues by Doctor Ross, Sammy Lewis, Little Milton, Rufus Thomas, Roscoe Gordon and Little Junior Parker; country by Johnny Cash, Earl Peterson and Slim Rhodes, and rockabilly by Jerry Lee Lewis, Carl Perkins, Roy Orbison, Warren Smith, Billy Lee Riley and Ray Harris. Astonished, I immediately sent him another sixty bucks: '*If you want the Elvis records, they'd be ten dollars a pop,*' he wrote. I considered that too expensive and declined his offer. Yeah, I know.

By the time I had absorbed all this, I was left with a fascination for the Sun label – something a lot of people have had over the years – and I determined to compile a proper and complete discographical listing. There was a limited one available in a publication called *Blues Research*, an occasional journal dedicated to blues discography, but I wanted to take it further. With the unassailable assuredness of the eighteen year old and the unstinting help of Dave Sax, Terry Marshall and a clutch of older London rockers – colourful figures including Rockin' Gus, Railhouse Jock, Hot Rock Ford and two unwashed, nylon-shirted herberts who actually co-owned a record collection and a 1956 Ford Zodiac – I assembled as much information as I could.

By the time I was done, there was enough for a booklet. I decided, therefore, to become my own publisher. With seed money from my father, I approached Steve Lane, the jazz trumpet-playing printer who produced *Vintage Jazz Mart* on his ancient Roneo machine. For an agreed price, he would print my epic production. I laboured throughout the summer on an old typewriter to produce the original copy, which in those days had to be cut as stencils, page by page. Bill Greensmith took photos of record labels on a blistering hot day on Wimbledon. I had *The Sun Legend* ready by September – some seventy pages of badly typed fax'n'info. I set about marketing it with adverts in *Blues Unlimited, Melody Maker, Record Mirror* and other journals, and putting it into Dobell's and elsewhere on a sale-or-return basis. To my astonishment – and my father's relief – it took off like disorder at an anarchists' meeting.

Chapter Four

1968-69: I THOUGHT YOU WAS A NUTTER

Somewhere around this time I connected with live blues again because Bill Greensmith phoned me one night and said: ' 'ere mate, Freddy King's playing at the Toby Jug in Tolworth. Coming?'

You bet I was! Tolworth, just outside south-west London, was a long way from my patch, and I prepared for this adventure like an anthropologist being sent up the Limpopo: 'I'm stepping out for a while. If I'm not back by Wednesday, send my papers to the British Library.' The Toby Jug was a huge old boozer with a back room usually devoted to wedding receptions and meetings of the local Chamber of Commerce. This particular evening it was, instead, swarming with the broad slice of blues-obsessed British society that I was growing used to: hairy fribblers in greatcoats, proto-skinheads in jeans that stopped dead above the ankles, hippies in sunburst tie-dye, suedehead soul boys, teachers in comfy pullovers and corduroy slacks, mods and rockers clinging grimly to an arranged truce for the duration, and blokes like me, with sufficient lack of dress sense to eschew any group identity. If there had been a deconstructionist fashion movement at that time, I would have defaulted into it.

We saw Freddy King perform that night on a postage stamp-sized bandstand lumbered with a pair of war-weary Vox amplifiers and a rotten five-quid-a-gig local group, who had perhaps mastered their third and final chord only that afternoon. He was wonderful. Just a year or two later he would join Leon Russell and Shelter records to become part of the overblown 1970's touring rock band syndrome that spawned a thousand self-indulgent twenty-minute guitar solos. In the Toby Jug he was still, essentially, in his 45 rpm Federal mode, and he blasted us at staggering volume with classic hits like 'Hideaway', 'San-Ho-Zay', 'The Stumble' and 'I Love The Woman'.

Sweating profusely, he played his guitar behind his neck, between his legs, with his teeth and one-handed, swinging it by the neck over the audience. He did splits, leaps and, considering the circumstances, a very creditable duck-walk. He shouted his songs directly at us, grimacing and smiling, eyes closed, then wide open, mouth pouting then gaping; he had the most mobile features I had ever seen. Close up and very personal, to the point where his sweat beads could have been collected in a jar by the front row revellers, we saw a show that, in essence, may have been as close as any of us had ever got to a juke joint, if you accept that we stoked ourselves not with chittlins and Early Times bourbon but Smith's crisps and Watney's Red Barrel ('Your turn in the barrel,' grinned Bill when my round was due).

The audience was ecstatic. I saw immediately the advantages of experiencing live blues in intimate circumstances rather than vast halls or cinemas. Meanwhile, a bespectacled man dressed like a classic bank clerk was going nuts at the back, jumping up and down, sweating, laughing, whooping, clapping his hands, shouting 'YEAH, FREDDY! ALL RIGHT, FREDDY!' and was finally overtaken by his own enthusiasm. He failed to realise his belt was losing the battle with his trousers and he fell over backwards in sudden, deep surprise with his pants round his ankles. It turned out he WAS a bank clerk.

Occasionally I would hook up with Trevor Benwell, ex-RAF fighter pilot, collector of early jazz and editor of *Vintage Jazz Mart*, and we'd go drinking somewhere in Harrow or Pinner, his old haunts. He knew a wide variety of eccentric people and we were always running into them in pubs. One was a tax inspector who really wanted to be a house painter and would take on all manner of redecorating jobs because he felt it to be his true calling. But he was dreadful at it, often getting into trouble with clients for putting the wrong paint on the wrong surfaces. 'They never complain, though, when I tell them what I really do for a living.'

Another was a fellow called Bert, who had spent his considerable inheritance collecting vintage motor cars and had a garage with a Hispano-Suiza, a Morgan and two Bugattis in it that he would happily display to the right kind of plump young lads who took his fancy.

And then there was a man known only as Happy Harry, a gifted and enthusiastic inventor of his own Cockney Rhyming Slang. He created new phrases rather than use established argot, and a monologue from Harry could begin: 'So, there I was driving me Haddock and Bloater dahn the 'ands and Feet when the old girl ups and Shepherd's Pies on me...'

On a cold night when we had finished drinking and Trevor was taking me back to where I had parked my car, we came down King George the Fifth Avenue in Harrow in his AC Aceca, an aluminium-bodied racer that was always demanding attention. He switched on the heating and it immediately malfunctioned, filling the interior with black smoke and sparks. As he hit the brakes he said, urgently: 'Cockpit's on fire, old chap. Bale out!' and we ran for it, not knowing if the car would merely smoulder or be engulfed in flames. It sat by the road quietly smoking while we sat on a grassy bank doing the same. I turned to Trevor and asked him if he knew what he'd just said. 'Yes,' he replied in distant wistfulness: he had been shot down twice in his RAF career and in that first moment was in a Hurricane over the Channel, rather than an Aceca in Middlesex.

The London School of Economics was, at this time, a hotbed of alternative politics, radical thought, Left Wing think tanks and generally bolshy attitudes. Everyone was a budding Dave Spart, which also meant they collectively looked upon a blues gig as an ideal supplementary flag to wave. It would, indeed, have been a perfect rallying point for them in the autumn of 1968, had it been almost anyone except Champion Jack Dupree that was appearing in their hallowed halls. Jack had settled in England in the early 1960's, making a home for himself in Halifax. 58 years old when he played the LSE, he had more energy than many in the audience. It was what he did with it that rattled the cages of those who saw a direct connection between Applied Alternative Geo-Politics in the Post-War Global Forum and a jolly evening of barrelhouse piano.

I arrived early enough to help two Sparts shove an ancient upright piano into position in the large common area that had been allocated for the night's entertainment. Like most British Upright Pianos of the period, it had been carefully tuned by soaking it in a solution of chip fat, beer and fag ash for a decade, then left out in the rain for a season. The finish was peeling nicely, the keys were a dirty yellow colour – all of them – and one of the feet had to be replaced by a phone book. When Jack sat down and attempted to get the feel of it, I swear I heard it cough. However, he had mastered less healthy instruments in his career.

The moment that the audience had settled and Jack reappeared from behind a curtain, he was completely and thoroughly on.

'Shakespeare, he say: "Two beers, or not two beers?" Ha!'

Then he sat down and assaulted the piano with 'Dupree Shake Dance', stomping his feet, grinning, pounding the keys with all the finesse of the boxer that he had once been. He never actually finished one number and began another, he simply clambered from tune to tune across a bridge of jokes, turning to the audience as he played the final bar of one song to announce

'Shakespeare, he say: "It's better to have an old hen than pullet." Heh-heh.'

At which point he lost several Sparts and Spartettes, possibly members of Orwell's Anti-Sex League. The noise they made in leaving was drowned by Jack's immediate launch into a whomping version of 'Cabbage Greens'. He grinned, mugged, waved his hands, rolled his eyes, laughed, gurgled, shimmied his shoulders, shouted the blues and told outrageous stories. Extreme lefties who had expected someone blind, crippled, raggedy, terminally depressed and perhaps even prepared to die on stage began retreating in order to re-examine their socio-political relationship with the blues. Jack, meanwhile, halted the proceedings to take a break and play a tape of his own recordings, a wide-ranging anthology of issued and unissued stuff.

'This one was made when it was 110 in the shade. Phew! That's why it's so *hot*. Har!'

He then proceeded to blatantly offer the tape for auction, eliciting bids from the audience. I went up to the seven quid I had on me, but was beaten by a man with one arm and a left-handed cheque book. Several more members of the Lenin Appreciation Society elected to vacate rather than be sullied by this indecent process. Jack returned to the piano to play 'TB Blues', which cheered up the surviving Marxists somewhat, and this morphed into an extraordinary version of 'Goin' Down Slow', to which Jack attached so much feeling that a loose pillock who appeared at my shoulder said: 'Wow, man, you can tell he wrote that one from direct experience. That's, like, real death-bed stuff man. Oh wow.'

Jack closed with an astonishing version of 'Smokin' Reefers', during which he produced and lit a pre-rolled cigarette and took long luxurious drags on it. Probably Old Holborn. His was the most authentic barrelhouse piano blues performance I've ever seen live. Or ever will, given that Winifred Atwell is now dead.

My working life continued as usual, with an average of 60 hours a week and, generally, without incident. Generally. I was crossing the busy and relatively narrow main street one morning, having delivered something to someone, swinging a keyring on my finger the way that nineteen year old herberts will. This bunch contained keys for the shop, alarm system, safe, stockroom, both cars, the garage and the outside toilet. All crucial stuff. It suddenly flew off my finger and lodged with a heart-sickening clunk in the back bumper of a slowly passing Humber Snipe. The traffic jam that it had been a part of then immediately dispersed and the Humber gracefully picked up speed, with the keys to my world hanging on its bum and the driver oblivious to my plight.

In those days I could run very fast if I had to, but never had I run quite this fast. I pounded after the car, shouting and waving, people on the pavements turning see a large, frantic youth weaving dangerously in and out of traffic. I finally caught up with the driver at the first set of traffic lights which had, with great fortune, turned red on him. I appeared in his open side window gasping, dishevelled, crimson-faced, hair like an explosion in a mattress factory, dribbling on his side mirror and attempting to explain why it was necessary for him to stop. He quickly grasped the situation and pulled to the side while I rescued the keys and displayed them as evidence. 'Sorry mate,' he said. 'I saw you all right, but I kept going 'cause I thought you was a nutter.'

I got invited, along with Bill Greensmith, Frank Nazareth and their Wimbledon mate Pat Grover, to go and see Bruce Bastin in deepest Sussex. The reason? He had just returned from the States with vast quantities of blues 78's that he was prepared to sell. Say no more.

On a Sunday morning I drove over to Wimbledon, hooked up with Bill and Frank, and we then went to find Pat, who possessed the old lorry we would travel down in. There was only room for one other person in the cab, and Bill, in his Dickensian period, with mutton-chop sideburns and heavy winter coat, won the toss ('That's because you're a very practised old tosser,' quipped Frank). Frank and I rode in the back with the tail-board down so we could make obscene gestures at old dears in Morris Minors who couldn't get past us. The lorry, lacking any workable suspension system, jolted and bounced us to the point where Frank observed: 'Cor, you wouldn't have to move much to fuck in here, would ya? Just relax and let the lorry do it for you.'

I had not met Bruce before. I was amazed, as were the rest, at the size of his collection. Six-foot racks filled with 78's stood either side of his huge and VERY SERIOUS mono hi-fi system. There were supplementary stacks all round the room. We began with vast quantities of freshly-brewed tea, cakes and shellac. Bruce played us stuff we had not only never heard before, but never heard OF. His knowledge was immense, his dedication total and his track record impeccable. A decade older than us, he had started earlier, seen Muddy in 1958, and been amazed by the event.

'It changed my life,' he said. 'Never before and seldom since has anything affected me as much.'

From 1964, he had spent more than a year in the USA on an exchange programme, lived and travelled in a converted ambulance, discovered and interviewed blues singers, found the holy shellac grail, and hauled it all home to Sussex. A total hero.

'Back in those days, I was buying 78's at a hundred dollars a ton in Georgia,' he grinned, pulling yet another Ralph Willis record I'd never seen from the rack. 'It's got more expensive this last couple of years.'

It was at this initial session that Bill coined a phrase which entered the lexicon of our circle. Barely tolerating a rockabilly 78 that Frank had requested, Bill declared that he had no interest whatever in hearing 'that fucking...' – he grasped for an adequate description – 'fucking *poodlestabbin'* music.' From that moment on, all rockabilly activity was known as 'poodlestabbing'. We began inventing records like 'Stab That Poodle With A Cast Iron Noodle' by Wally Helmet & His Twilight Poodle Assassins on Dead French Dog records out of Knees Bend, Arkansas.

Finally, we got to the records Bruce had for sale. Box upon box of post-war downhome blues. I completed my Muddy Waters Chess collection that day, and got a long way towards the entire Little Walter as well. I don't even want to think about what I missed through ignorance. Average price? Ten bob each. I spent thirty quid and came home in total sensory overload. 'Enjoy yourself?' asked Dad, turning from the TV to greet his pale and trembling offspring staggering through the door with three large cardboard boxes. 'Muddy... Walter... Bruce... Wolf... Elmore... Lightnin'... Bill... old lorry... Ten bob... Corblimey... you wouldn't believe.... amazing... yeah, fine thanks... see you later... gonnaplayrecords...' More of Bruce later, also.

'If you had 34/6 to spend on the last weekend of September, and more than a passing interest in popular music, there was what seemed like a difficult choice to make about how to spend your money. From 7:00 pm to 7:00 am Sunday, the Jefferson Airplane and the Doors were playing at the Roundhouse; and from 10:00 am Saturday to 5:00 pm Sunday, with only a nominal break through the night, the blues were being talked about, sung, eaten, smoked and played with very little pause in most of the halls and chambers of Conway Hall.'

– Charlie Gillett, *Shout* magazine (October 1968)

Throughout the summer, Chris Trimming and other members of the National Blues Federation had been laying plans for an autumn convention that many thought doomed to failure. Personally, I bought my ticket out of a sense of duty. When you're nineteen you do things like that. Support the blues at any cost – even 34/6! Then something called 'involvement' happened. About three weeks before the event I got a call from Alan Newby, who was one of those organising the convention. He explained that a recitalist had dropped out and asked if I would like to take his place? 'You can talk about anything you like. As long as it's blues, of course. Ha-ha.'

I don't think for a moment I was the first choice for a replacement; probably the last. However, flush with thoughts of fame, riches, big women, Mackeson, chicken sandwiches and my name in print I readily agreed. I decided to call my recital 'Pre-War Country Blues Obscurities'. Snappy title, huh? That's the sort of recital an intense nineteen year old tends to give. I set about diving through my collection and made up a tape of my rarest 78's. There was no way I was going to take precious shellac into the degenerate mêlée I felt sure I'd find when I got there.

Saturday morning, 10:00 am, I arrived at the Conway Hall armed with notes, tape and sandwiches. ('If someone offers you any strange pills or cigarettes, you won't accept them will you?' my mother had said before I set off.) I met several other convention-goers on the tube including a group from Switzerland, identified by their plastic Dobell's record bags. 'The blues is in this direction?' they asked, pointing variously. By 10:30 things were under way, with a recital by Mike Vernon (the man who is not my brother).

'Mike had opened the Blues Convention with a rather charming, lazy selection of records he'd produced, establishing an atmosphere of sympathetic appreciation of opposing opinions which lasted throughout the weekend. While we listened to him, we took stock of the scarcely credible efficiency with which Chris Trimming had organised the event; I had just time to notice with wonder that we even had a biro to make notes with, before I lost it. I couldn't handle that kind of systematic consideration of my comfort.' – Charlie Gillett

The next recital in the main hall was 'Screening the Blues' by Paul Oliver, but I had to miss it because I was doing my own recital in the North Room. With competition like that, I fully expected to spend a pleasant hour playing music to myself, but surprisingly I gathered an audience of some thirty people, to whom I was introduced by Simon Napier, whose tape recorder I was using, and who was probably there to see it didn't get swiped, rather than listen to me.

'An irritating young American in shades chattered through Paul's records and talked about "Spade Music". I later discovered he was Nick Perls, to whom we are all grateful for his part in finding Son House and others. But I couldn't help wondering why he was interested.' – Charlie Gillett

Reeling from the fact that I had finished my hour without anyone from the BBC offering me a job on *Late Night Line Up*, I wandered around in the foyer chatting to friends and collectors. A *Blues Unlimited* stall selling books, records and magazines had been set up by the side of the stairs and seemed to be doing brisk business. In the opposite corner, Mike Rowe had a small table from which he was attempting to sell, for 2/6d each, some of the 400 copies of the Bobo Jenkins 'Fortune' 45 he had had specially pressed. I asked him how he was doing. 'There don't seem to be many Detroit people here today,' he answered.

A largely liquid lunch was followed by a film show. This turned out to be less than successful, because the main hall was equipped with large skylight windows and no way of blocking them off. I sat up in the gallery to try and see Big Bill and Bo Diddley, but in the end gave up and again talked matrix numbers and general bollocks with other collectors until Simon Napier took the stage. In his *Shout* article, Charlie Gillett says that Simon talked about Post-War Country Blues Field Researchers, but I cannot remember much about this hour. This was possibly due to my having just met a girl in a tight leather dress that I was desperately trying to impress. I failed.

An auction followed in the main hall. This was, to say the least, a strange affair. 78's and 45's were offered from the stage by Mike Leadbitter. I bought a Jimmy Rogers Chess 78 for 12/6 and a George Smith 45 for ten bob. Someone bought an Arthur Gunter 78 for 3/6. In all I think they made about eight quid in 45 minutes.

Only during a British-organised *Blues Convention* could you find yourself in the middle of a tea-break. But following the auction, that's exactly what we got. A catering staff was dispensing tea, sandwiches, buns and biscuits for the hour preceding the concert. Tea is so ingrained into British life that even those anarchic bearded hairies of the late Sixties, espousing freedom and liberation for the soul, stopped to take a plastic beaker of the liquid gold.

The evening concert was largely British groups. The acoustics of this venerable old pile were never built to cope with amplification of this power, so within a few minutes the purists (including me) had repaired to the pub across the road, in much the same way some critics had spent time in the bathroom during Muddy's first British concert. The difference being, of course, that we knew we were right and that they, back then, were wrong.

The pub, full of collectors, loonies, Ray Bolden, Big Henry and Indian Arthur was more entertaining anyway. Arthur performed his usual party trick of suddenly falling down and remaining there.

A little later we made our way back to the hall in time to catch a new blues band called 'Free' make its first public appearance. Mike Raven, who was emceeing, strode onstage dressed entirely in black, with a huge golden medallion on his chest and said: 'All right you lot, belt up and listen. The management has received complaints about people pissing through letter boxes. Would you please use either the toilets provided, or, failing that, each other?' Having missed Jack Dupree, who we had assumed would be on last but wasn't, we went back to the bar, stepping over Indian Arthur as we did so.

Sunday morning. I decided that, as traffic would be relatively thin and trains even thinner, I'd drive up in what passed for the car I owned at that time, an ancient Ford Anglia. As a result of taking several wrong turns, I missed the opening lecture and have now forgotten who was giving it. In the club room Mike Leadbitter was playing a selection of post-war obscurities and asked me to operate the somewhat antique record player. A large hangover and an unsteady hand ensured that several of the records received less care than they were due, and I had the job taken away from me.

The atmosphere on Sunday was more relaxed, if that's possible, than the previous day. Mike didn't even attempt a theme, he just played stuff that pleased him. Lurking at the back was a complete wally who played atrocious harmonica throughout it all, and put his hand up, schoolboy style, at the end of each record to enquire about the catalogue number and whether it was available in stereo. Mike played records by, among others, Lightnin' Slim, Doctor Ross, Elmore James and Frank Frost ('I knew 'is bruvver, Jack!' yelled the wally).

Mike's session went on all morning and the euphoria gathered momentum. Lunch was an exceedingly relaxed affair. So much so that many people fell asleep during the early part of the afternoon, but were woken up by what I considered to be the most interesting recital of the weekend. Charlie Gillett had been given the opportunity to play what he called 'Rocking Rhythm & Blues'. You may find this hard to believe, but until that moment I had never heard Wynonie Harris' 'Bloodshot Eyes' before. It knocked me out, as did Amos Milburn's 'Chicken Shack Boogie'. It was probably the one event of the whole weekend that got people's feet tapping rather than their heads nodding.

This was followed by David Evans, who attempted to discuss what he called 'Some Blues Myths'. I was still attempting to impress the Blues Myth in the leather dress, and so missed much of what was said. Later, however, Dave was joined onstage by Mike Leadbitter and Canned Heat's Bob Hite, and the whole session slid into a freewheeling gathering of friends, most of whom ended up onstage doing whatever they felt like. By that time few people cared, and those that did were up in the gallery reading the *Sunday Times* anyway.

As the convention drew to a close at 5:00 pm, we drifted out into the warm autumn sun. The weekend had been pronounced a success and it had certainly produced its own magic for me, but as an incurable romantic, that was hardly surprising. Five of us clambered into the Anglia (no small achievement, I can tell you) and chugged off to visit Dave Sax's record and brown ale collection for the rest of the evening.

Hot on the convention's heels, the annual *American Folk Blues Festival* appeared in October, again at the Hammersmith Odeon ('*up the Rappa-Hammersmith,*' quipped Simon Napier in *Blues Unlimited*, parodying William Moore's 'Old Country Rock'). This year we were offered Curtis Jones, Jimmy Reed, Eddie Taylor, T-Bone Walker, Big Joe Williams, John Lee Hooker and Walter Horton. I was still very keen, but also continuing to question the concept of allocating small amounts of time to a large, disparate group of artists in an unsympathetic setting. Surely the way to go was to present one or two related artists in more intimate surroundings?

Nevertheless, you haven't managed to get your arse into South Side Chicago or the Delta yet, have you, Vernon? Buy your ticket and shut up... Everybody I knew was there (all right, not my Aunt Daisy from Neasden, but she often wasn't well, as my Uncle Bill's libido would readily have attested). And being there for and with each other was almost as important to some as the music. People loudly and grandly aired their egos in the pubs before and after the gig, talking about not only the music but what rare records had been recently amassed ('I just got the Andrew Dunham on Sensation. Do you know how *FEW* copies of that there are?') and also about each other's unreasonable behaviour ('He had a mint copy of J.B. Lenoir's 'Eisenhower Blues' with a glossy label. I offered him my mint matt label copy and 2/6 thrown in, and the bastard WOULDN'T TRADE!!!'). One of those people, of course, was me.

That night, Jimmy Reed was very drunk (as he often was), and Eddie Taylor quietly and solidly supported him, rescuing the situation as he often did. When it came to his solo spot, Eddie sang 'Bad Boy' and to me he sounded just the way he did on his classic Vee-Jay sides. Eddie Taylor was a man for whom I had the utmost respect. Those few commercial recordings were, in my opinion, among the best of all Chicago blues. That he was not a greater success was, I thought, a tragedy directly related to his role as Jimmy Reed's sideman. I'm probably oversimplifying the case and I'm probably wrong as a result, but that was how it struck me then and it still does. Eddie was, for me, *the* consummate Delta-based Chicago blues singer. To see him perform one song that night was like being offered half a wine gum. I wish I could have caught him in different circumstances.

Big Joe Williams was described the next day in the *Sun* – still a decent liberal newspaper at that time – as '*a short, squat barrel of a man*' by someone obviously used to grinding out tripe in a bar late at night and then phoning it in. However, a national daily paper had actually deigned to carry a review of a blues gig – something that surprised me and, that morning, bolstered my already unshakeable belief that the music would one day be seen worldwide in its own right, standing gloriously unshackled from the needs of old farts in sports jackets to regard it as no more than the foundations of jazz, or viewed by ignorant headbangers as rock's essential basis and little else. Raise the flag higher! Buy more Arhoolie albums! Canonise Gus Cannon! We are righteous and we shall prevail! Mike Leadbitter for Home Secretary! Let our swords remain unsheathed until duty is rewarded by victory! We will die wholesale and bloody in wet muddy fields protecting our belief that Charlie Patton is the purest source for all of the deepest blues! Onward, ye bold crusaders! Subscribe to *BU*!

'Your eggs are ready, dear.'

'Oh, ta.'

And so 1968 begat 1969 with my libido still unstretched by use. The records continued to pile up regularly, however, with boxes of 78's and 45's arriving from Sweden, France, America and around Britain. *The Sun Legend* had sold out, all 500 copies, and made a profit I split with my dad, who went out and bought a secondhand banjo with his cut. 'That's nice dear' remarked my mother as he bounded up the stairs with it and immediately began to demonstrate just how loud an instrument it could be. The other legacy *The Sun Legend* provided was my bombardment with additions and corrections from people that even I regarded as anally retentive:

Now, item 27 - this is very interesting; it turns out that the Rocking Stockings' Christmas 45 is actually Billy Lee Riley under a pseudonym, and that promotional copies were pressed on a special festive red-and-green label, which you unaccountably failed to note in your book. The matrix numbers remain unaltered.

Yours sincerely,

U.B. Doobie,
The Old Police House,
Letsby Avenue,
Basildon

Then, sometime in the last days of winter I met a girl called Glenys. She had long hair, dark eyes and a large collection of extremely short dresses. We became a couple instantly and my off-duty habits altered as a result. We lasted until late autumn, and she brought me many new experiences, including the final one of being unceremoniously dumped because I never went dancing with her. I was still thick as two short planks.

Thicker yet were the occasional loonies who drifted into our shop. We averaged some 600 transactions a day – we knew this because the cash register had a mechanical counter built into it – and the law of *that* average clearly stated we were due a nutter at least twice a week.

On a quiet afternoon, as I busied myself restocking shelves for the next burst of activity, a dishevelled and unshaven 40-something man strolled up to the counter and belched directly at me. I recognised the delicate aroma of stale egg mixed, oddly, with an overtone of hair oil, as he said, without any warning:

'You know, they still haven't replied. I mean what's the point of having a Royal Family if they don't respond, eh?'

'Can I help you, sir?'

'I mean, it's been over a month since I sent my postcard. If only they would listen to me, their problems could all be solved.'

'You're probably right. Now, what can I get you?'

He picked up a large bag of wine gums and fished in his coat pocket for that daft little horseshoe-shaped leatherette change purse that people insisted on carrying in those days. I hated him just for that. Pedantically he counted out the 1/3 and then suddenly and violently opened the bag, scattering perfectly innocent confectionery across the counter. He picked up gum after gum from their resting places and stuffed them in his mouth as he continued to speak, the twinning of mastication and mumbling producing a stunning visual side effect as multi coloured drool began the journey down the twisting paths of his unshaven chin.

'I KNEW...' (glomp) '...they'd have the silverware if they weren't...' (ga-chook) '...watched. I mean, you can't...' (schplut) '...trust them, can you?'

'Er... anything else we can do for you?'

'No, but there is something I can do for YOU!' (Oh shit, is this where we get the unstoppable religious tract?) 'I note that you peddle stationery, and I am in the process of divesting myself of a lifetime's collection of good quality pens. Let me show you.'

He opened his greasy light brown coat to reveal row after row of half-chewed ballpoints taped to the lining. There must have been at least fifty. He stood there holding his coat open, grinning like a flasher in a nurses' dorm. Inspiration descended.

'Look, I've got plenty of stock right now', I said, 'but I know a man who really could use what you have. Let me give you his address.'

'Ah. Inside information, eh? Knew I'd come to the right place.'

I jotted down the name and address of another newsagent a mile down the road, and Pen Man left to pursue his mission. About a week later, at a cash and carry wholesalers, I ran into my colleague.

'Cor', he said, 'I had a right bleedin' nutcase in the other day, tried to sell me a fuckin' used biro collection. I told 'im to piss orf. So *then* he takes orf 'is trilby, fishes into it and offers me 'alf an egg sandwich covered in fuckin' stale Brylcreem. I chucked 'im out.'

'There's a lot of it about,' I answered quietly.

———————————

In April 1969, B.B. King appeared at the Albert Hall. His supporting acts were to be Sonny Terry & Brownie McGhee and Fleetwood Mac. Why didn't the promoters do an upright job and include Mrs. Mills and Tommy Cooper as well? Nevertheless, we were going to see the King Of The Blues – a very big deal, especially for Bill Greensmith, who had been B.B.'s biggest British fan for some years, as well as the compiler of the original discography upon which all others are now based. Bill and I had front row seats for this, booked weeks earlier.

Brownieandsonny appeared first, and were thoroughly and completely Brownieandsonny. They always were, no matter whether they played the Albert Hall or a tweedy back-room folk club. I had seen them before this night and would see them again, and they remained one of the most thoroughly professional acts in the blues. They also, of course, detested each other, but they knew each other very well too, and as a result their music spoke with one voice. Like performing twins who accepted that their fate brought them their fortune, they could predict each other's moves and weave in and out of them seamlessly. When Sonny performed the extraordinary harmonica and vocal whoop, 'Hootin' The Blues', Brownie's guitar was watching his back every step of the way. Listen to any Brownieandsonny performance and the thing you'll never hear is a missed beat.

Fleetwood Mac was, by 1969, in an awkward phase of transition. Having been launched by Mike Vernon's Blue Horizon label as a blues band wedded to the Elmore James sound, and having travelled that route via the Chess studios in Chicago and segued into their Top 20 period with 'Albatross' and 'Man Of The World', they had a heavy foot in both camps when they stepped on stage at the RAH. What were they going to do as the warm-up act for The King? Their answer, sensibly, was to produce a splendid, no-nonsense set of knockabout rock'n'roll classics. They performed 'Long Tall Sally', 'Maybellene', 'The Girl Can't Help It' and others with an enthusiasm that spoke perhaps of an awareness of their predicament, but they pulled it off and managed to exit stage left with integrity.

Now it was time: B.B.'s band appeared on stage first, beautifully suited-up like London gangsters on a Sunday outing with their mums. They played the warm-up set and then the barracking began: 'Ladies and Gentlemen, put your hands together for the KING OF THE BLUES, the one and only MISTER BEE BEE KING!'

And, to a staccato accompaniment, our man strolled on stage with Lucille, his guitar, strapped across his chest to greet the awestruck applause. Without further preamble he launched into 'Paying The Cost To Be The Boss'. I glanced at Bill. If he'd beamed any broader the top of his head would have fallen off backwards. B.B. finished his opener. I asked Bill what he thought so far. 'Cor... *FUUUUCK!*' He always had a way with words.

And so it went, one searing classic after another, with B.B. wailing in his open-throated gospel voice that had learned its craft at the feet of the Fairfield Four, and pulling a swarm of stinging notes from Lucille that both

The Sideburn Brothers waiting for B.B. King:
Me outside the Royal Albert Hall with Frank Nazareth and his wife, June.

underpinned and highlighted it. His voice and guitar were like Brownieandsonny insofar as they *knew* each other, but they were more intimate lovers than competitive twins. There was a *simpatia* between voice and instrument that flowed directly from B.B. and arrived at our ears welded into the fluid sound of The King Of The Blues at the top of his game.

Suddenly, a string on Lucille broke. The audience gasped in sympathy in the same moment that B.B. said 'Oh-oh!' Accepting the situation and stepping close to the microphone, he began to speak; to tell a story as if he were addressing just one person instead of an Albert Hall-ful. As he did so, he reached into his pocket for a fresh string.

His story went more or less like this: 'Well, this here is Lucille, my guitar. Let me tell you about her and how she got her name. A lot of years ago I was playing in a little club somewhere down South, and there was a fight. Two guys got into it, and in the fighting, the old kerosene stove that

93

heated the place got knocked over, started a fire. So, people started runnin' for the door. B.B. King started runnin' for the door too *[laughter from audience]*. Then, when I was part-way out the door, I remembered I'd left my guitar back on the stage, so I went runnin' back to get it. Pretty foolish, huh? *[more laughter]* So, later I found out that the fight was over a woman called Lucille. I figured if they were stupid enough to get into a fight and start a fire over a Lucille, and I was stupid enough to run back in, I'd better call my guitar Lucille. And here she is.' ...by which time he had re-strung and re-tuned, and immediately launched off into 'Don't Answer The Door'. It brought the house to its feet in a roar of amazement. We had no idea this was a rehearsed schtick, we just thought he was being a thorough professional. As it turned out, he was. We just didn't know how much.

Because Bill had credentials as a photographer, he managed to get backstage after the gig to take a few Cartier-Bresson snaps. I trailed along posing as his caddy, very aware of the privilege. B.B. was relaxed but stoked; the gig had gone well, and he was sitting on a chair, with an unplugged Lucille, just fooling around and talking to people. As Bill pursued decisive moments with his camera, B.B. started explaining the various guitar styles he admired and who had influenced him. He has always been open and generous about guitar players he admires: 'Here's T-Bone,' he said, emulating T-Bone Walker's groundbreaking single-string style. 'He's the guy who started it on electric guitar.'

'Here's how Blind Lemon sounded,' and he pulled music from Lucille that could have been trucked in directly from the Paramount studios.

He demonstrated another style: 'This guy was a genius, anyone know who I'm talking about?'

'Django Reinhardt!' I and another guy immediately said.

'Riiiight... Django. He was just great. I really admired what he could do.'

Opening the door of opportunity a little further, I asked B.B. how he'd first come across the Manouch Gypsy.

'Army guys coming back from Europe after the war; they brought the records in. I listened and was just... amazed. Oh, I've been a Django man for 25 years or more.'

I told my father this story over breakfast the next morning, and he smiled and said: 'You'd better play me some B.B. King then.'

I took a vacation for a week in Newport, Monmouthshire. Not an obvious choice for traditional holiday delights, but I'd been invited to spend time with some friends who shared a house; the connecting tissue being that we were all blues enthusiasts. Dave Williams, Adrian Tolchard, John Hart and a ferule little geezer called Barney lived together, bloke-fashion, in a decaying old Victorian property on the edge of town. I took a train down, found the house and knocked. A bleary young herbert with a cigarette in one hand, a beer bottle in the other and half a sandwich in his mouth opened the door, wearing only socks and sunglasses. It was Barney. He managed to share some of his sandwich in greeting me and I took my bag up the gritty stairs to the main front room which contained two sofas, a large hi-fi, hundreds of records, a deeply unclean carpet and the remains of a fortnight's snacking. It was very relaxing.

Later Adrian, Dave and John returned from work and, in a kitchen that only blokes would set foot in, we set about creating the kind of meal that only blokes are good at: vast quantities of overcooked bacon, greasy eggs, carbonised sausages, fried bread, tomatoes, a hundredweight of baked beans, a bucket of chips and a garnish of mushrooms, all deliciously smothered in brown sauce, served with extra white bread and butter, optional Marmite and gallons of tea. For dessert, cigarettes, beer, blues records and a very lengthy farting contest.

Each man had his own room and the 78's were kept in them, but albums and 45's were stashed in the front room and the combined collections offered a staggering choice of music. At 8:00 am or 2:00 am the house would shudder to the sounds of Magic Sam or Jimmy Reed or Son House. Locals would come and go – I never knew who they were – and we picked our way over bodies, beer bottles, fag ash and old newspapers to reach the kind of bathroom that only blokes are good at keeping. If we survived this experience we could be rewarded with more beer, fags, music, crisps, Mars bars, and an occasional doobie. The sounds of carnal activity issued from every room. I loved it.

———————————

Fred McDowell came back to Europe, his first overseas tour in almost four years, and his first on the folk-blues club circuit. Excited beyond measure (imperial or metric) at the prospect of seeing one of my all-time favourites, I was even prepared to venture into uncharted wastelands to do so: the Elephant and Castle, in East London, and the dusty upper rooms of an old pub that served as the base camp for Jo-Ann Kelly's blues club.

An extraordinary woman, Jo-Ann was the possessor of a voice that could not possibly have been further from her image. She looked like a thousand other young English women at the time, in granny specs and a big hat planted across her uncoiffured hair. But she could sing like her heroine, Memphis Minnie, and she could play guitar with the deepest Delta commitment. In the often chequered arena of British blues interpreters, Jo-Ann was the hugely talented exception, and her untimely death in 1990 an even greater loss.

The evening was opened – or rather torn asunder – by a set from Brett Marvin & The Thunderbolts, about the noisiest bunch of oiks on the folk-blues circuit at that time. Music to drink Watney's Bleedin' Red Barrel to. Jo-Ann appeared, played an engaging set including a *tour-de-force* 'Ain't Nothing In Rambling' and introduced Fred McDowell. I had stationed myself as far up front as possible; there was no stage, Fred would simply occupy a chair in the window of this huge, crowded old room, and I wanted no-one to block my view. When he sat down, I was within three feet of him, directly in front of the machine-head of his beautiful red-bodied electric guitar. If anyone in the audience cared that this Mississippi bluesman had gone electric, they didn't shout 'Judas'. We'd have duffed them up if they did. Fred plugged in, looked across the room, smiled a smile I recognised from 1965 and said it again: 'I want y'all to know that I do not play no rock and roll.'

A beer-swilling, righteously folky in-oneness-with-you-brother cheer rippled through the room. Then Fred just leaned into it and blew us out of our British minds.

He opened with 'Shake 'em On Down', as he probably often did, and I reconnected with the version he had played in Croydon four years earlier, the difference for me being that this time I was three feet, rather than fifty feet from him. I had never heard this depth of Delta blues this close before, and the music swallowed me whole.

He played scorching, power-laden slide guitar with the nonchalance of a man waiting for a haircut. No grimacing, no mugging, no airhead banging, just Fred and a guitar he knew well, doing what he was supposed to do: play the blues like no-one else could. Fred McDowell's style is unique. You cannot point to even the most obscure 78 rpm disc and say: 'Aha! Blind Boy Migraine on Gennett! That's where he got it from.' A CD called *The Roots Of Fred McDowell* would be completely blank. Followers there are, but predecessors none. All this – except the bit about the CD – was rammed home to me that night.

In between songs Fred would talk to the audience with an easy, winning charm, as if he'd known us for years. Then he'd reach back in and pull out 'Kokomo Blues' or 'You Gonna Be Sorry'. His slow-burn blues were just as intense as his country dance party tunes, and I remember the rising astonishment we all felt that night as he wound deeper and deeper into his thoroughly reworked edition of 'Worried Life Blues'. It soared and dived, glided from stanza to stanza, rose into the air again, swooped back down and hovered above us until Fred ended it with a final glissando. By the time he had played the last note, the tension was wound so tight that, had the wild burst of cheers, whoops, rabid applause and exhalations not happened, the place would have imploded and none of us would ever have been seen again. Just a huge, cumbersome ball of fused energy harbouring home-knitted socks, partially digested lentils, sensible sandals, half-full tins of Golden Virginia, startled looks covered in facial hair, Fair Isle sweaters and real ale in dimple mugs would have been all that was left for someone to have to roll home to Mum with a bizarre explanation.

My father, perhaps the most industrious man I ever knew, decided that running a shop for ninety hours a week wasn't enough. He therefore underwent and passed the Advanced Motoring Test, took out extra insurance, bought a decent secondhand Austin 1100, fitted it out with a set of 'He-Man' manual dual controls (I'm not kidding about the name) and began advertising. That was all you had to do in those days to become a driving instructor. Was life simpler? In some ways, yes; there were fewer rules. To my mother's surprise, it actually fitted into our lifestyle quite well. He got fairly busy, and so we hired another part-timer to stand behind the counter while he was on the road. The empire was expanding.

Three streets up from the shop was a garage, owned by a Jamaican called Ken. Large and successfully busy with all manner of repairs, it was therefore able to support several apprentice mechanics, also mainly Jamaican, who had been told by Ken that (a) they would be more useful to him if they passed their driving tests and he could therefore pay them more, and (b) he was willing to fund the costs involved if they agreed to stay at least a year after they passed.

This was Dad's initial customer base. Because they were young, keen and motivated, all four candidates were model students, passing their tests first time round. At the testing station Dad built a fast reputation among other, more conservative, driving instructors as an upstart specialising in blacks. His response, typically, was to ignore them and get on with it.

Not everyone was as ideal as the apprentices. He struggled for months to train a middle-aged man, a deeply religious soul who crossed himself every time he drove past a Catholic church which, in suburban North London was quite often. He sometimes took both hands off the wheel to do so. 'Do that once too often and you'll *need* to cross yourself,' Dad reminded him.

The guy who finally convinced him that perhaps the business wasn't all it was cracked up be was the young construction worker who he instructed, on the A41 at Mill Hill, to 'go straight over the roundabout', a simple enough manoeuvre that everyone in those days understood. Except this bloke. Responding with a dramatic and serious 'Right, guv', he suddenly sped up, cut across traffic and headed straight for the flowered island that connected four major roads, eliciting some very interesting gestures from other motorists. He bounced over the cement surround, climbed the slight hill, swerving to avoid a tree, and had mowed down the council-owned flowers before Dad could recover from his shock enough to apply the 'He-Man' brake system, reach for the ignition key and disable both car and student in mid-island. 'Sorry guv,' he apologised when reprimanded in old British Navy language by Dad, now furiously smoking at least two cigarettes, 'but you did say "straight over the roundabout".'

Now in it's seventh year, Horst Lipmann and Fritz Rau's *American Folk Blues Festival* was both an integral grid in the European blues map and, increasingly, an anachronism. The History Of The Blues In One Evening had been fine in the early days, but it was becoming frustrating to see legendary figures, for whose first 78's one had perhaps just traded a limb or two, sit down on stage barely long enough to get their bums warm. HOWEVER... what else you gonna do with your evening? Huh? Besides, this year looked much more promising. Horst & Fritz (which is *not* Cockney rhyming slang for 'Blitz', but could be) had gone and seen Chris Strachwitz, and were bringing in an impressive roster of mostly Arhoolie-related artists. Chris was there too, as a sort of road manager, translator and general harried gopher.

Thus we got to see Juke Boy Bonner, Alex Moore, Clifton Chenier, Carey Bell, John Jackson, Earl Hooker and Magic Sam. Juke Boy opened, always a difficult task on nights like this, and, soon after, seeing him in much more intimate surroundings, I was even more divided about the *AFBF* philosophy. The Chenier brothers were almost certainly the first zydeco band to step into the European arena. Some people, who hadn't yet focused on this genre, wondered openly what an accordion was doing on stage; until, that is, it began to move under the expert hands of Clifton Chenier. He kicked off with 'Squeeze Box Boogie', and it made eyes pop all across the hall. The Albert Hall had been there a long time, seen and absorbed a great deal since it was first erected, but I don't believe it had ever encountered an accordion and rub-board boogie before this night. The resonance in the instrument was astonishing, and the old pile filled itself to the rafters with the glorious, swooping, fluid sound of rocking accordion backed by the crazed rattle of the metal rub-board. They finished and, I swear, there was a three-count pause of astonishment before the audience broke out of its trance and into its applause. The Chenier brothers grinned broadly. But then they always did.

My memory of that night was that everyone was good. Alex Moore brought over forty years of Texas barrelhouse piano experience to the party. John Jackson eased that warm, archaic Virginia accent into our senses and then prodded it home with guitar picking that sounded to me like the spirit of Blind Blake had finally extracted itself from under the streetcar that felled him and descended onto the RAH stage. (Another wine gum sir? Thank you no, I've probably had enough.)

But the star of my evening was Magic Sam. Young, good looking, very hip and VERY hot, he knew full well, I think, that his career was taking off in directions he seriously wanted it to go. If ever a man exuded the expectant glow of immediately impending success, it was Sam that night. Accompanied by his bassist Mack Thompson, he opened with a stinging version of 'All Your Love', faithful to the original Cobra recording from more than a decade before, yet also fresh, exciting and vigorously performed like a newly-written song. As the closing bars echoed over the audience and we responded with our applause and cheers, Sam turned to Mack and asked him what they were going to play next. The taciturn bass player grunted and shrugged. 'Speak up, man,' chided Sam, 'you're over here now, not over there' – a remark that was met with the thunderously self-righteous applause that only a white liberal European 1960's audience could have produced. Did Sam really believe that it was better here than there? I had no idea, and no chance to consider the many implications, for he immediately launched into his instrumental classic, 'Lookin' Good'.

If you didn't see Sam in the flesh, the best way to get a feel for this particular performance is to listen to the version on the *Live At Ann Arbor* CD at full volume, then allow for the fact that you really had to be there anyway. I'm sorry to appear smarmy (no, I'm bloody not), but Sam's performance was so whole, so intense and also so visual that sound was not the only element; his guitar was more an integral part of his soul than anyone I've ever seen except Son House. He rocked the Victorian hallways with an energy that came from deep inside and simply found its way directly to the strings. 'Looking Good' is a very simple boogie pattern, repetitive even, but the sheer swing that Sam imbued it with took it to levels that few others could reach. He really was that good, and that he died at age 32, even before the fast-closing decade was gone, is one of the great tragedies of blues history.

Duke Boy.

'And what of Earl Hooker?' I hear you ask.

I missed him. Glenys threw a sudden wobbler that I simply failed to understand and demanded to leave as Earl was setting up his guitar. I drove her home in a very loud silence and she got out without a word. The next day she sawed off the pair of short planks she had been stepping out with for the last few months and I never saw her again. Frank Nazareth asked me a week later what I'd thought of Earl Hooker. I told him my story and he jokingly remarked: 'You'll be sorry you did that if he dies next week.' A few months later, Earl Hooker was dead. 'I'm not opening me gob again,' said Frank when I reminded him of his prophecy, 'unless there's money in it.'

Juke Boy Bonner stayed on to fulfil a solo tour of London gigs, and I took agreed random time off from the business to concentrate on this. Juke Boy and I had been writing to each other for close to two years, I had amassed every record I could by him, lusting only after the Irma 78, his first. I was ecstatic at the thought of spending time with him.

Juke Boy played his first gig at the 100 Club in November, an excellent, tight, cohesive set. He was comfortable there, in intimate surroundings – and also warm. His entire tour was plagued by a deep cold snap, with sharp frost on the morning ground and intermittent but heavy snow. Bill and I spent a great deal of time with him, and, by agreement with the promoter, undertook to pick him up from his hotel and spend the day with him providing we further undertook to deliver him to the night's gig. We did this more than once.

On the first day that we called for him, we were delighted to find Otis Spann sitting in the lobby. While we waited for Juke Boy, we chatted with Otis and I believe this was the occasion that Bill established the presence of B.B. King on Otis' one Checker release, 'Five Spot'. In fact, Otis had forgotten he'd cut it until Bill reminded him.

We took Juke Boy out to Bill's Wimbledon flat to talk and play records. He was astonished at how much Bill had that was both familiar and unfamiliar to him. Bill played him Jimmy Rogers' version of 'Sloppy Drunk', which he had not heard before, and he loved it immediately, asking to listen to it three times. As the afternoon continued, Bill's wonderful mum appeared at the door with trays laden with tea, toast, jam, cakes and biscuits. Juke Boy looked at this cornucopian apparition, then at his watch. 'Hey,' he said, 'the English really DO take tea at four o'clock, huh?' That night, in a pub in Hammersmith, he sang a word-perfect version of 'Sloppy Drunk'.

I missed Otis Spann's performances at Ronnie Scott's because we were with Juke Boy, and it's one of my two 1960's regrets. Bill and I went everywhere Juke Boy went. On another occasion when we called for him at the hotel, he was ensconced by the lobby fireplace, sharing a pot of tea and a plate of fairy cakes with a delightful old couple from Hurstpierpoint in Sussex, up in London for the shopping. They had connected with him the previous day, and had taken an immediate and deep interest in him. As we approached, they were asking him how the previous night had gone.

'The "gig" you call it, yes, Mr. Bonner? Or may I call you "Duke Boy"?' said the wife.

'Yes ma'm, call me Juke Boy.'

'Kind of you, Duke Boy,' chipped in the husband. 'So you're happy with your reception here?'

'Yes.'

'Good, good. We like to support the Arts, you know.'

As we approached he rose to greet us with an outstretched and manicured hand. 'And you gentleman would be Mr Bon... er, Duke Boy's entourage I take it?'

Juke Boy had a contract to cut an album for Liberty while in London, and so, on a bitterly cold November morning, we all gathered at the Regent Sound studios. He was to be accompanied by members of the Nighthawks, perhaps one of the best and certainly most dedicated British blues bands then active.   Bassist Bruce Langsman was a collector who, on stage, would announce the title of their next tune followed immediately by the catalogue number of the original release: 'Now were gonna play Arthur Crudup's 'I Wonder', Ace 503. Thank you very much.'

People arrived complaining about the cold. Mike Leadbitter came in saying he'd gone deaf from the screams of all the brass monkeys out in the street. Someone else arrived to be asked how they were.

'In a word, cold.'

'And in two words?'

'*Fucking* cold.'

'Thank you, that's what I needed to hear.'

Juke Boy came through the door obsessed by the disaster that had befallen him that morning. The hotel laundry had lost every last sock he had.

'Hi! How you doing, Juke Boy?'

'They lost m'goddam socks, man.'

'Fancy a cup of coffee?'

'I need socks, man, socks.'

'Here, have a chair.'

'Shit, it's cold when you ain't got socks.'

Someone found him a pair. The session got under way and lasted until early afternoon. By the time everyone was done, the sun was starting to go down – it was almost 2:00 pm – and, following a quick pint and a brief street photo-shoot at which the subject of socks was again raised, Bill and I dragged Juke Boy off in search of replacement soft furnishing for his feet. We headed out for Wimbledon and the Hand-In-Hand pub, stopping off in Tooting at a gents' outfitters that Bill knew. We all three entered this genteel, old-world establishment looking like the trio of heavyweight boxer and two minders that the staff assumed we were.

'Can I help you, gentlemen?'

'Yeah, I need socks before I loose my toes to frostbite, man.'

'Walk this way, please.'

'If he could walk that way, he wouldn't need socks,' I said, seizing the opportunity.

'May I ask where and when you are next appearing, sir?'

Juke Boy looked to Bill for an answer.

'Fulham, mate,' Bill replied.

'Ah, I didn't realise there was an arena there.'

Turning again to Juke Boy he continued: 'Tell me sir, have you ever met Mr. Ali professionally?'

On a quiet Sunday afternoon I drove up to Juke Boy's hotel, picked him up and brought him back out to Cricklewood to listen to records. Our shop closed early on Sundays, at 2:00pm, so I presented him to my parents at mid-afternoon, and again, he was immediately smothered with motherly tea, crustless ham sandwiches, fairy cakes, chocolate eclairs and more tea. I showed him my collection of Lightnin' Hopkins 78's which he viewed as something beyond surreal.

'These are Houston records. How d'you get 'em?' and he sat listening to his good friend Lightnin' play the blues long-distance at him in a London flat.

My father asked him if he'd ever heard Django Reinhardt and, when Juke Boy said no, explained that what he was about to hear was produced by two fingers and a thumb, then stuck 'Dinah' and 'Sweet Georgia Brown' to him. Juke Boy, like any decent musician, was awestruck. He then took up my father's offer of his electric guitar and played some Sunday afternoon blues; after the first number, Dad quietly reached for his old acoustic instrument and gently joined in on rhythm. It is my other 1960's regret that the tape recorder was no longer functional. For Juke Boy's own comments on his British experience, listen to 'Childhood Dreams' on Arhoolie CD 9040.

And so, the Sixties drew to a close. Were we, in that moment, aware of how special they had been? Only partly, I think. For one thing, not a great deal altered between 31 December and 1 January, nor did we expect it to. We hadn't gone decimal yet, we weren't in the Common Market and we still had a bunch of daft sods in Parliament who thought they knew what was best for us. Things were going to change radically, as we now know, but at midnight on 31 December, as I played the decade out by lowering the needle onto the groove of Muddy Waters' 'You're Gonna Miss Me', hindsight was nothing like ready to be interviewed. Why was I not cavorting in the fountain at Trafalgar Square? Because I had to get up at 5:00 am to schlep newspapers, that's why. Welcome to the new decade, mate.

Chapter Five

1970-75: YOU *SURE* YOU'RE NOT A ROZZER?

The next thing that happened to me in January 1970 was a day off. I returned to my familiar stamping grounds like an odd lemming drawn to a Cliff Richard, to see the lunchtime crowd at Dobell's, eat cheap spaghetti and talk bollocks with some of them at the very loud and cheerful little Italian restaurant a few doors away. Over heaped plates of Bolognese, Clifford Martin was acting out the recent acquisition of another rare record. Imitating the polishing of his fingernails, he said, as if to himself, but loudly: 'One of the chosen few, you know. Ha!' The faux polishing continued.

'Yes, Clifford, I know you're Jewish. So was my great-grandfather. What of it?'

'No, no... one of the chosen few who now owns a mint, original copy of the VERY RARE John Lee Hooker LP on King. I suppose you, like everyone else, have the nasty reissue on Ember?'

I nodded a pasta-filled head.

'Did you know the original is called *Every One A Pearl*?'

No, the pasta agreed, it didn't.

'That's because ONLY the original, which I now possess, has that title, and only a very few CHOSEN ONES possess it.'

'Clifford', I said, 'you're a wanker.'

'So are you,' he retorted, unmoved, 'but I'm physically smaller than you, which makes you a *MUCH BIGGER* wanker!'

He had me there.

Leaving Clifford to devices I understood well, I swanned through Zwemmer's art-book store across the street, peering again at images created by Dali, Magritte and Man Ray, then bought a cigar from the extraordinary little tobacconist's shop next door.

To enter this emporium was to step back in time. The pungent aroma of tobacco blending deliciously with the visual pleasure of its gleaming, finely-balanced scales, and the rows of polished glass-jarred pipe tobacco that served them; the display of exotic cigarette packets from Turkey, Greece, France, Spain and America, and the ranks of new lighters in glass cases, standing ready to ignite the contents, all spoke of a quickly vanishing, unhurried era. The equally extraordinary pair of old men who ran the place were natty little geezers who seemed to be on loan from the 1930's, in brown shop coats covering pin-stripe shirts topped off with bow ties. They looked and sounded like Henry Crun's younger brothers: 'Ah, yes, a Cuban cigar young sir, certainly – an excellent choice and most satisfying, I think, if you will excuse an opinion. Shall I cut it for you?'

Smoking luxuriously, I queued to see a new movie at Leicester Square in the afternoon: *Bullitt*, starring Steve McQueen, was opening that day. As I waited in line, an odd thing happened. A worried-looking young man who could have been an extra from *Get Carter* approached me and asked if I was a policeman. No, I replied, I was just waiting to see the film. He beetled off, only to return from an alleyway huddle even more perplexed.

'You SURE you're not a rozzer?'

'Look... no... I'm not, I assure you.'

'Oh, okay.'

Away he went, to reappear once more, now VERY harassed: 'Look, chum, you got any ID on you? My mates want to start a find-the-lady game and they think you're marking them.'

'Look, I'm NOT a bluebottle; I'm a tobacconist. Here, I've got my Tobacco Retailers' Federation membership card – have a butcher's. In fact, take it over there and show them.'

'Right, ta.' He presented the card to the two other skittish Carter lookalikes who studied the document, then peered in my direction and back at the card again. Finally, the messenger returned.

'All right mate, we reckon you're straight. Sorry,' and he disappeared. I cannot explain why this happened, except that possibly my dark blue serge trousers, light blue shirt, black knitted tie, size eleven black boots, short hair, six feet and 14 stone might have given them the wrong impression. But I always dressed casually on my day off.

By now I was a fully integrated member of the circle of blues collectors who infested and penetrated outward from London. There was nothing especially organised about us, we were just a group of like-minded souls who knew, communicated with, and visited each other, and who gathered, druid-like, at important occasions such as the acquisition by one of us of previously unheard and rare records. No harm in it. In fact, it prevented us from snatching old ladies' purses or publicly humiliating fat, spotty boy scouts with undropped testicles and high blood pressure. As my wife said recently to the complaining wife of another obsessive collector: 'Be glad, it keeps them off the streets.'

In addition to Bill, Dave, Frank, Clifford, Terry and Bruce there was Mike Rowe and Barbara, his delightful wife, who then lived in an ancient apartment in Lewisham, the kind with creaking wooden staircases and a timer on the stairwell light that always cut off even the most fleet-footed in mid-climb. Most of Mike's living room was taken up with metal shelves filled with records. Like Bruce, he had been bitten by the music earlier, had one of the better collections at that time – he still does – and it was at his place that people often sat cross-legged and facing east while considering the cosmic implications of the latest rare 78 to have arrived, via some complex private deal, from Hastings or Maxwell or Dowling Street. He had, by this time, just written his classic history of Chicago Blues, *Chicago Breakdown*, which, almost four decades after publication, is still the best single account of the early post-war Chicago sound. More of him later, also.

Then there was Frank Weston, a warm, open man with a an easy laugh, a black beard and piercing eyes. A contemporary of Bruce Bastin, he had seen Big Bill live in the 1950's, and in the early 1960's had worked for a London theatrical booking agency. He had been responsible for looking after Little Walter during his 1964 tour – no easy task, apparently. Walter was loath to rise from any bed he happened to be in, and was *not* a morning person. Oscar Wilde's remark that only dull people are bright in the mornings is one with which Walter would have thoroughly agreed, if perhaps in different words. It was Frank who accompanied him to a London tailor's to acquire the suit he appeared in on his two TV shows, and it was Frank who saw him come offstage, chug a half-bottle of gin followed by a mouthful of Coca-Cola then promptly hit the floor.

Frank also looked after Buddy Guy, and perhaps still possesses the audio tape of the 1965 discussion and jam session that Buddy and he enjoyed in Frank's apartment. Frank's agency promoted tours by Josh White, the Weavers, Pete Seeger, Jack Dupree, Jack Elliott and Chris Barber, fostered the careers of Long John Baldry, Cyril Davies, assorted Scottish folk singers and the Spanish act Dorita y Pepe. Frank was often plagued on the phone by a star-struck fan, Charlie Nash, who would call him to enquire about the weekly activities of this or that artist. One day he phoned and said: 'ere, yew got any pichers of Doreeta-why-Peep?'

Frank's very beautiful wife, Sylvia Pitcher, was a professional photographer, and a good one; her work often adorned the covers of British-issued blues LPs in the 1960's and 1970's. I was especially struck by one example, which simply and starkly portrayed the classic Southern image of a rural shotgun shack, overhung by ancient trees and surrounded by long-unattended grass.

Where, I asked, had she taken this stunning Cartier-Bressonesque image? Mississippi? Arkansas?

'Essex,' she replied, 'just outside of Basildon, actually.'

Peter Brown was tall, light-framed and handsome. My mother thought so, anyway. 'What a GOOD looking fellow,' she would say, and then proceed to feed him vast quantities of chocolate éclair cakes to fatten him up. Pete had a heroic track record none but Bruce could boast of. In the early 1960's, he had taken himself off to the US, landed in Chicago, got a job with the Jazz Record Mart store, out of which Delmark Records operated, and in his spare time went junking for blues 78's. Serious, knocking-on-doors-in-likely-areas junking. It was Pete who first discovered the Ora-Nelle 78's by Little Walter, Othum Brown, Johnny Williams and Johnny Young, buying them directly from the original store on Maxwell Street. If he hadn't, maybe they'd have been dumped and we wouldn't have ever known about them. By the time Pete returned to England in 1966, he owned a considerable collection, plus a whole pile of goodies to dispose of. In 1968, he put the best of his pre-war collection on his own 'Down With The Game' label, five groundbreaking volumes of random, but well-chosen and nicely-mastered pre-war blues. He also issued two pioneering EPs of post-war rural gospel. I once spent an entire evening offering him combinations of everything I owned for his copy of Tommy Johnson's 'Cool Drink Of Water' on Victor, even though I knew I had nothing to match it. Like the true gentleman he still is, he diplomatically refused my every desperate overture. Bastard.

I also got to know Paul Oliver, although on a different level. I was first invited to his house one evening as part of the group he gathered to welcome the visiting Dr. Harry Oster and his wife Caroline. To me, this was somewhere above the level of an invitation to the Queen's garden party. As well as being the doyen of all British blues experts, Paul was a lecturer in architecture, and his wonderful open-plan, split-level house in Harrow reflected his other major interest. I well remember being astonished at how many books and records he had, and that his living room area had been built with custom-made shelves integrated into the roughly pentagonal space where he and his wife Valerie entertained guests. Harry and Caroline Oster arrived last, to be met by the gathering as early Christians would have greeted an original Apostle. He sat and told stories of his exploits in field recording in Louisiana, and I listened especially to his tales of Robert Pete Williams. Had it not been for Dr. Oster, Robert Pete might have festered and died in Angola. And he certainly came across as a lot less insensitive than John Lomax. But then so did Ian Paisley.

I think it was on this evening that I first met Tony Russell, an erudite Oxford man who has continued over the years to staunchly choose the blues, jazz and hillbilly path, and whose contribution to our knowledge today would require its own chapter to sufficiently recount.

Tony perhaps rues that day, for he issued a generous invitation to me to come round and listen to what he had – an offer I took up and then perhaps abused when I discovered that he had a rare post-war record I especially lusted after, the Slim Pickens on Holiday – Eddie Burns' pseudonymous first recording. I offered him money immediately, and he refused. I questioned him about how often he would play it, and, in desperate justification, quadrupled my own listening estimate when I got his response. I badgered him for weeks, at one point sending him a letter every day for a fortnight requesting his capitulation in as many ways as I could cook up. Eventually I took delivery of a pile of what were then desperately rare early hillbilly 78's, and traded most of them to him for that one record. Obsessive? Moi?

Incredibly, he still talks to me.

I had taken a visitor to Paul's house on that Oster evening, one who happened to be staying with me at the time, Bengt Olsson. Bengt was Swedish by birth, but spiritually a Memphian. He had gone South in the mid-Sixties, hanging out in Memphis and the Delta as a teenager, in the course of which he interviewed and listened to everyone, drank moonshine in alleyways with Charlie Burse, was arrested by the Memphis police for suspected pimping and released again for being Swedish, made superb field recordings and scarfed up a significant collection of 78's. By the time he arrived in Britain, he had written his book, *Memphis Blues,* and was narrowing his area of specialisation down to the jug bands of Memphis and was prepared to trade anything he had to get what he needed.

He needed the Ben Covington Paramount which I happened to have and offered me a landslide trade I simply could not refuse: I wound up with eight rare post-war downhome 78's for the one Paramount! I thought he was mad. So, I think, did Paul Oliver when Bengt's first words to him that evening were: 'I understand you have the Mobile Strugglers on American Music?' Yes, Paul replied, he did. 'Then I will give you an Ishman Bracey Victor for it,' he answered, bluntly. Paul look stunned for a second, suppressed a laugh then warmly agreed.

Outside of his obsession, Bengt was a riot. His British English was as perfect as his American English, and his jokes were non-stop ('It's nice out isn't it? / 'Yes, but the policeman made me put it away again', etc). But the accent would still get in the way on occasion. He enjoyed calling anyone who displeased him, from an uncooperative record collector to a slow barman, a 'mootherfooker'.

There was also Tony Trent, a lanky, hairy fellow with a serious sinus problem and a deep interest in Leadbelly, someone who in those days, like Blind Lemon, Big Bill and Sonnyandbrownie, was often ignored simply because the old jazzers had overemphasised their contribution to the foundations of jazz. Every group held prejudices, and ours were definitely showing. Tony would appear at every live gig, always ebullient, always ready to talk over a pint before and after, always sharing any ideas that alcohol delivered to his head.

'Have you ever considered the life of a milkman?' he asked me.

'No, I haven't. Why would I?' I'm sure I replied.

'Well, think about it: you get up really early every morning before the sun rises and, no matter what the weather, you load up your milk float and you trundle off through mean and narrow streets anonymously delivering dairy produce. All day. Tout les bleedin' jours. Six days a week. Collecting profit for the man. For you, a sharecropper's pittance. Unable to break out of the vicious cycle, you go home each night exhausted, feeling trapped, very depressed by your life. Now, if you simply switch the milk float for a mule and the streets for forty acres, and transfer the whole thing to Mississippi, then you've got the essence of a blues life. So why don't British milkmen sing the blues, eh? I mean, they live 'em, don't they? Your round while you're considering it, mate – mine's a light and bitter.'

We all gathered whenever a blues singer appeared in London, which was surprisingly often in the early 1970's and almost always at the 100 Club in Oxford Street. It had been a jazz club since the 1940's, gone through many changes, and survived them all. The entrance was a narrow, bland, blink-and-you-miss-it doorway that lead down an ugly hallway and descended via shadowed stairs to the basement. At the turn of those stairs sat the combined entry lobby, cloakroom and ticket office. Then, to the left, a pair of double doors, the entrance to a low-ceilinged arena with a long bar stretching across the right-hand end, a centre-set, low, open stage backing the far wall, and an almost-always closed Chinese restaurant at the opposite end. It was dark, muggy, smoke-filled and noisy. I loved it. To enter the 100 Club on a blues night was to walk directly into much of the real meaning that the world then held for me.

I had been there as early as 1967, and in the spring of 1969 had witnessed the extraordinary evening when Lowell Fulson, whose gig it was, invited a member of the audience onstage to jam. B.B. King, having just played that week at the Albert Hall, stepped up and accepted a loaned guitar. As I watched the two previous Kent Records artists perform together, I remember wondering how much combined royalty income they were owed by the label's owners, the Bihari brothers. A truly anal notion, considering I was being entertained by two of the great post-war guitar stylists.

Blues gigs in the early 1970's were often operated by the extraordinary Ron Watts, a Victorianesque barrel of man with a handlebar moustache and a head-on approach to life. He brought in Lightnin' Slim, Big Boy Crudup, Tommy Tucker, J.B. Hutto, Freddy King and the Johnny Otis Show. Images of many of these nights flow into one another – this was my drinking period – and I was a royal pain in the arse to Ron.

A generally easygoing man, he would often allow a few of us to crowd into the tiny dressing room that sat adjacent to the toilets, to chat with whoever was preparing to play that night. He bawled me out, quite rightly, for buying Lightnin' Slim a pint ('You can't fuckin' do that, I control the artistic beer intake here, not you, you arsehole!') and also for answering the dressing room phone and giving information to punters about upcoming gigs in an over-the-top Flaming Queen voice ('Any more of that "Effie Dropbottom" nonsense and you're out on your fuckin' ear, mush'). Yet he always forgave.

I clearly remember Freddy King jamming with Stan Webb, staging a guitar battle that ended with Stan bested, but loving it; I also vividly recall members of the Johnny Otis show almost unable to play because they were laughing so hard at an image that erupted in the audience in front of them.

The old teddy boys and rockers had come out to pay homage to Johnny, and during 'Willie And The Hand Jive', a perfectly-attired three foot high midget teddy boy was hoisted onto the shoulders of a rocker twice his size and sat there, his size three blue-suede-shoed feet dangling across his partner's lapels, while both of them executed a complex and synchronized hand jive.

There was also a night when a visiting Belgian jazz fan and I struck up a pre-show conversation about the history of the club. He and his alcohol became quite excited about being in such a historic setting and he wandered off for a refill and a think. He reappeared to ask me if Dizzy Gillespie had played here.

'Not sure,' I replied, 'but possible.'

'Alors!' – off he went again.

Moments later, he loomed up out of the dark in front of me, grinning with the delight of fantasy. Had Stan Getz played here?

'Very possible,' I said, now beginning to wish I hadn't started all this.

'Oooohhh, zutalors! I – 'ow you zay – unclog mah nostreels weez delight!'

Back he came from the lavatory with another thought: 'Louize Harmstronghe, deed 'e plai 'ere alzo?'

'Oh, yes, he jammed with Lester Young back in '49.'

'Argh! Merdalors!! And 'ere I yam in zee prezzence of hall zees eestory. Deed... deed... Sharlee Parkair evair...'

'Yup, 1947. He jammed with Hot Lips Page and Django on that very stage. Bill Coleman joined them half way through the set. Charlie Mingus was on bass. Not a lot of people know that.'

'Oooh! Argh! I weell keel mahself wiz plezure!' and he went scampering off again to get more ale.

I moved my position and spent the night avoiding him.

There were other turns that we saw in this remarkable establishment – not blues, but a great deal of fun nevertheless. Bob Kerr's Whoopee Band, a kind of jazz-oriented Bonzo Dog Band captained by Kerr, himself an original Bonzo, appeared more than once. The night that pokes sticks in the mind's eye, however is one when saxophonist Jim 'Goldenboots' Chambers, rising to take a vocal refrain, was confronted with a blown mike. We heard it pop as he reached it. Without skipping a single beat he changed horses mid-stream, and wordlessly mimed his way through with exaggerated silent-movie gestures, turning a potential embarrassment into a glorious sight gag. He sat down again to a storm of applause. Bruce Bastin turned to me, beaming with delight, and said: 'WHAT a trouper!'

A similar group who seem to have fallen off the edge of the earth's memory are the Amazing Mad Gas Medicine Show & Junk Band. Like the Bonzos and the Whoopees, they specialised in parody, but employed a wider brief: blues, jazz, vintage rock'n'roll, doo-wop, pop and country were all legitimate targets. There were at least five of them, possibly more, and their version of Jerry Lee's 'Breathless' involved the pianist being lifted up on the shoulders of the bass player and turned backwards while still playing. He never missed a note, and I still don't know how they did that.

Much less amusing was a trio called Something Else, three old rockers from (probably) Essex with unreconstructed haircuts and attitudes, who performed extraordinarily good rockabilly versions of classic tunes by Eddie Cochran, Carl Perkins, Elvis, Billy Lee Riley and others, but who also used the stage to air their political views ('Vote for Enoch Powell', 'Join the National Front', etc), causing a dissent among the divided-camp audience that rose to almost Red Alert level as the fuel of alcohol was poured across the embers:

'Oi! Wannapunchupthefroat?' enquired a huge, wobbly-drunk rocker of a lean and protesting hippie.

'No thanks, man, I roll my own,' he replied, ducking and weaving as he spoke.

Somewhere around this time, probably in May 1970, when he was in London to record, I also saw Howlin' Wolf at the 100 Club. I have no recall of who backed him, but it was a probably local band. He, however, was extraordinary.

Wolf was a *BIG* man, and his presence, too, was huge. The only artist to challenge Muddy in Chicago, he had similar charisma and power, and, despite their sometimes fierce competition, one was not better than the other; they were both unique. Wolf was playing harmonica that evening, roaring into it in a way I've never heard anyone do before or since. He had enormous lungs, and when he blew through his gob-iron it rattled and hummed and damn near exploded under the force. If Robert Crumb was drawing it, the harmonica would be bulging under the pressure of air pouring through it.

He sang his classics, and to watch him perform 'Smokestack Lightnin'' or 'Forty-Four Blues' or 'I Ain't Superstitious' was, for me, to reconnect with the rush of enthusiasms I had had back in 1963. Wolf was the first electric bluesman I happened to hear, and, although first encounters generally bite deeply, I think if I'd not heard Wolf until later, he would still have blown my Y-fronts off. Of course he bloody would, he was The Wolf. He ended the evening with his khaki shirt bathed in sweat, smiling, ready – it seemed to me – to go again. A giant.

The 100 Club night I recall most vividly, however, was the one on the final day of June 1970 when Son House played to a room more packed and sweaty than I had ever sweltered in before. My previous experience of seeing him live, at Hammersmith in 1967, had been frustrated by my distance from him and his lack of onstage time. On this evening, I bought three pints immediately and commandeered a table at the very front of the stage. I had a sturdy bladder in those days. No tarty pre-gig flitting from conversation to conversation for this lad tonight, Son was serious stuff, and I was staking out my territory. I was joined by a couple of regulars, Tony Trent ('ere, mate, have you ever paused to consider the life of a trainee proctologist?') and Ray Bolden ('Good evening, *wankers*'), but that night, as far as I was concerned, it was just Son and me.

He was 62 by the time he was rediscovered, and this was almost six years beyond that. We might reasonably have expected him to coast a little. Frankly, he could have just broken wind and left again, and I'd still have applauded him simply for being Son House, with all that that meant. Here was the man who played and knocked around with Charley Patton and Willie Brown; here was the man Muddy Waters stood in awe of and was prepared to say so; here was the man who had set foot in the Paramount studios way before most of his audience was born and created a small body of music so powerful that it continues to reverberate throughout the blues today. Here, in a nutshell, was a pure source of the blues, a surviving essence. I was sitting six worshipful feet from him.

He clambered slowly onto the stage, taking his time getting seated, and then somebody handed him his guitar – the beat up old National that you see in all the photos and films. With a benign, quizzical smile he looked around him at a sea of expectant, largely white, faces – an audience he had grown used to in his new career. He began to talk, and as he did so the buzz from the crowd fell away, shepherded by a shushing that began at the front.

He talked quietly, gently, like a benign grandfather addressing his many offspring on matters of importance. His manner was sweet and retiring, almost shy. He rambled some, but it didn't matter – this was Son House. Then, having finished what he had to say about the blues not being about jumping a rabbit and running him a solid mile, but about a man and a woman in love, he struck a chord on his guitar as if to wake it and took off into 'Death Letter Blues', his audience now only a fog as his deep sense of The Blues suddenly and completely overtook him.

He became a different person when he sang, and he did it immediately. There was no gentle transition from the quiet speaker to the man possessed by his subject; it was as sudden as a door slammed shut. His whole body moved with the music, he and his guitar inseparable. His eyes were closed and he just wasn't with us any more, nor was he singing for us. He was somewhere else in his life, singing to himself and for himself, in the deepest recesses of his being. We were simply observers of the complete baring of a soul.

This was not entertainment in the way that J.B. Hutto or Lightnin' Slim were. Watching Son House sing the blues, you had to witness it for what it was: a private catharsis made public. When he finished singing, he seemed to come out of a trance, a look of surprise on his face. 'Oh, yes, I'm back here. Of course.' For several minutes, he had spiritually left the building, leaving his body to transmit to us, via remote broadcast, what he was experiencing. When he returned, he was exhausted, as if he had just completed a long and arduous journey, which indeed he had.

Then he would do it all again for 'Empire State Express' or 'Preaching The Blues'. He was the most extraordinarily deep bluesman I ever experienced. Electrifying, in a real sense. Being in Son's presence while he sang made me tingle. It sent involuntary shivers through my body and tears welled in my eyes, as they still do when I visit his recorded and filmed legacy. I saw him several times during that tour, talked to him at length one afternoon at a press reception I simply dared to walk into, and shook his hand on more than one occasion. I needed to do all that, to listen to and talk to and clasp the hand of the man who was, in every sense, the greatest surviving original blues singer. In doing so, I connected with the deepest of Delta Blues on every level I could. What a privilege.

Out of the blue one evening I got a phone call from a man with an American accent. Clearly, it wasn't my great uncle Ted, my paternal grandmother's brother from Detroit, who had run away from his London home at the age of fifteen in 1908, joined the merchant navy, jumped ship in New York, made his way to Montana, worked as a barman in a town where they still checked guns at the door, survived the Roaring Twenties, the Wall Street Crash and the subsequent Depression, drifted to Detroit and into the motor industry where he got a job and built a career as a paint specialist, married, raised a family, returned home for his one and only visit in 1960 dressed in the loudest suit and matching hat I'd ever seen, chomping cigars, draped with cameras, dispensing ten bob notes to me at the drop of a hat and calling me a 'cute little booger' as he did so. No, he was dead.

This American voice belonged to Bob 'The Bear' Hite, lead singer of Canned Heat, a successful-enough Californian rock band riding their hits 'On The Road Again' and 'Let's Work Together'. The reason he was calling was not because I was the secretary of CHAPS (the Canned Heat Appreciation and Publicity Society), but because he and I had been writing to each other for some years, trading blues 78's and fax'n'info. Bob, more than anything, was a collector. A serious, 100% manic, certifiable madbugger shellac and vinyl junkie. He now used Heat-generated cash to continue funding his obsession and also poured money into *R&B Collector,* a dedicated collectors' magazine. He wanted to chat about blues records, and he had called to invite me to the hotel he was staying at, somewhere in west London.

I left immediately, and arrived to find his vast, friendly, hairy bulk spread across one of the two double beds in the room. With him were Henry Vestine, a sleeping Al Wilson, and sundry other California types I neither knew nor needed to (they weren't blues collectors, were they?). Bob offered me a joint. I took it and, without thinking too hard, gave it a decent toke. Now, you have to remember that in England throughout the 1960's, if you smoked dope it was – unless you were very rich or dead lucky – low grade stuff sprinkled into regular rolling tobacco. What Bob had just handed me was pure California grass. And there was a LOT of it. Within minutes (or was it hours?) I was more stoned than I had ever been in my life.

I got the munchies and the giggles about the same time, consumed a vast plate of offered food, and sat in a fast-expanding universe, the epicentre of which was the hotel room I happened to be in. How very cosmic! The hotel room I happened to be in was the epicentre of the world!! And at that epicentre the conversation was about rare blues records!!! So, like, *BLUES RECORDS* were, in fact, at the very epicentre of the world!!!! And I was, gosh, a *BLUES COLLECTOR!!!!!!* And so were *THEY!!!!!!!* And it was *US* at the centre!!!!!!! Wow, what luck!!!!!!

We talked for hours (or was it minutes?) about rare records: 'Jeez, you have the Freddie Spruill Paramount? Shit, I *NEED* that fuckin' record!'

'Make me an offer then. I'd accept a lifetime's supply of this funny green stuff.'

Then things fell into complete fantasy as Bob and Henry got to wondering what VERY early 45 rpm records might look like if they had existed.

'What would an Aristocrat 45 look like, man? Green or white?' – Henry (toke).

'Hey, I've got one. A fuckin' Old-fuckin'-Swing Master 45 by Man Young! Ha!' – Bob (toke).

Going in the opposite direction, I began thinking up very late pressing 78's: 'How about the Eddie Taylor Vivid, huh? A white label deejay copy pressed in pure vinyl' (toketoketoke).

With the sense of perspective that very good grass can sometimes offer, Henry said: 'What th'fuck are you talkin' about LATE 78's for? This is a fuckin' EARLY 45's thing we got going. Don't bum me out man... Oh man, now I'm bummed out (toketoke). Oh, okay, now I'm not.'

I left around 3:00am, in a stupor, took the elevator all the way to the unfinished basement in the same condition, got out and realised I had gone too far. I turned to get back into my new friend, Ernie the Magic Time Travel Box, but he had closed his doors and left. There was no call button. I finally found a window (minutes? hours?) climbed out, fell into a taxi and arrived home slightly ahead of it.

'How much?' I asked of the cabbie, possibly in fluent Tagalog.

'Two quid, but I'll trade it for some of what you've had tonight mate.'

I didn't even bother getting into bed. I just started making up the newspaper rounds, writing the addresses in a variety of interesting colours. Only around 10:00 am did I realise that my car was still parked in west London.

———

We closed our shop in the summer of 1970 because the local council was redeveloping the area. They paid us a compensatory price that our solicitor fought for and won, and we decided to go and do other things. We bought a house at Mill Hill, the furthest-flung corner of north-west London.

My father began work as the London representative for the Memorial Company of Worksop, Nottinghamshire, which made, engraved and erected gravestones.

'It's a dead-end job,' he quipped, as did just about everyone else who met him. As usual, he made a success out of it. My mother took a position as a receptionist-and-telephonist in an establishment called The Cottage Homes, a managed retirement village for spinsters and widows from the drapery trade. Despite being offered a position teaching English in Kampala by the

Ugandan Ambassador, then a customer of ours, I decided I wanted a career in the music business. What I got was a job at Imhoff's.

Imhoff's was five floors of records, hi-fis, televisions, radios and accessories that sat just inside New Oxford Street, a mere rock-chuck from my beloved Charing Cross Road. I began working in the popular record department in the basement, christened, by some executive Vera Lynn fan in the early Fifties, the 'Melody Bar'. It paid fifteen quid a week and I had to fund my own travel, so my lifestyle would not be quite so grand, but I felt it was a move in the right direction. To some degree, it was just like being back in the newsagent's trade. The loonies still came through the door:

'I heard a tune on French radio last night. Do you have it?'
'Would you know the title, sir?'
'No.'
'Could you hum it?' (Several bars of tuneless crap follow.)
'I'm sorry sir, none of us can identify it.'
'And you call yourselves *professionals?*'

'Hello. I'm looking for a version of 'Elizabethan Serenade', in English, NOT German, thank you, largely instrumental but with a vocal chorus and, if possible, bells in the orchestration.'
'Where have you heard this sir, on the radio?'
'I haven't heard it at all, I'm just describing what I want.'
'I see.'
Incredibly, we found a version that fitted his needs and sent him off to a listening booth. He emerged glowing,
'Yes, yes, the very thing. How much is that?'
'One pound sixty-five pence, sir.'
'ONE POUND SIXTY-FIVE?'
'Yes, it's an LP.'
'But I don't *NEED* an LP. Haven't you got an EP thingy or something?'
'No sir, it hasn't been issued in any other format.'
'Well... why NOT?'
'I can't say sir, that's not our decision.'
'Well, I'm certainly NOT paying the price of a decent plastic mackintosh for a piece of music. Good-day to you.'

But we also got lots of very reasonable people looking for the week's Number One 45, or the current hit LPs, or an oldie they had missed out on. Imhoff's had an extraordinary 45 rpm back stock that would be worth a fortune on eBay today. I played willing fisherman for serious soul and R&B freaks with carefully researched lists of obscure 45's they were trying to track down:

114

'Got Sue 317?'
'Nope.'
'Okay, how about London 9330?'
'Yup.'
'Great! Er, Atlantic 4027?'
'Yes.'
'Right, I'll have that then. Try R&B 502.'
'Got that.'
'Shit! You've GOT that? Er... how many copies?'
'Two.'
'Can I have 'em both?'
'Yes,' etc.

We also served the needs of Viv Stanshall, vocalist with the Bonzo Dog Band and the oddest fish I've ever encountered. He was genuinely, wholly, completely and wonderfully eccentric. He would appear in a baby blue crocheted one-piece jumpsuit with huge bright orange octagonal specs and a clockwork laugh machine in a knitted bag. His wants were simple: 'The Laughing Policeman' by Charles Penrose. We had that. He then told me the tragic tale of how Penrose came to obtain his wonderfully infectious laugh. It had been bestowed upon him by trauma, following the accidental drowning of his son. Stanshall often came at quiet times when he could listen to arcane recordings for whatever project was cooking inside of him, and we gave him the attention he deserved. He was a lovely man and a gentle soul with true wit.

I discovered that if you ordered something from the suppliers by catalogue number, you could sometimes get it even if was officially deleted, simply because it still sat on their shelves. It was in this way, as late as 1970, that I procured the final eleven stock copies of *The Dance Album of Carl Perkins* on London, which sold out in a week because I peddled them privately to a captive audience of collectors for five quid a throw.

By the time I had been at Imhoff's a few weeks, I could pick my lunch hour, and so went to Dobell's and the Italian spaghetti house every day, instead of once a week. The money wasn't as good as it had been, but the times were fine. And the experience that it gave me, a thorough grounding in how to professionally file, track, order and display large quantities of stock, was to be of greater value by far than the salary. However, after a while I got to the point where I realised I was in a dead end, as much fun as it was, and took a local job for twice the money, managing the shop floor of an electrical store in Mill Hill.

That year, Muddy Waters came back to London. Not only that, I heard the whole band was coming with him; only not that, he was appearing relatively locally to me; that not only, he was going to be in residence for a week.

Opposite Belsize Park tube station, at the very top of Belsize village, adjacent to Hampstead, stood a small parade of shops. Behind them, down a narrow drive, lurked the Country Club. Everybody and anybody played there. I have no idea now who promoted the week-long gig, but I offer them my undying gratitude. It was a unique experience to see the founder of Chicago blues play for seven consecutive nights. Like probably every other fan in London and beyond, I figured out how much I could afford to spend in seeing him seven times and then went way beyond my budget. It was worth every overspent penny.

The interior of the Country Club was a simple box, with a large stage at the very end facing rows of seats giving way to floor space that ended at the bar. Down the right-hand side was a narrow walkway leading to the toilets. On the left of the stage there was a small booth equipped with a turntable, amplifier and microphone, from which a disc jockey could play pre-gig music. For the week we were about to experience, Ian Cole, one of the London Blues Circle, and possessor of huge quantities of obscure 45's, served as the very willing and enthusiastic disc jockey. So good was he at his job that, as the week progressed, band members turned up early just to listen to what he was playing.

The advantages of playing a week-long gig were obvious: the band could leave their equipment on stage; the acoustics the club offered were sound-checked once, at the beginning, and left alone. The band quickly got used to the ambience of the place and could relax for the week; there was no kit to schlep at the end of the night, just the precious guitars. They were staying in a good hotel and spending their days relaxing and exploring all that London could offer. We the audience would benefit greatly from this unique opportunity. And we were, night after night, the same audience.

It only took me 25 minutes to get there from home. Bill Greensmith and Frank Nazareth travelled an hour or more from Wimbledon every night. Bruce Bastin came up from Sussex seven nights running. ('How could I POSSIBLY be doing anything else?' he remarked, with images of 1958 flooding his frontal lobes.) Others trekked in from even further afield.

Muddy was in the final stages of recovery from his awful car crash the previous autumn. He was also playing guitar again, something he had not done for a while. I now realise that we saw him at a cusp of change in his career, settling into his final decade's-worth of playing to international audiences with a newly constructed band, and concentrating on his guitar technique in a way he hadn't done for perhaps ten years.

The memories of six of those seven nights collide, and I cannot place specific incidents in specific evenings. Early in the week, possibly the first day, Bill and I had somehow managed to gain an audience with Muddy in his hotel. In those days it was not impossible, although Bill's photographic credentials certainly helped.

We turned up to find him holding court from his bed; several band members, a roadie or two, and Mike Rowe, attempting a serious interview, were already there. To say I was excited would be about as accurate as describing the Battle of Hastings as a scuffle. My two-short-planks'-worth simply erupted into the room with the enthusiasm of an untrained Labrador puppy. In doing so, I interrupted, without thought or even a vague awareness, the delicate discographical proceedings Mike was conducting. That he still speaks to me is proof only of his forgiving nature.

As the afternoon became the early evening, Muddy prepared to leave for the gig. Mike and I offered rides to other band members. I had Pee Wee Madison and Sammy Lawhorn in my car with Bill, and Mike followed with Willie Smith and Sonny Wimberley. Muddy and the other band members rode in a chauffeured Daimler. We followed this sleek and powerful vehicle as best we could. It took some doing: I jumped more than one set of lights, and Mike, following me, did the same, but with considerably greater danger to life and limb. The gods that protect blues fans and band members, however, were on duty that night, and we pulled up outside the club, adrenalin surging like an uncapped oil well, to see Muddy step elegantly out of the Daimler.

Sets opened with the band playing a warm-up instrumental or two. During this time, a low murmur from the audience was still in evidence. Drinks were still being ordered, seats still being vacated and reclaimed, quiet chat still being offered at the bar. When Muddy came on stage the mood altered. The audience concentration was total. We were in the presence of The Man, and we knew it. Muddy had the kind of commanding personality that simply overrode his surroundings. When he was in a room, he was the centre of it. His charisma, for that is what he most certainly had, was completely and wonderfully obvious. In 1970, he had abandoned his process hair style for a conservatively short and gracefully natural Afro. It suited him well. He appeared to be in generally good shape and was still looking incredibly sharp. By this time, I was familiar with every issued recording he had made. I knew the Muddy songbook as well as Bruce, Bill and many others. Yet to see him appear in front of us was to experience something far deeper than a live reading of old classics. Like most great musicians, every time he played a song, he found something new to insert into it.

He especially proved this one evening by setting the band to one side, sitting down with his guitar and simply going back twenty years to play 'Walking Blues'. He had us spellbound. We were witnessing not a recreation, but a virile reading of a seminal performance, one that not only reached back through Robert Johnson to Son House, but forward to the Chicago blues sound Muddy himself founded and beyond to the global impact of the Rolling Stones, and all that followed. We were privileged that night to see a performance that was pivotal; an example, as Worth Long once said, of something so central to blues history that its absence would be unimaginable.

We sat and listened, night after night, to 'Walking Through the Park', 'Long Distance Call', 'Mean Mistreater', 'They Call Me Muddy Waters', and all the other classics. There was an evening however, that outshone the rest, and it was the final one. Why? I can't say for sure. Perhaps the band felt they had really come to know the club and its audience. Perhaps because it was the last night, and time for all the stops to be thoroughly pulled out. I'm just glad I was there. When Muddy began 'Long Distance Call' we knew we would get a stinging bottleneck guitar solo in the middle. We were not, however, prepared for what happened.

'Long Distance Call' is a very slow blues. If you know it at all, you know when the guitar solo is about to happen and you have time to prepare for it. It arrives, naturally and obviously, introduced by a short bridge. As the band was crossing that bridge on this Saturday night, something happened that even they didn't see coming. Perched on a leather-seated bar stool out front, legs wrapped around the bottom struts, Muddy was gliding towards the solo when he suddenly announced 'Now I'm gonna kill it' and proceeded to play the most intense, taut, blues-soaked solo I have ever heard him execute, on or off record or film. As he did so, he rose from his seat, legs wrapped around the bar stool struts, bending himself upwards, as he stared intensely at the fretboard, completely absorbed in playing a solo that left even the band in amazed awe. We saw them clearly exchange: 'What th' *FUCK*??' glances with each other. The crowd, us, Bill, Bruce, Ian-in-the-box, me, gulped and gasped, held our breath as if to assist the length and intensity of what was occurring and then, when it was done and the band dropped back in behind him, roared and rolled and screamed with orgasmic fervour. Astonished, Bruce and I exchanged glances that said '*Corfuckingblimeydidyoucopthat*?' and similar scholarly observations.

Muddy had come and gone. Over a third of a century later, those events, though chronologically confused by time, remain crystalline for many of us who were there. I had seen him before, and would see him again, but never under such perfect circumstances.

In January 1972, Eddie Burns turned up in Britain for a tour. This was the man whose first record I had so severely badgered Tony Russell for a few months earlier. I simply HAD to meet him! In fact, Bill Greensmith, Bruce Bastin and I kind-of took over being his minders for the duration. Eddie played a splendid gig at the 100 Club, ably backed by the Brunning-Hall Sunflower Blues Band, and appeared on the then still-not–quite-moribund BBC Radio One with the same group, where his version of 'Wig Wearing Woman' was announced, in all seriousness, as 'Wigwam Woman' by the presenter. He and Brunning-Hall also recorded an album for Action Records which probably bears reissuing, and he played a few solo gigs. Bruce and I drove him to one at some university or other, possibly Reading, where we were immediately assumed to be his roadies and ushered into the dressing room while, out on stage, we heard the distant sounds of some local herbert attempting to be Robert Johnson. Okay, where's the free drinks then? Eddie played a nice set of acoustic blues that night and, as a result of his encounter with Bruce, we all met up again at Bill's flat a few days later. Bruce brought along his Complete Eddie Burns Original Pressings Collection, and we sat

Bruce Bastin, Eddie Burns and yours truly.

with Eddie while he listened, remembered and reminisced about his Hastings Street days. Another splendid privilege.

Exactly when and where the spirit of the 1960's began and ended depends, I believe, on your experiences inside of it. Most would agree that it didn't really begin in Britain until at least 1962, possibly 1963. For some, it dead-ended in 1970 on a London rooftop when angry Beatles poured their energy into 'Get Back' – ironically their finest moment, if you'll excuse an old tobacconist's opinion. Others might point to the curse of decimalisation or the arrival of the 'three-day week' as late as 1973.

For me, it altered slowly. Throughout the rest of 1970 and into 1971 things chugged along happily. I worked my workaday job, bought more records, visited with Bill, both Franks, Peter, Bruce and others, or had them visit me. I continued to attend the National Film Theatre to see things denied me by commercial cinemas; read the *Guardian* and my books; watched my preferred TV shows, most especially *Monty Python*; listened increasingly to Radio 4, and was on my way to becoming a young Old Fart when I met Linda.

We connected because she had a Saturday job in the newsagent's from which I ordered my monthly magazines. She worked for Barclays Bank during the week as a cashier, and was a bubbly and good-looking woman four years my senior. We began dating in the autumn of 1971 and married a little over a year later, as soon as we had found a decent flat to occupy. For the next two years the focus of my life altered.

First, I became Joe Serious, with plans to Get On In Life, Build A Career, Begin A Family and Be A Success. To fund all this, I sold my 78's and 45's, parting with nine years' accumulation. Old friends saw less of me, I changed jobs to begin the climb up the ladder, and then one day Linda and I received a remarkable offer from my parents.

They had decided they missed the shopkeeper's life and wanted to get back in the game. A local shop with great potential had just come on the market. It had one of those classic enormous apartments attached. Would we like to pool our resources and go into business with them? We could have the flat, we could start the family we said we wanted, we could all enjoy a reprise of those glory days. Want to do it? We thought about it for the length of a pot of tea and said yes.

In January 1974, we all quit our day jobs and Linda and I moved in above the shop. Six weeks later, on St. Valentines Day, my father's car was broadsided by a six-wheeled truck. It broke every bone in his body on the right-hand side, from skull to ankle, and for ten days his life hung in the balance. My mother was consumed with grief and worry. Linda was thoroughly frightened by the events. I was just in shock. But the show called 'The Shop' had to go on.

Dad began a slow and painful recovery, but was never going to be the same man again. His hair had turned white, his walk was now a limp, pain following him in everything he did. But he was alive. As he turned the corner to recovery, Linda became pregnant. At the end of January 1975, Matthew was born.

I still recall the moment that fatherhood arrived. I stared at his hand for the first time and was astonished by how perfectly the fingernails were formed. It was love at first sight. We took him home, where my father's first words to his only grandson, spoken in a cold back yard where he had waited to greet our return from hospital, were: 'I love you, Matthew.'

Only six weeks later, Linda returned from the local doctor with the news that the painful lumps on her neck needed a biopsy. When the tests were completed, we were called to the hospital, where it was bluntly explained that she had contracted Hodgkin's Disease, a cancer that attacks the lymph glands. Chances of survival were less than fifty-fifty, complex operations would have to begin immediately. For the first two years of Matthew's life, she would fight both the cancer and the string of nasty side effects caused by the treatment. With a sick wife, a new son, a damaged father, a harried mother and a 90-hour-a-week shop to run, I had no time for anything but the most immediate concerns. I peered into the entrance of my long dark tunnel and wondered how long I would be in it.

Chapter Six

1975-79: BLOODY OLD RATBAG

In the middle of the darkness, a small light appeared, although at that time I had no idea what it would lead to. Sometime in the spring, a fellow my age came in to the shop to place a card in our advert window. Among the ads for rotting cars for sale (*'Good runner, used daily, needs new tyres'*), free kittens and offers of babysitting, he wished to insert the sale of his record collection. I read the card he handed me, which said something like:

```
For Sale: 200+ 45 rpm records, 1963-66.
Many great oldies, original sleeves, some
EPs. Stones, Kinks, Who, Animals, Chuck
Berry, Otis Redding etc. Good condition
throughout. £40 o.n.o..
```

On impulse I said: 'I'll buy them', and took delivery that afternoon. Through a network of locals that I knew, I sold less than half of them for more than twice my investment. I had become a record dealer!

It was a small beginning, but a good one. Dad took an interest in this, and we agreed that the business could fund any further purchases and running expenses until the experiment either took off or could be called a failure. It was to be a great source of therapy for him.

I began reading the *Exchange & Mart* 'Records For Sale' section, and had some good luck very early, buying two nice jazz LP collections for reasonable prices. Dad and I kept the few that we fancied, and I re-subscribed to *Vintage Jazz Mart*, typed up my lists, submitted them and awaited developments. By the time we had finished, there was a reasonably good-looking profit grinning at us. We also began placing 'Records Wanted' ads in *Exchange & Mart*, and expanded into buying 78's, including one or two splendid collections of pre-war British pressings. Then, one day I received an extraordinary phone call in response to one of our adverts:

'Mr. Vermin?'

'Er, *Vernon*, yes.'

'I hear you buy old records.'

'Yes.'

'Well, I've got lots of them.'

'What kind of records are they?'

'Old ones.'

'I understand, but what style of music are they?'

'Oh, VERY mixed, all sorts.'

'Look, tell you what, have you got the records there with you?'

'Yes, they're all here'

'Well, could you just grab a handful and read me what's on the labels?'

'Oh, I don't think any of them have labels, dear.'

'It's the bit in the middle that's printed.'

'Ooohh, all right. Good idea.'

I sat holding the phone imagining the Bings and the Franks and the Tommys and the Veras I was going to have to refuse.

'All right, dear, here we are. Now, this first one is Cook's Dreamland Orchestra and the label says it's Gennett.'

'Eh?' I looked down and realised the tea in my mug was shaking.

'Here's one on the Victor label by a feller called Benny Moten. Wasn't he a comedian?'

'Uh...' Okay, now the tea was slopping over the brim.

'This one's very pretty. Its label's called QRS.'

'Er, how many do you think you've got?' I said, trying to quell the castrato trembling in my voice.

'Ooohh... HUNDREDS, dear.'

'I see. Any idea what you want for them?'

'No dear, but you'll know when you see them won't you? I can have my lad deliver them to you tomorrow.'

And so he did. All 600 of them. It was an extraordinary collection of classic jazz, mostly early British and European pressings, but including a handsome sprinkling of American originals and early reissues.

Did I buy them? No, I didn't. What I did instead was to tell the old dear the truth that she had a fabulous collection worth some thousands of pounds, and that, rather than buy it, it would be a lot fairer if I sold them for her on commission. She laughed, thanked me for my honesty, called me a stupid twit into the bargain, and we hammered out a simple deal. She made her several grand and I made my commission. Taking commission deals became a key element in my fast-expanding sideline.

'How did she come by such an extraordinary collection in the first place?', I hear you plead. She was the owner of a stationery shop and had a tenant in the flat above who was found dead in his bed one morning. The records were his, and he had no family. After the funeral, she cleared his rooms, with a view to chucking everything out, including the records. She almost did, until her son suggested they might be worth a few bob to someone. He was right. I still sometimes wonder who the victim of the Dead Man Blues was.

The shop remained our main source of income and, as Dad slowly improved, so some of my mother's fears and worries abated. Linda was still very ill though, so all of us, including Linda's mother, took turns looking after Matthew. We were coping.

None of this, however, discouraged the loonies from coming through the door. Why was it always the early afternoon that they presented themselves? What did loonies do in the morning? Prepare hat-transportable sandwiches for other loonies?

This one, though, was a little less benign than most. He looked normal; they often do. As he stepped through the door, I glanced at him, in the way that retailers glance at everyone who comes in, just to size them up. He was white, English, medium build, middle aged, middle class, dressed sensibly in casual middle-class middle-age English clothes accompanied by out-of-fashion specs and a hat that probably should have been shot a decade earlier. Perfectly normal.

I continued filling cigarette shelves and saw him go to the far wall where all the weekly magazines lay, and pick up the *Baptist Times*. No problem, he'll come over here in a minute for a small Cadbury's Fruit & Nut bar and a pocket pack of Kleenex. Then I saw him shake loose a copy of the *Jewish Chronicle*; okay, so he was buying for a neighbour. Then he snapped up the *West Indian World*, *Gay News*, *West African*, *Private Eye*, *Catholic Herald*, *New Musical Express*, the feminist *Spare Rib*, and the far-left *Morning Star*. He approached the counter and handed them to me with a thin smile. I gave him the price, which he extracted from his little leather horseshoe (I should have guessed that one). As he passed me the exact money he said confidingly: 'Just keeping an eye on what their little minds are up to,' then turned and left.

We drifted into 1976 still trading in newsprint, tobacco, confectionery and jazz records. Then, one day I got a phone call from an old chum I hadn't seen for some years, Chris Reichardt. Chris had been in the blues collectors' circle since the late 1960's. His family had money, and so he had taken the opportunity to visit the US in 1969, returning with an extraordinary starter kit of downhome blues 45's, mostly culled from Randy's Record Shop in Gallatin, Tennessee and Stan's Record Shop in Shreveport, Louisiana. To this he added albums, 78's and more 45's throughout the next few years. Now he was getting married and wanted to sell. Was I interested? I offered him the commission deal and he accepted it. There were probably 600 records, all of them good, some of them amazing. But clearly, I had to do more than just put them through *VJM*. With the willing assistance of several other collectors, especially Ian Cole and Bill Greensmith, I scraped together a basic mailing list of potential customers. As I was preparing the auction list, Ian, Bill, and a few others I had now reached asked me if I would put some of their unwanted records into the same list for the same terms. 'Sure, why not?'

In the late spring of 1976, I mailed out about 200 copies of a privately-printed list. The results were spectacular. Chris Reichardt got his money and so did everyone else. I clearly needed to do this again. I therefore approached everyone within striking distance who had bid and offered them the commission deal. It was enough to launch a second list, and from these and the several others that I ran in the following two years grew an odd nodule called *Sailor's Delight*. But we need to step back a little because in the meantime there was also a lot going on back at the ranch.

Linda and Dad were both steadily getting better, but my parents had had enough of the shop and London, and were starting to make retirement-to-the-coast noises. The record business was doing well, I felt that there was potential to expand it, and was willing and eager to try. The shop was in good saleable shape, so we decided to up sticks all over again. In January 1978 we disposed of the shop, my parents sold their house, and with the money from both, my folks moved to coastal Sussex and Linda and I put a deposit on a Victorian row house just round the corner, at Brockenhurst Gardens.

I was now trading under the name 'Sailor Vernon'. This was not my invention. Following the premature death of Mike Leadbitter in 1974, *Blues Unlimited* had been sold on by its surviving founder Simon Napier to a consortium that included Bill Greensmith, John Broven and Mike Rowe. Getting mellow on something one evening, probably Lucozade Slings, they began dreaming up soubriquets for their friends. For reasons none of them can now recall, mine was 'Sailor'. Without telling me, they impishly altered my standing advert in *Blues Unlimited*. The next issue read: '*Want good Blues record auction lists? Write to 'Sailor' Vernon. All the nice guys bid with Sailor!*' People in Japan, Norway and Wigan, not knowing the difference, began addressing envelopes to 'Sailor Vernon' and I quickly realised that I had been handed a great trading name. My lists, which had increasingly become filled with all sorts of jokes and arcane rubbish as well as the records, started to go out under that name. The odd nodule would eventually morph from these lists. Look, it wasn't MY fault...

In early March 1978, armed with 1500 quids-worth of dollar travellers' cheques, a ticket for a rental car and a new credit card, I stepped outside of Britain for the first time in my life. I was going to see if I could acquire enough records to kick the business up a notch or two. If it failed, I'd have had an adventure and I'd get a day job. If it succeeded, I'd be on the path I had wanted to take since I had stood in that rare patch of Kilburn sunlight listening to Ralph Foxley's stories and advice. It was worth a shot.

I arrived in New York to be greeted and swept out of the airport by Dave Sax, who had emigrated with his wife Patsy six years earlier by accepting a job with Bell Telephone. He took me directly to Harry's Steak

House and I consumed my first vast American hamburger among the hubbub of a late Friday night crowd. I was here! The land I had dreamed of since, oh, I don't even know when, perhaps since I first saw the Lone Ranger or Laurel & Hardy. I'd been an Americanophile most of my life. Now, in this late-night hamburger joint on the road to Dave's Long Island home, I had my first genuine taste of America, in more ways than just the one. It was warm, comfortable, loud, fast, friendly, unceremonious and great tasting. I finished falling completely and forever in love with America there and then.

After a weekend with Dave and Patsy, catching up on old news and listening to records, I took to the road in the huge, electric-everything Chevrolet bestowed upon me by Dollar Car Rentals. For someone whose then-current vehicle was a biscuit-tin sized Mini Traveller, it was amazing. I played with the NASA-like control panels, watching windows and seats and rear view mirrors jump to my command. I turned on the ignition and listened to the quiet but powerful roar of its V8 engine. I stepped out to admire its sleek design. It looked like a silver bullet (Maybe the Lone Ranger's silver bullet? Tonto would know.) I *wanted* one. 'Get me the Loan Arranger – and Pronto!'

On the Monday morning I took to the road. An Englishman on the New Jersey turnpike for the first time. Was I mad? Was this real? Or a dream I would awaken from to find myself consoled with a pot of tea and an afternoon rain? It was real. I turned on the radio, watched the aerial climb up through the wing and heard Dolly Parton's 'Jolene'.

My first stop was Philadelphia, where I was to take up the kind offer of a place to stay made by Russ Shor, with whom I'd been communicating for a year or more. He lived on South 48th Street, and I came over the Walt Whitman Bridge, landed on North Broad Street and pulled into a gas station to ask directions. I expected a vastly complex set of instructions that included references to landmarks I had no idea existed. I would, being a bloke, simply listen to all this, nod like I understood perfectly and set off. Nobody would ever see me again. Years later, a rusty car containing a grinning, tea-stained skeleton would be discovered somewhere deep in the Amish countryside... but the guy simply said, in a broad Philly accent that I would come to recognise: 'Okay, thisiswhachadoo: this is North Broad, runs all the way to City Hall. Go round City Hall, it becomes South Broad. You want South 48th, right? Count 48 blocks after y'get past City Hall and hang a right. That's it.' And it was. Try getting from Neasden to Tooting with instructions that bald.

Russ's house was a grand old Victorian nestling serenely in the leafy street of a real neighbourhood. He welcomed me in, fed me, played me extraordinary records from his fabulous 78 collection, gave me a bed and saw me off the next day on my way South. I turned onto Interstate 95 at 8:00 am filled with excitement, wonder and Jimmy Dean breakfast sausage. I was, to borrow one of Bruce Bastin's phrases, 'bug-eyed and headed South'. My plan was simple: I would pop down Interstate 95 to Florida, where my aunt had offered me a place to stay, and from which strategic location I had promised my mother I would report by phone; it meant a lot to her that I would see and be with her favourite sister. Then, I would head back up and inland through the mid-South, stopping off at places I had been told would have old records for sale. Whatever else I picked up on the way was gravy. Then, back in New York, I would cut deals with collectors who knew I was returning. There was no Plan B. It was that loose.

I was out there alone. I had a month, a car, money, changes of clothes, maps, some addresses, 40 packs of the British menthol cigarettes I was hooked on, and a need to succeed. I floored it, exceeding the speed limit whenever I felt safe to do so because I wanted to have that experience I had seen so often in the movies. At one point, when I crossed the state line into North Carolina, I actually had sufficient romantic gaucheness to shout 'YEEEHHAAA!' No-one was listening except the seven year old inside me.

Before long, I began to grasp the sheer *size* of America. It took me two days to cross the Carolinas, stopping only for gas, food and lodging. I was high on the mixture of fresh experience and the odd ersatz déjà-vu of having seen visions of all this before, in movies and on TV. Broderick Crawford was still out there somewhere, saying 'Ten-Four'. Bonnie and Clyde were only a mile or two ahead, hiding out from the law behind a thicket. Steve McQueen would come hammering past me any minute in a Thunderbird chasing two geezers waving a shotgun back at him. Laurel & Hardy would flag me down from the roadside to point out that their Model T had been sawn in half by a bizarre accident. And any minute now Big Joe Williams' hitching thumb would bring me to a halt. I popped another wine gum from the stash I had snuck through customs and flipped on the radio. 'Jolene'. Dolly Parton was clearly intent on accompanying me into the South.

It took me four days to reach Sarasota from Philadelphia, including a few stops along the way to gawp bovinely at this, that or the udder. My aunt greeted me like the long-lost relative I was and celebrated my arrival with a barbecue on the back lawn, including in it every last extension of her family: her three sons, two daughters, their wives, husbands, boyfriends and neighbours.

I stayed a week, including an overnighter to Miami to check out one of those leads I had. I came back with several hundred original Vee-Jay 45's and the experience of having driven Alligator Alley, the two-lane, shoulderless, gas-station-free highway that cuts through the Okeefenokee swamplands to Miami. I was told that it got its name from the alligators that lay in wait just feet from the roadside, ready to make lunch out of any pasty-legged fool like me who might want to get out and have a stretch. Oh, and the mosquitoes... don't drive with the windows down, you'll get eaten alive. At the midway point, as I checked my gas tank level for the umpteenth time, I realised very fully that this was not the A41, and that there was no turning back.

After a final celebratory party in Sarasota, I departed to head up into the lower and mid-South. I would turn left at Tallahassee and head for New Orleans. In Mobile I got lucky and found a juke box distributor in the phone book who responded to my call with a 'Come on down and buy', so I spent a jolly afternoon leafing through browser bins, turning up a healthy mix of blues, R&B, old rock and country. He charged me 50 cents a pop for the several hundred 45's I found, but pulled the Hank Williams and the Bo Diddleys back out with an apology: 'Cain't sell 'em to ya, waytoo valerbel.' I didn't argue. I had just found, among other things, an *effluentpile* of silvertop Chesses.

I arrived in New Orleans on Good Friday evening, barrelling in off Highway 10 West. As I crossed the bridge that led to the twinkling lights of the city, I kick-started the radio to find that Dolly had been replaced by the remarkably welcome Fats Domino singing 'Walking To New Orleans'. What a wonderfully appropriate entrance! If life is all about detail, this serenaded twilight entry was a small jewel to always treasure.

I spent Easter in town, just gawking as much as anything; I played tourist on Bourbon and Canal Streets, avoiding a plethora of Japanese camerakazi pilots, and enjoyed an evening with Terry Patterson, a local collector who seemed to have every worthwhile New Orleans 45 on an original pressing, and who introduced me to Billy Tate's 'Single Life Blues', which is still somewhere in my all-time Top Twenty. I left without having bought much, but I sure had a nice weekend. However, it was time to get serious and go to Athens, Georgia, where Bruce Bastin had said I could get some real nice stuff that he had left behind. Following the speed of the CB-linked trucks, I floored it out of Louisiana accompanied by a hellfire radio preacher.

Bruce was right. In the upper floor of a side street record store in this neat college town, I found just what I was looking for. 'Any friend of Mr. Bastin is welcome here,' said the owner, unlocking the stockroom door to my future. Bruce had taken just about all the downhome stuff, but there was a ton of steaming R&B and I took all I could cram into the car: trunk, back seat, floor, front seat, under the seat and back parcel shelf. I threw out everything I didn't need including spare shoes and dirty laundry to make more room and began the long slow trundle back up to New York. I was about a day later than I wanted to be and I had a scheduled plane to catch and still a lot to do in Philadelphia and New York.

I left Athens at five in the evening and drove fourteen hours straight, arriving bleary but stoked in Philadelphia at seven the next morning. It was too early to go to Russ's and I needed sleep, so I checked into the Starlight Motel, and fell into a short coma. When I woke, I strolled into the lobby looking for lunch, was directed through a door by a clerk whose surprise I failed to understand until I opened the door. It was as if I had walked through a western movie's swing doors to find that I was the cause of the piano ceasing to play. All eyes turned on me. This was clearly a VERY BLACK neighbourhood. Would I be welcome?

Using my best loud BBC voice I offered salutations and requested a menu. The mood relaxed, the hubbub regained its voice and I sat at the bar. A couple approached and began a conversation. Where was I from? Why was I here? How long would I stay? What was London like? Had I ever met the Queen? I began to realise that, although I was white, I represented no threat because I was from somewhere else and, to a degree, was an object of curiosity who, in passing through on a limited time frame, could be interviewed about life outside their immediate experience. I was having the tables turned on me for all those times British blues enthusiasts sat down with a visiting musician, opened a notebook and said: 'So, Lightnin', tell me where and when you were born...'

I got back to New York, 7000 miles motoring behind me, dumped my stuff off at Dave's and we both went to see a number of other New York collectors who might have some 'interesting things'. It turned out they did, and in a manic weekend that turned my legs to noodles, I concluded several handshake agreements to sell on commission. By the time it was all loaded into boxes and consolidated with my other stuff back at Dave's, I had amassed something like ten thousand 78's and 45's, and a small clutch of rare albums. Using an air-freight company I would do business with for the next few years, I took delivery in London three days after I got back myself. Explaining to a protesting Linda that we *needed* to do this, I inserted the dining room furniture into the lounge and turned the newly-emptied dining room into a stockroom, office and packing station. I would work out of this back room for the next six years.

The arrival of ten thousand records peaked some interest among the London blues mafia. In the first few days I was overrun by excited visitors who shuffled through shelves, cackling, gasping and drooling, listened at full volume to sound after sound that they'd not heard before, talked loudly with me and each other in colourful language, joined me in filling the room with smoke and fag ash, drank gallons of tea, consumed pounds of chocolate biscuits, pissed inaccurately in our one toilet, broke wind – sometimes including several bars of a recognizable tune – shouted, laughed, argued over who was having what, scribbled frantic discographical notes, parted with their money and left way late slamming doors and gunning engines. All of them were, of course, blokes. Except Cilla Huggins, who I'm sure was never guilty of bathroom abuse, but rather a victim of it. Linda viewed all this quietly and at a distance. Other than making me clean the toilet, she rarely told me what she thought of it all, and, to be honest, my two short planks rarely stopped to ask. I was already on an ego roll that would last over half a decade.

As I was preparing the next auction, the increasingly complex appendices of jokes, off-the-cuff editorials, sidelines and arcane rubbish that I had been tossing in for a couple of years somehow became the first issue of *Sailor's Delight*. Much of the energy needed to push *SD* out of the womb came from Dave Clarke and Gary Atkinson. Dave was – and still is – a keen and

The very first *Sailor's Delight*.

knowledgeable R&B fan who also happens to be a talented cartoonist. Like everyone else I was starting to know, I met him because he was buying records from me. He offered me several very funny blues- and R&B-related cartoons that were just too good to go unpublished. Gary, now director of Document Records, was at that time a thin, callow Northern youth in a hand-me-down flat cap and often little else, which is why the police were so constantly interested in his every move. Seeing the error of his ways, he began dressing in sufficient quantities of re-woven reject lint to travel to London and visit me. He had – and retains – the most extraordinarily agile mind that harbours a wild sense of humour Spike Milligan would have applauded. He wrote complete rubbish that was so hilarious I simply had to publish it.

The banner head and cartoon logo that adorned every issue's front cover was created for me by Cilla, whose business of graphics and typesetting, coupled with her knowledge of and enthusiasm for blues, ensured her key involvement in *Blues Unlimited*. Cilla was not your average anything. Strong, intelligent, witty, assured and very committed to her chosen path, she was Howlin' Wolf's principal discographer, a specialist in post-war Memphis and Delta Blues, an early appreciator, along with Bill Greensmith, of Ike Turner's crucial role in post-war blues, and the possessor of a pair of jeans-clad legs no-one except her husband Mick ever saw. 'I think I might have a dress somewhere,' she once said when invited to a fancy-dress party.

To add to all this activity, I also invested in video. I had wanted a video recorder since about 1962, when I happened to see a demonstration on TV. The ability to record television! It captured my imagination thoroughly and, when the VHS system first became affordably available in Britain in the late spring of 1978, I was somewhere at the front of the queue. It captured Matthew's three year old imagination as well. When he came home from

Great cartoon humour from Latchford Slim *a.k.a.* Dave Clarke.

kindergarten the new machine was sitting above the TV.

'Wossat?' he enquired.

'Watch,' I said.

Taping about thirty seconds of whatever happened to be on, I rewound and replayed it. His face lit up like a Guy Fawkes' Night sky.

'We can record television?' he gasped. (He was quick on the uptake – still is). I nodded.

'Can we start a *Tom & Jerry* collection then?'

We did. Almost immediately, I initiated a another 'serious, balanced archive' (I could hear Roger Blanton's awful warnings echoing down the years) and began the wholesale and frankly illegal taping of movies, music, animation, documentaries and anything else I either wanted myself or could use as trading beads with other collectors worldwide. In league with other early enthusiasts, including John Goldman and a number of contemporary rock collectors, I willingly participated in the theft of intellectual property and its consequent dissemination to the Great Unwashed Public at 25 quid per three-hour custom-made tape including postage. We're talking not about *Deep Throat* or *Star Wars*, but things like *Good Morning Blues*, *Reet Petite And Gone*, *Go Johnny Go* and *Three Songs By Leadbelly*. I bootlegged video for six years, quickly going international and expanding the collection almost weekly. Andy Silvester of the Big Town Playboys told me that the band grew

out of watching Amos Milburn videos I had supplied them, and I supplied many other people with hours of innocent entertainment. So sue me. (I am now married to a woman whose job requires her to lobby various world governments to combat intellectual property violations. Go figure.)

Subsequent issues of *Sailor's Delight* were a vast improvement on the first. They could hardly have been any worse. Dave Clarke, masquerading as 'Latchford Slim', and later 'Duncan Disorderly' – his brilliant pseudonym that few people appreciated – provided desperately funny cartoons from his own ideas for every issue. Gary Atkinson contributed further wonderful rubbish and we were joined by Dave Wood, one of the most inventive writers whose work it has ever been my pleasure to mangle insensitively with terrible typing errors. He still wrote for me almost every issue, despite the huge cock-ups I inadvertently planted in everything he gave me.

The humour in *SD*'s parody articles was not just mine. Dave Clarke and I would spend entire evenings on the phone cooking up jokes, one-liners, gags and other silly stuff, laughing ourselves daft in the process. Then, while I strung the gags into a narrative, he would set about creating the extraordinary fake record labels that added such an important dimension to the text. His comic imprint was everywhere in every issue. I cannot imagine *SD* without Dave's contributing genius.

Glen Stapleton *a.k.a.* 'TV Slim', was the serious brain of the outfit. He and I had been sharing video enthusiasms since the machines arrived, though he himself was a fan, not a Nasty Ole Bootlegger. His enormous intelligence and acute critical factors were a joy to be with on any of the evenings we frequently shared while copying over newly-acquired video goodies. He

Some of the wonderful spoof labels produced for *Sailor's Delight* by Dave Clarke.

wrote thought-provoking and witty articles for *SD* on blues on TV and on aspects of pre-war blues. He also possessed a small but frighteningly good collection of pre-war 78's: most of the Robert Johnsons, including genuine factory tests, a Tommy Johnson, an Ishman Bracey, Blind Joe Reynolds' 'Outside Woman Blues' and other goodies.

Bill Greensmith, under the guises 'Douglas Dragonfly', 'Auntie Murder' and 'Reggie Mental' also contributed photos, gags and ideas. A little later, we would be joined by Keith Briggs as 'Uncle Charlie Briggs', contributing very funny articles in his inimitably Briggsian style. His tale of Robert Johnson's exploits is still one of my favourites. Later, too, Dana Gillespie loaned her persona and photographic images as 'Dyna Flo', acting as a foil to 'Juke Box Lil', whose alter ego was, of course, an Old Sailor. Others, including the Snackbar Brothers, Basil Trublu and Ernest Bluesappreciation were, essentially, also me. Then too, *SD* had fantastic feedback, and much of the one-off-the-wall material that turned up was simply turned in by willing readers. In short, *SD* was the product of all who contributed to it. I was simply providing a conduit.

I also got very cocky very quickly, because success was immediate and sizeable. I felt I could do anything I wanted, and often did, to Linda's frequent exasperation. The seeds of later downfall clearly were sown early. In the meantime, however, I was both having an odd-shaped ball and privately amazed that it was all going so well. But I needed to keep stoking those boilers if success was to continue. In early 1979, I had an offer from a record dealer in West Virginia to come and help myself to his 78 stock at very reasonable prices. He had good stuff, he said, and it would be worth my while. I approached Bill Greensmith with a deal: if he would come with me to help out, share the driving, the sorting, the packing and the loading, I would pay for everything except his own day-to-day expenses for food, drink and liquorice kazoos. He agreed, and we left in early February, in the middle of the miners' strike, on what we expected would be a simple mission followed by a few days touring. It couldn't have turned out more differently if Salvador Dali had planned it with a Greek Ouija board.

We arrived in New York and were out again like greased fish fingers, on the road to Philadelphia and Russ Shor's reprise offer of a place to stay. It was the weekend, so Russ took us to the fleamarkets where we met an acquaintance of his, a street-level record dealer who Bill immediately dubbed 'Mike The Shouter', for his need to deliver all he had to say at several decibels above normal: 'HEY, YOU GUYS FROM ENGLAND, HUH? OK, I GOT LOTSA BOXES, JUST LOOK AROUND AND SEE WHATCHA NEED. SO, ANYHOW, LAST SUNDAY THIS CREEP COMES ROUND, HE'S SHUFFLIN' THROUGH THE BOXES LIKE THE *DOUCHEBAG* HE IS, AND HE GLOMS ON THE THREE-BUCK PRESLEY SUN BOOTS. I SEE HIS EYES KINDA SWIVEL AROUND, Y'KNOW, HE BUYS 'EM AND GOES SCUTTLIN' OUTTA HERE. COUPLE HOURS LATER HE'S BACK FUCKIN' HOLLERIN AT ME I SOLD HIM GODDAM BOOTLEGS. I SAID: "LOOK

James Walsh at home, 1979.

BUDDY WATCHA EXPECT FOR THREE BUCKS, FIRST FUCKIN' PRESSINGS?" HE SEZ: "YOU RIPPED ME MAN, GIMME MY MONEY BACK." I SEZ: "AHGETTHEFUCKOUTTA HEREASSHOLE" – BY NOW I'M REALLY *HOLLERIN'* AT HIM Y'KNOW? – "YEAH, GITOUDDAHERE AND DOANFUCKIN COMEBACK." OH, OK, YOU GUYS DONE? LESSEE WHATCHAGOT...'

Russ decided he would join us for the trip down to West Virginia for company, and also to see if there was anything in this promised stock he fancied. Along the way, we stopped for lunch at Vinton, Virginia. At the diner's counter we got into conversation with the affably curious waitress and, when she heard we were interested in old records said: 'There's a guy here in town with a houseful.'

'Oh, really? Where might that be?'

She pointed out the window and up the hilly street to a vast old Tennessee Williams-style two-storey wood-frame house. 'Go and see Mr. Walsh,' she said.

We approached the decaying old pile on foot, feeling like unnamed and expendable extras in the preamble to a horror movie. We roused Jim Walsh from a post-lunch slumber and explained ourselves. He invited us into the most incredibly filthy house I've ever set foot in – and I'm a *bloke!*

Jim Walsh was an expert – no, THE expert – on early American vaudeville. He wrote regularly in *Hobbies* magazine about the subject, and had done so for years. He and his nine cats lived alone together in what he termed 'scholarly squalor'. He had not allowed the house to be cleaned in more than twenty years. As we crunched across dried catshit and fought giant cobwebs, he took us on a tour. Every room was filled with records, overfilled cat boxes, books, piles of magazines, overfilled cat boxes, catalogues, boxes, phonographs, typewriters, old telephones, overfilled cat boxes, framed portraits of vaudeville artists, and posters – including a huge one above a fireplace that had hung there so long the bottom was integrating into the wall. Everywhere we stepped, a dust pile rose to greet us.

He sat and played us records, explaining the who, the when the how... We stood, grinning thinly and staring about us in appalled awe. No blues records, though. Finally we had to leave, horribly fascinating though it was, to get back on the road. As we climbed back in the car Bill said: 'Blimey, that place is so dirty I bet even the rats wear overalls.' From that moment on, anything that was just a shade too dirty, or old, or stale, or dusty became 'walshy': 'Cor, this coffee's a bit on the walshy side', etc. Years later, engaged in research at the Smithsonian Institute, I came across box after box of ancient US record catalogues, each one bearing the rubber-stamped name '*James Walsh*'.

When we got to West Virginia and the stock, it quickly became apparent that most of the promised goodies had been sold before our arrival; what was left was crap. 'Hey, I wouldn't cross the street for this shit,' remarked Russ. He was right. We dropped him off at a bus station and went to find a motel. We were feeling lower than buried flyshit. To add to our woes, the motel was way below standard, with sagging beds, a non-functional bathroom and a dodgy old TV (I forget his name). We called it 'The Walsh Motel'. We sat on our beds depressed. Maybe we should call it a day. What else could we do? I faced ruin. All my current plans were tied to this. To leave now, which seemed the only option, was to return out of pocket and empty-handed. Could I get a job at Woolworth's, I wondered.

Then, brightening up, Bill looked at me and said: 'Listen. We've got four weeks, right? And the car's paid for. And you've got the money you WERE going to spend here. There's two of us, so let's just go South and see what we can find. I bet there's stuff out there. Double or nothing, mate. You up for it?' His speech and the willingness that fuelled it snapped me out of my depression and we turned to the Rand McNally to create the Plan B I had neglected.

We left the next morning for Tennessee, hitting Johnson City as it began to snow, and finding little to buy. As we crossed the state line into Alabama, we spotted an abandoned building hiding in a grove of shaggy trees. It was an old roadhouse, the kind that sat just inside a 'wet' county to accommodate liquor-seeking customers from the neighbouring 'dry' county. Long unused, it snoozed in the late afternoon sunlight quietly awaiting an eventual bulldozing. But on this day, and at the time we found it, the photographer's light was perfect. Bill spent maybe twenty minutes taking pictures, and as I watched him my mind's eye also saw the now-ceased activity it had possibly hosted. I heard loud, raucous juke-joint bottleneck guitar, I saw people weaving in and out laughing, shouting, smoking, dancing. I watched old pick-ups lurch across the uneven gravel driveway, filled with good time expectancy. Three guys pulled up and unloaded National guitars, laughing, whooping, calling each other 'Son', 'Charlie' and 'Willie'.

I quietly chewed my wine gums and watched Bill work. When he had done, and the small window of perfect light he'd recognised was fading, he explained the theory of available light and the crucial difference it can make to a good image: 'It's *all* about light, mate,' he remarked. I hadn't seen that before, but I could see it now. We also recognised something else.

'Listen,' I said.

'I don't hear anything,' Bill replied, quite correctly.

'That's the point. It's DEAD quiet. Nothing. All you can hear is air moving.' And we played mute audience for some minutes to that rarest of all commodities: absolute and complete silence.

We moved on through Alabama, driving hard and fast through deeper and deeper images of 'blues' country. At one point we reached the brow of a hill to discover that the path was now a long, deep dip in the sunlight-dappled road, bottoming out in mid-view and climbing steeply again to the horizon. It was completely empty and looked exactly like the Danny Lyons photo on the cover of an LP called *Memphis On Down* that we had been staring at for over thirteen years. Bill and I both saw it immediately. We were about to drive into one of Mike Rowe's LP covers. 'I hope he doesn't want a toll fee for this,' quipped Bill. 'We won't tell him,' I answered.

Reaching Birmingham in early evening, we spent some quiet research time with motel phone books looking for record stores and juke box distributors. The next day, our luck began to change as we hit a one-stop distributor and spent a long morning pulling 45's. We had broken our duck and I began to exhale just a little. We burrowed further South, headed for Jackson, Mississippi.

Refreshed the following morning by a lack of Marmite for breakfast, we set out to find Sammy Myers, the blues singer whose classic, 'Sleeping In The Ground', was a favourite anthem of British blues collectors. To experience a room full of slightly drunk young Englishmen, grasping brown ale bottles and rocking back and forth on upright chairs to the rhythm of this tune was to be assured that all was well with our world. No matter how long it took, or to what lengths we had to go, or what energy we expended, we simply *had* to find this heroic singer and photograph him, for the lads back home were depending upon us! It wasn't difficult; we had his address. Bill interviewed him for *Blues Unlimited*, took the photos, and we left with an invitation to see him perform that night at the local juke joint. We hung out in downtown Jackson and then, as the sun removed its afternoon cap, we went and found Richard's Playhouse, where Sammy had said he'd be.

It was a long, low, dark, narrow and deafeningly noisy juke joint. You HAD to shout to be heard, thereby adding to the cacophony. Boy Scouts would have had to use semaphore to offer Bob-a-Job Week services. I don't think they bothered. We took seats up front, near the shoebox-sized bandstand and watched the band set up. Bill recognised the guitarist, King

Edwards, and introduced himself. We were joined by the tenor sax player, a guy called Cadillac Shorty, who immediately told us he'd been on every Little Richard record ever made. The drummer chimed in to inform us that his was the insistent beat we heard on Isaac Hayes' 'Shaft'. If we wanted big-time bullshit, we'd come to the right place. When they kicked in, however, they were good and the place suddenly exploded as the tight little dance area in front of us quickly filled with a motley selection of interesting characters. A pot-bellied mid-life guy with a pork pie hat and a chomped cigar dancing with a woman twice his size. A tall, lanky solo dancer was doing limbo moves without a pole, and getting deeply into it. We never saw him again. Two large and tightly-clad women danced around each other, followed by many eyes linked directly to libidos. We sat, whitely, and observed.

Sammy came on stage and played a solid, very loud set of blues. His voice was still good, his harmonica playing still sharp, the overall sound thick, woolly and chugging. I'd never been in a juke joint before; the pace was frantic, the noise deafening, the edge palpable. The owner, a tough-looking woman in the middle range of her life, tolerated neither trouble nor the seeds of it. Yanking one guy out the door with just one hand, for crimes we didn't understand, she shot a glare across the room that indicated immediate rough justice for anyone else who might get above-station ideas. When the set had finished, I went to take a leak in the snug little Men's Room behind the bandstand. As I was standing at the wall, Sammy Myers appeared at my side. His very limited vision and the dark that we stood in immediately colluded in his dampening my jeans and shoes. I came out shaking drops off my leg and squelching ever so slightly, explaining to Bill what had happened. 'You lucky sod,' he laughed, 'you'll dine out on that story more than once.'

We arrived in Bossier City, Louisiana late the following night. Bossier is the adjunct to Shreveport that sits two miles up a straight, two-lane highway from the town's edge. The next morning, we washed the previous days' 25,491 dead bugs from the front of the car.

Greensmith:	'What's the last thing that goes through a bug's mind when it hits the windscreen?'
Vernon:	'I don't know, what is the last thing...' (etc)
Greensmith:	'Its arse!'

Turning on to an already steaming highway, we found a whole shooting gallery of juke box distributors strung along it. We hit one after another, pulling records and becoming heady with success. In one, we were invited into the back room of the family-run business by the daughter, and after an hour's digging, realised that the further back we physically excavated, the older the stock was getting. Then the Old Mom, a fierce-looking woman who reminded me of an enraged, pallid hen shoved unwillingly into a floral-print gunny sack, appeared at the door and asked us to cease. I had just found the Calvin Frazier J-V-B.

'Ya'll goan hefta leave. Mah doughta shoodna letcha in ina firze playce.' We protested vigorously, pleading to at least buy what we had found so far. 'Naw, I gotta book tells me alla th'pryces on alla th'rekids an' besahdes 'at, mah howse burned las' naght an' ah ain't got th'time to deal wit' ya'll.'

We left, with Bill in a greater temper than even I was. 'Bloody old ratbag!' he shouted, as we stalked briskly across the parking lot. 'I'll drive.' He got in, started up and shot off the lot onto the highway considerably faster than Little Noddy being chased by Mr. Plod. 'Her house burned down, eh?' he continued. 'Pity she wasn't fuckin' *in* it!'

Nevertheless, by the time we left Shreveport three days later, including a very useful run through Stan's Record Shop at 728 Texas Street, we reckoned we'd done well. We headed north to Texarkana. I was breathing easier every day. On the way, we attempted – as we had done in previous days – to squeeze something more out of the car radio than disco or country. It was always a dismal failure and we quickly reached the point where, as one of us punched the 'Off' button, we would both, loudly and in perfect unison, shout 'BOLLOCKS!!!'.

Lots of similar stuff occurs on a long road trip. Bill and I talked about everything: the past, the present and the future. We cracked gags, told stories and also invented characters, fictional archetypes born of and on the road. One was 'A. Liberace':

> 'Er... hello, Liberace's the name.'
> 'What, *THE* Liberace?'
> 'Er, no, A. Liberace.'

This in turn morphed into:

> 'Hello, my name is J.P. Taylor.'
> 'Not *THE* J.P. Taylor?'
> 'Sadly no. Merely A.J.P. Taylor.'

and

> 'Achtung und guten tag Kamerads! Mein name ist Dolf Hitler!'
> 'Surely not *THE* Dolf Hitler?'
> 'Gott in himmel, Tommy Schweinhundts! NEIN! Ich bin *A*. Dolf Hitler, dumkopfs! Donner und gerfuken Blitzen!'

We were STILL reading far too many *War Picture Library* magazines... but that's where we learned all our German.

We reached Texarkana in 100 degrees of clear heat – a very different gaggle of goose droppings from the snow of Philadelphia and Tennessee or the muggy clouds that hung over Shreveport. We found little there, and so

A rare pic of my mate Bill,
who is usually behind the camera.

we began the journey that would drop us back down to Little Rock, Arkansas.

On the way down we skimmed into East Texas, and along the flat, hot highway saw a ramshackle old clapboard house with a sagging porch and a dusty front yard filled with sun-baked appliances and signs that read '*COME ON IN, STUFF FOR SALE*'.

Of course we stopped. We clomped across the deep boarded porch and pushed the screen door open. Inside was the most singularly overwhelming Aladdin's caveful of alarming old rubbish either of us had ever laid eyes on. Two huge, ugly white couches faced each other in the main room, each creaking gently in their clear, tight PVC covers like a scrawny old fetishist in his back bedroom on a wet Saturday afternoon. They were surrounded by just about everything it was possible to manufacture and still shove through a door. Beads, curtains, pillows, tableware, linen, rugs, jars, decanters, lamps, old newspapers and magazines, paperbacks, screen-printed framed artwork, canned food... and sitting among all this was the family whose living was made principally by selling everything and anything they had.

The TV they were watching had a price on it. So did the perversely creaking couches. Each room was filled with more and more stuff. One back bedroom gave itself completely to cheap costume jewellery, another to slap-happy make-up and miniature bottles of Raid and Pine-Sol masquerading as perfume. There was a six-foot stack of slightly water-damaged Roach Motels. No useful records though. The head of the house followed our every amazed move with clear satisfaction.

'Impressive, huh?' he chortled. We nodded.

'Hey, lemme show you this.'

Clearly, from the important position it occupied in the centre of the mantelpiece, sitting on its own miniature rug, this was the very pinnacle of the inventory. Gingerly, and with great reverence, the piece was taken down and demonstrated to us. It was an eighteen-inch high hand-painted glazed china Elvis-In-Vegas liquor decanter that played 'Love Me Tender' when wound, and required that the King's head be removed in order to gain access to the contents. The old fellow gently decapitated the Colonel's boy, revealing not a red neck, but a cork one, and cackled with delight. He wanted eighty bucks for it and he wasn't joking.

'Er... actually, me Mum's already got one,' said Bill quickly. I bought a Velvet Elvis balsa-framed picture for $1 which I handed to Bill outside as a consolation prize. 'Oh, thanks mate,' he replied, breaking it over his knee.

In Little Rock that evening we found a motel and did what we had been doing in every motel since Johnson City, which was to test the beds by leaping at them from as great a height as we could manage and landing in full belly-flop position. If we hit it just right, we could sometimes bounce back off and land heavily on the floor. It was our new hobby.

Bill had a phone number for the blues singer Larry Davis, and we connected with him the morning after we arrived. He graciously spent the ante-meridiem with us, Bill interviewing him for *Blues Unlimited* and taking photos. Larry took us to a local recording studio he used and played us a lot of very good Larry Davis. Over lunch, he invited us to his house that evening to sit in on a band rehearsal. We felt like lottery winners!

In the afternoon we poked about the town, found a secondhand furniture store and went in. It was full of secondhand furniture. However, sensing it was worth asking, I enquired about shellac of the leather-faced owner, to be told there MIGHT be some in a wardrobe out back. I picked my way through the stock, found a likely wardrobe and opened it. Several feet of badly stacked 78's blinked in the unaccustomed light and immediately started begging to be sorted. I'd come to the right place.

Meanwhile, Bill had got into conversation with leatherface, the usual 'where-ya'll-from-what-ya'll-doin-here-were-just-touring-the-South-mate-nice-place-you-got-thanks-buddy-well-y'all-come-back-y'hear?-sure-we-can-bring-the-wife-and-kids-next-year-they'd-love-to-see-all-this-it'll-make-a-change-from-Frinton' stuff. Having brought that to its logical conclusion, Bill wandered back to see how I was getting on. Sweating buckets and breathing hard was how.

'Anything good mate?' he enquired lightly.

I waved the third Willie Nix and a Big Boy Spires at him, pointing to a growing pile on the table. We took our stash out of the furniture store. 'Pay Your Furniture Man!' I remarked, invoking the famous Reverend J.M. Gates recording, and fell into the car giggling.

Our luck held. Within an hour we were inside an extraordinary old junk store; actually, more of a barn. The owner sat behind a huge central table cleaning a large and varied collection of handguns. Spread around him on trestle tables was all manner of old tat. It was dank, dim, grimy, and supported by a dirt floor that crunched as we walked on it.

Bill started turning things over while I was drawn deeper in, to a far wall where several low stacks of records sat. There was the usual stuff, tatty albums by Dolly and Frankie and Ricky and, as absolutely-bloody-always, anywhere from Little Rock to North Watford, a wrecked copy of *The Sound Of Music*. Then, I found a small heap that gripped my stomach muscles tighter with every turn of a label: Will Ezell, the State Street Boys, Charlie Spand, the Hokum Boys, Barbecue Bob, Leroy Carr, Georgia Tom, Frankie Jaxon, the Mississippi Sheiks... Bill appeared at my shoulder, saw what I'd found and quietly backed away. He returned seconds later with a box full of extraordinary old rubbish. A few photos, a Coca-Cola advert, some old magazines.

'Get a price for everything,' he whispered.

I did. It was about $4, I think. Outside Bill said: 'If we'd JUST bought the records, he might have sussed us.' I believe he was right. It was in this store that Bill found what was to become the fake Robert Johnson photo, of which more later.

Two prime quality British herberts presented themselves at Larry Davis' house around half past six. The tight little living room was filling up nicely with guitars, amplifiers, mikes, leads, neighbours and Larry's old mum, seated on the couch. We found places to squat and just quietly watched. There was a second guitarist, who introduced himself to us as 'Bubba', whose un-named but clearly eccentric brother took a seat next to Larry's mum. The bass player acknowledged us, and told us his name was 'Leroy'. They were offering pseudonyms. I don't blame them; we could have been the IRS for all they knew. Tuned up enough to let one go, the three guitarists began to play. Someone was out of tune... the music stopped while it was fixed, started again, drifted a little. Then Larry asked where in hell was the drummer, and it suddenly struck me what was missing. Halfway through the next number, he and his kit fell through the door. He set himself up in record time and joined in. As he did so, the music suddenly took off, like a seaplane given a final boost to free it from choppy waters. As the sound climbed and flew, it got tighter, harder, Larry's vocals suddenly became serious, his picking meaner and more stinging. The music took him, he rose to the occasion from his chair and stood to play, smiling with satisfaction. The rehearsal had become a gig, and we its audience. Larry sang song after song, each framed by the now closely-knitted instrumental support, and as he did so, his voice got more and more in touch with his soul, until he had lost himself in it all, singing with eyes closed, sweat beads tap-dancing across his forehead. I looked at Bill, wearing the same rapt face I'd seen at B.B. King's Albert Hall gig a decade earlier.

When it was over, we sat around and chatted. The atmosphere was relaxed, congratulatory and satisfied. Bubba's brother was a talkative, ebullient man who had clearly had too much of something even before he'd arrived. He chatted constantly to everyone and no-one. Turning to me he said: 'I used to be a good blues singer y'know, until I lost my voice.'

'Oh, really, how'd that happen?'

Outside the recording studio with Larry and his wife.
Yeah, I know about the flared jeans. It was 1979, OK?

'Eatin' too much *pussy!* Hehehehehee.' Then he went back to his serious business of playing air guitar to the tunes in his head. We went to a late-night diner with Larry and his wife, chewing the fat until perhaps 2:00 am (it was woefully undercooked). Why can't every day be that good?

The following morning we drove to Helena via Pine Bluff. We wanted to see Helena because of its association with Sonny Boy Williamson, a regular broadcaster on station KFFA, whose image still graced the bags of cornmeal that sponsored his early career. We found KFFA and also the Gist Music Store across the street, where the owners were happy to talk to us about Sonny Boy, but added little we didn't already know. We then went to the grocery store down the block, looking for Sonny Boy cornmeal bags. We found them in every size from Jolly Handy to You Expect Me To Lift That? We bought several examples of the Jolly Handy size and then blew the cashier's mind by asking her for a plain brown sack, carefully emptying the contents into the sack, even more carefully folding the empty bags and offering her the debagged cornmeal as a gift for her next regular customer. We were not the first Mad Eurobuggers to do this, nor would we be the last. Frank Weston has a lovely tale to tell about emptying cornmeal into a brown bag in the same store, being approached by the janitor and asked if he was Swedish. No, Frank replied, he wasn't, why? 'Well, only last month a coupla guys from Stockholm or somewhere was doing the same thing you're doing. What I gotta know is... WHY?'

We departed Helena to head for Mississippi, and as we did so we drove past a craft store displaying hand-woven baskets. 'They must be the Helena handbaskets everyone says this country's going to,' I remarked. Bill, driving, reached over and viciously slugged me with a badly damaged Velvet Elvis.

We zig-zagged through Mississippi on our way to Clarksdale. We had to, for we kept encountering signposts for places that our fantasies had fed upon for years. Muddy's birthplace, Stovall – nothing but a grocery store at a crossroads now; Friars Point, immortalised by Robert Lee McCoy – a ramshackle town where wood-frame houses wound in and out of each other in eccentric patterns; and Henry Sims' Farrell, merely a signpost by the roadside. It took most of the morning, and it was wonderful. It was odd, though, to take this tour through a light carpet of snow; my fantasies had always coupled the Delta to hot, steamy days where road mirages implied water on the tarmac and dust rose gently from worked fields, not crunchy ice and visibly exhaled breath.

It was early afternoon before we arrived in Clarksdale and began looking for Sixth Street. We found it with little difficulty – it's not that big a place. Sixth Street was our goal for the simple reason that this was where Wade Walton's 'new' barbershop was located. In 1960, Paul Oliver had recorded and photographed him at his original premises on Fourth Street. I guess I could have wished that Wade hadn't moved, simply so I could actually step into one of those familiar photographs, but I wasn't complaining too hard when we got there because it looked right. A single story brick building with a large plate glass window and Wade's old, well-kept Chevrolet parked outside.

Wade's Barber Shop was much more than just a place to get a haircut or a shave. That was in the front. In the back, accessed via a doorless frame, was a dark bar populated by a few quiet drinkers. Behind the bar

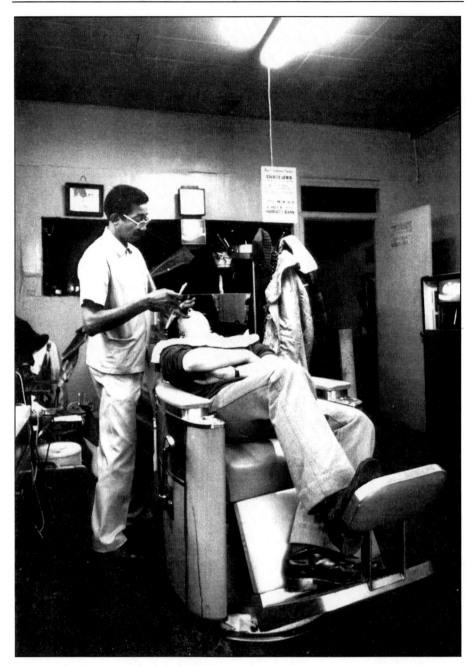

A close shave for the Sailor.

Mrs. Walton was sound asleep in an old barbershop chair. Wade was there also, talking to friends when we walked in. He had been used to blues tourists since Don Hill's 1958 visit, and had the clippings to prove it, but in 1979 it was nothing like as hectic as his final decade of fame.

We wandered back into the shop, Wade talking constantly but quietly about the blues, which he deeply loved, and about his other life as a barber. We sat and listened as he embarked upon a short illustrated history of the blues. I'd heard his records on Arhoolie and Bluesville, but I'm not sure Bill had at that time. Wade played and sang a lovely, gentle 'Rock Me Baby' on acoustic guitar, switching it to above-the-head and behind-the-neck positions; he took up an electric to play 'Dust My Broom'; he blew deep blue harmonica, bending notes through cupped hands, then he took out his cut-throat razor, grabbed the free end of his leather strop and reconstructed the wonderful 'Barbershop Rhythm' that Paul Oliver and Chris Strachwitz had first recorded nineteen years previously. I was ecstatic. I'd listened to that recording many times and now I was a few feet away from the live version. I heard Bill's camera shutter working overtime but I didn't see it; I had gone into hyperfocus. All I could see was Wade making extraordinary, rhythmic patterns with a steel blade and a piece of leather. In short, quick strokes back up and down the strop, he produced an airy, agile, walloping, soft-blues-shuffle that no-one else has ever attempted. There are no rare Paramounts even remotely like it; Joe Von Battle never hosted a strop-player in the back room studio of his Hastings Street store, Harry Oster never found one, nor did either Lomax. While this one-man blues festival was in progress, customers drifted in and took seats, expanding the audience. No-one seemed pressed for time, but eventually Wade realised he needed to take care of business and began cutting hair.

Conversation continued as he did so. Customers, mainly older men, reminisced about seeing Jimmy Reed play black high school dances round town in the late 1950's, and about the legendary Son House, who everyone knew of, but none had seen. All the while, Wade snipped, razored, shaved, brushed and trimmed. A man trailing a small, unwilling boy entered and plonked him in the chair for a cut. When Wade was done, he asked if it was okay. Dad replied he thought maybe the boy's mother wanted it a little shorter. Wade responded with a thirty second powercut that left the lad's head, at least, ready to join the Marine Corps. Amused by this, Bill leaned over to me and whispered 'bootleg haircut'. I couldn't resist; I had a three day road-beard and asked Wade for a shave. Clambering into the chair and being lowered into the prone position under a hot towel I heard two sounds. One was Bill laughing at what he saw as a wonderfully absurd situation; the other was that razor strop. I didn't shave again for two days; there was no need.

In the spring of that year, I published Bill's photo of this event on the front cover of *SD*. All you could really see was a set of nostrils and an unshaven chin, attended by a Sweeney-Toddishly grinning Wade. That's the kind of power being your own publisher gives you. Several years later, the same photo appeared in the *Radio Times* as an illustration for one of Francis Wilford-Smith's wonderful *Aspects Of The Blues* programmes. You could still see my nostrils perfectly.

Wade's bar contained an old Rock-Ola 45 rpm juke box. As I left money for a beer, I wandered over, *very* clean shaven, to check it out. It had obviously held its contents for an extremely long time. I pushed a quarter in, punched a number and Muddy's 'Forty Days and Forty Nights' pumped its lush way up through the speakers.

'Juke box guy comes in here every month, wanting to change the records on my box. I won't let him,' remarked Wade.

I drank my beer, listened to Muddy, looked around me in the dark bar and beyond to the bright front parlour and wished I could just be here forever.

The following day was a Sunday. Bill had a Clarksdale address for Raymond Hill, one of Ike Turner's old Kings of Rhythm, and an early Sun Records artist. He took some finding among the cloned blocks in the housing project he lived in, and somewhere along the way Bill spotted a beautiful poster advertising a live Little Milton gig; one of those classic tri-colour ones that haven't essentially altered in style since the 1940's. We pulled up. 'I'm havin' that,' Bill said in his best wide boy voice, and got out to appropriate it. Sitting at the wheel with the engine running, I lit a cigarette and watched. Capturing it was more difficult than Bill had imagined: there were perhaps eighty heavy staples pinning it to the wooden telegraph pole. I could hear Bill grumbling to himself as the staples fought hard for every inch of ground, ripping fingertips and nails as they held fast: 'Sod it. Balls! Ah, *bollocks*... shitlegs... fuck... gosh, how frustrating... SHITE! Ah, shitdamnfuckbollocks...'

While Bill was engaged in this Herculean endeavour, a Sunday Morning Drunk strolled past. He stopped, and I saw him look at Bill, hear the stream of consciousness delivered in the deepest of South Wimbledon accents, then blink, shake himself and wander in closer. Either Bill didn't hear him come up behind him or he didn't care. The drunk continued to observe Bill's highly engaging performance. From inside the car, I continued to watch and listen to them both. At length, when Bill was perhaps 75 percent done, the drunk spoke.

'Zat your poster, man?' he enquired, unsteadily gesticulating.

'It will be when I get it off this bleedin' post, mate,' replied Bill, still working.

'Oh, okay, jus' checkin',' and he wandered off.

We eventually found Raymond Hill, who agreed to an interview despite his wife's dire warnings about how many times he'd been ripped off. Then, duty done, she offered us coffee. We accepted, and Bill began talking with Raymond about the old days. Bill has a very winning way as an interviewer. He is naturally charming, sympathetic and knows exactly what he's talking about. He could sometimes prod a musician into remembering a long-forgotten detail by mentioning a small, arcane info-nugget that made his subject realise he really *did* know his stuff. Raymond Hill talked for perhaps two hours while I quietly fed the worst coffee I'd ever encountered to an innocent rubber plant at my immediate left. I hoped it would survive, but at that moment it was either it or me.

The following morning, Monday, we hit Greenville. There's an old Willie Love song called 'Nelson Street Blues', celebrating the joys of this thoroughfare; how you can zip in and out of the DeLuxe Café, the bars, the suit-pressing shop, how you can laugh and talk with the folks you meet. It had once been a nerve-centre of black life in Greenville. But Willie Love had sung about it in 1952. Over a quarter-century later, in a Monday morning rain, Nelson Street was about as engaging as Tooting Broadway on early closing day. Another bubble burst, we pointed the car in the direction of Memphis.

On the road to Memphis, another in-car character was born. His name was Eric. He was a south London rocker, thicker-planked than even me, obsessed by rockabilly in general and Sun Records in particular.

'ere, we're gettin' close to Memphis, ain't we? Cor... good 'ere innit? I mean, Tennessee Cotton Country mate, them fields was probably full of rockabilly singers back in the Fifties; I mean, if you'd stood 'ere in 1957, I bet you could have 'eard slap-bass playing right across them fields. Blimey.'

We pulled into another motel just inside Memphis. We gave the beds the damn good thrashing they so richly deserved, and our thoughts turned to the possibility of hearing some live blues. We washed up and headed for Blues Alley on Front Street. We had no idea who might be appearing, but it seemed the best shot we had. It turned out to be Laura Dukes, Big Sam and Sonny Blake. Neither Laura nor Sam were especially good. Laura, to be blunt, for all her connections to the final years of the Memphis Jug Band, was dreadful to the point of being surreal. Sonny Blake, however, was another matter. While the band that backed him were journeyman quality only, Sonny himself was in fine form. He played sharp, full-toned harmonica straight into the microphone, producing a sound not unlike Little Walter on, say, 'Hate To See You Go'. His technique was simple; he broke no new gob-iron ground, but what he played was pure, straight blues. His singing was smoky, relaxed, and intimate. He came across to me as one of the most engaging and pure blues singers I'd ever heard.

Meanwhile, an idiot white kid two tables away was attempting to accompany Sonny with his own thin, reedy little harmonica, interjecting comments like 'Yeah, Sonny' and 'Blow it man, I'm with you.' Of course! It was the legendary Memphis Harmonica Prick. Bill seriously wanted to go and fill him in. I dissuaded him by pointing out that he probably couldn't do much more damage anyway. I wrote a note and passed it to the Prick. It read: *'Greetings from England. Fuck you and the harmonica you should immediately shove up your arse. God save the Queen!'*

The next morning we went down on Beale Street. I remembered Jack Teagarden's voice from my childhood, and I started to do the Bedsan Walk. As it turns out, it's a bit like the Lambeth Walk only totally different.

There wasn't much of the old Beale Street left, but Sonny's Loan Office was still there and so was Schwab's. Schwab's was a department store that had operated on Beale Street for over a hundred years before we clomped into it that day. It had the feel of an old, original Woolworth's, but more downhome. We marvelled at the extraordinary mix of stock, everything you might hope to find in a locally-serving department store, but our attention fixed on the wonderful selection of Policy Number dream books and the counter full of packets of rabbits' feet, High John the Conqueror Root and bottles of love potion. This extraordinary display of folk-lore for sale captured our imaginations, and I was just completing my purchases when Bill found the owner, Abe Schwab. He was one of the most engaging men I'd ever met, and he immediately launched into a history of Beale Street, with Schwab's as the focal point. While he was doing so, a couple of his old cronies arrived; one was a pawnbroker who looked like Tommy Cooper with a more lived-in face. He immediately opened an ongoing salvo of gags:

'This man lies for a living,' smiled Abe.

'Right, I lie like a *rug*... Hey, listen, what's the definition of "mixed emotions"?'

Sensing a gag, we responded, in music-hall voices: 'We don't know, what's the definition of "mixed emotions"?'

'It's when your mother-in-law drives your brand-new Cadillac over the cliff'!'

He then went on to explain how sales promotion was carried out in the old days. If it got too quiet, he would send a couple of his guys out onto the street with a shotgun. One would chase the other up the block shouting: 'YOU'VE BEEN FOOLIN' WITH MY WOMAN, YOU SONOFABITCH! COME BACK HERE, I'M GONNA BLOW YOUR MUTHAFUCKIN' HEAD OFF!'

They would caper around the block some more, and finally run back into the store, with one still shouting and brandishing the shotgun at the other. By this time, they'd have gathered a large and curious crowd around them, who all followed them into the store. Then someone would lock the doors, and they'd start selling to the newly captive audience.

Sitting in Abe's office was a framed vintage photo of the famous disc jockey, Dewey Phillips, in his studio. This was the guy who had hosted the *Red Hot & Blue* R&B radio show in the early 1950's and was also the first deejay in the world to play an Elvis record. In 1979 no-one in Europe had seen this. Bill carefully took photographs of the photograph.

We left Memphis and took the road to Nashville; or, rather, to a small place just outside of it called Goodlettesville, where Doug Seroff lived. Doug was doing the same thing I was, attempting to wrest a living for his family by selling rare records. It turned out that he lived way up in the hills above the hamlet we were aiming for. We needed directions ('Okay, from this hamlet you take the right fork to Macbeth, following the Midsummer Nights road out of it and you'll come to Muchado. Ignore it, it's nothing'.).

Doug and his wife welcomed us, and for two days we drank their tea, ate their food, bought them dinner, used Doug as a guide and talked his head off. He took us downtown to Nashville, where we poked around the record shops and distributors, looked at the Grand Ole Opry and clocked all the hopeful wannabe country stars out on the street in big hats and boots, fighting light rain and heavy anxiety with fixed grins. It struck us as a shade tawdry, the rhinestone glitter turning to paste and board if you got too close. This was years before the country revival, and Nashville was then in something of a rut, clinging to that which was past its 'sell by' date and not knowing what direction to take next; I think we saw it at its worst. Doug and I sat and talked about what it meant to be a record dealer, and drew comfort from each other in the similarities. He was a wonderful host, a gentle soul who did what he did up in the wooded hills, because being a Nashville bus driver had driven him crazy. His wife was a schoolteacher, and between them they made ends meet by cutting their given cloth very carefully and were grateful for what they had.

Time was getting short and we had found enough records to rescue our trip. The Dodge Diplomat we had been living out of was riding low at the back; not only did we have several thousand records, we also had a blood-stained poster, tin trays, photographs and a huge curved enamel blood-and-bandage barbershop sign Bill had rescued from a wall one morning while I nervously kept the engine running. We headed north to St. Louis. As we did so, the weather began to turn foul.

We arrived in St. Louis in mid-evening, turning off the Interstate into the middle of a large and apparently well-organised street fight. We slowed down enough to avoid hitting anyone, but kept going, weaving through some dozen or more flailing bodies brandishing tyre irons and chains among gently falling snow. Don't mind us, we won't interrupt. No, please, carry on as if we weren't here. 'Welcome to St. Louis then,' said Bill wryly as we left the mêlée behind. The next day, the weather got worse and we had a ways to go, so we abandoned our plans to dig around St. Louis and got back on the Interstate heading east toward Philadelphia.

Bad decision. Within an hour we were embroiled in the worst snow storm either of us had ever seen. The Interstate was only just passable, but strong winds howling across open fields blew hapless Ford Pintos into the sides of eighteen-wheelers and then off the highway. Abandoned vehicles littered the roadside. The visibility was maybe twenty feet. The traction generated by a trunk full of records was what kept us on the road, but it was a very long morning. We pulled off around lunchtime for gas and food, and, as I got out of the car for the first time since the storm had set in, the wind sliced into me like an ice-cold meat cleaver. I had NEVER felt that cold before. Imitating the great Swedish runner, Bengt Duble, I hurtled towards the warmth of the diner.

Back out on the road again, things got worse. Average speeds were perhaps twenty miles an hour. Worryingly, vehicles MUCH bigger than my old uncle's caravan in St. Oseth's started sliding about in front of us. Oh shit. In the afternoon, the light gave way and took half our forward visibility with it. Exits were being marked as blocked, one after the other. We realised that we were stuck ON the interstate and our gas tank was now reading way below half. Steady, Carruthers, remember you're British... Where's your stiff upper lip? Er, just above this loose wobbly bottom one, actually.

Eventually, somewhere just inside the Pennsylvania state line, we found a clear exit ironically marked 'Summerton'. We cruised into Philadelphia the next afternoon feeling like heroic returning warriors. Russ welcomed our records back and sorted through them while we ate our way through his fridge; then we got on the New Jersey turnpike and headed back up to New York to keep our appointment with British Airways. On the way we were paralleled by a police vehicle with a loudspeaker attached to the top. Apparently, I was speeding.

'PULL OVER!' shouted the cop car in its best bullhorn voice.

'NOT WEARING ONE!' yelled Bill. We got a ticket and a lecture.

Using Dave Sax's house as a base, we took two days to pack, sort and get the airfreight ready. We gawked around Manhattan for our final day, going up the Empire State Building. No Fay Wray or King Kong in sight, just a couple of tired Brits. The adventure was over. We had driven over 6500 miles in less than thirty days, seen and heard and experienced more than we could have imagined, brought home the shellac bacon and the won the day's vinyl bread. Bill had rescued my arse by working his off on my behalf. You want to make a classic buddy-bonding movie? You just read the script.

Chapter Seven

1979-84: MINISTRY OF CERTAIN THINGS

Sailor's Delight was doing well: it expanded quickly into selling new albums, books and more video, but the basis of the business was always the expensive auctions and cheap set sales. Yin and Yang. Beluga and Bovril. Cannon and Balls. People frequently asked: 'Where do you get all this stuff?' and the answer was 'everywhere and anywhere'. To some degree, it was a self-fulfilling prophesy. The better-known you get, the more records come your way – often in great piles. People would simply call up and say: 'I've got piles.' I'd tell them they had a wrong number – the doctor's surgery was only one digit different from mine. Records came through the door at me, or I went out and got them. I travelled as near as round the corner and as far as Paris. To do so, I bought the first of a string of secondhand Volvo station wagons. The old ones were built like tanks and had the load bearing capacity of a small truck. My father agreed to be my accountant, providing I sent him LPs in return. I was paying the mortgage and the bills on time, I set my own agenda and suffered no fool gladly for long. I considered myself, once again, to be one very Fortunate Young Sod.

The foot traffic was always pretty heavy. I didn't just trade by mail, I actively invited people to come and rummage, which is how I came to meet Percy Miller. Percy had been in London since the early 1960's but, as a teenager growing up in Jamaica, he had been exposed to R&B by the proto-disc jockeys Duke Reid and Coxsone Dodd. He came to shuffle through 78's and buy, and he began telling me stories about the old days. Tales of huge mobile discos mounted on the backs of Trojan lorries (hence the early record label name); of amplifiers so powerful and of speakers so loud and vibrant they had to be tied down with guy ropes; of disc jockey rivalry, 78's with labels peeled away to prevent the competition figuring out what they were; of how Roscoe Gordon and his singular rhythm fathered ska, which became blue beat, which begat reggae.

Others who trundled through had less interesting tales to tell, but were no less colourful. Ray Topping was a regular. Almost always accompanied by his buddy and driver Martin Sachon, a Hatton Garden diamond merchant with a penchant for mint R&B albums, Ray's enthusiasm's for obscure records knew no boundaries. I once sold him an Andre Williams

45 that I knew was dreadful, and told him so.

'I know,' he replied handing over a fiver, 'but I collect the geezer and I need this for filing purposes.'

He was also occasionally responsible for the destruction of furniture. On a day shortly after I had returned from Paris with the second load of mint albums from perhaps the most comprehensive collection of rare blues LPs in Europe, Ray was sifting through the stock, reaching higher and higher up the steel shelving that they sat on. He stepped up onto a wooden folding chair to reach the top shelf and, finding the previously unseen Roscoe Shelton Excello LP, gave a leap of excitement. Ray was a big guy, so the chair did what chairs do when big guys jump up and down on them, and immediately gave way. Ray began to fall; Martin and I saw clearly how and where he would land, squarely on the carpet in the middle of the room. As Ray glided backwards to his fate, his right arm, with the hand still clutching the precious mint album, shot out in front of him to protect it. He landed full on his back, raising a light cloud of unhoovered dust, but still clutching his Roscoe at arms length in front of him. From this prone position, legs akimbo, Ray immediately said: 'The album... is it... okay?'

It was.

As Ray became increasingly involved in advising and then directing R&B reissues for Ace Records, so his visits, too, increased, rummaging my shelves for unheard stuff. He quit his day job and went to work for Ace full time. He would therefore be sent, at company expense, to the Modern Records archives in Los Angeles where he would forego the sun, surf, sand, soap-operas, sex, sleaze and social life for a fortnight in a dank basement chasing down obscure performances on acetate and tape, checking matrix numbers, scribbling fax'n'info in a book and listening, always listening, to unissued R&B and blues. Occasionally, he would emerge from this underworld and into Bob's Big Boy restaurant for food, requesting chips with everything and getting crisps instead of the French fries he lived on.

He also loved to play air guitar. If he was demonstrating a newly found unissued master to me, and there was a blasting solo in the middle, he would flail along on his imaginary Les Paul. He occasionally graduated to other instruments too. When he turned up with a test pressing for the reissue by harmonica player George Smith, he was explaining, as I listened, how and where he had found these gems, but his need to play air harmonica got in the way.

'Tell me later, Ray,' I said. 'Don't want to interfere with your playing.'

'Oh, right, ta,' he answered, closed his eyes and blew a devastating solo.

Then, one evening he turned up with a rare 45 by Clifton Chenier, the zydeco accordionist. 'Here, listen to THIS!' Only just in time did I get out the way of his much needed elbow-room.

I used to entertain Matthew, now about five years old, by telling him elaborate bedtime tales of Dr. Ray Topping's exciting exploits in Rhythm-&-

Bluesland. Matthew would giggle himself silly at all this, and we quickly arrived at a hook line which we chanted in unison at the end of every tale: 'Ray Topping is an *IDIOT!!!*' Then one evening, when Ray was in the back room with me, Matthew, fresh from a bath, looking angelic in red pyjamas, a dimple-cheeked smile and a mop of blonde hair, came through the door to say goodnight.

'Do you know who this man is?' I asked him.

He shook his head.

'This is Ray Topping!'

Eyes out like organ stops, Matthew turned to him with a huge smile and said: 'My dad says you're an idiot. Goodnight.' and then he turned and left. Ray looked astonished for a moment, then glanced at me and burst out laughing.

Despite his excesses, Ray was a likeable man who remained thoroughly committed to his path, and was a genuine expert in his field. Without his crucial input we would know a lot less about post-war blues than we do.

Sunday afternoons could often get very busy, with anything up to eighteen people barging about loudly in a tightly-fitting room, spilling out into the hallway or through the back door to the garden if it was pleasant enough. Regulars included usual suspects Bill Greensmith, both Franks (Weston and Nazareth), Bruce Bastin, Cilla Huggins and Mike Rowe, as well as Richard Johnson, Ken Martin, Dave Williams, John Broven, Johnny Jackson, Chris Bentley, Bill Pearson, Mike Yates, Ian Cole, and a local friend, Ron Stevens, who shared my experience as a son–of-a-newsagent and was also an old R&B and soul fan. He simply sat and watched, incredulous, while the enthusiasms of the afternoon washed over him.

These sessions were always at their most intense when new stock arrived. It brought out the best character disorders in everyone. I would pour fuel on this by providing beer, tea and a large assortment of junky kids sweets; fruit lollipops; sherbert-filled Flying Saucers; bright pink chewy shrimps; Blackjacks, Fruit Salads and Mojos; jelly worms; red liquorice string; Blo-Pops; Chupa-Chups, Gummy Frogs and Jelly Babies. Watching someone like the huge, enthusiastic, balding yet long-haired and vastly red-bearded Richard Johnson, occupying rented space somewhere inside one of his enormous, shapeless woolly jumpers, chugging down jelly worms while discussing gospel quartet rarities with Ken Martin was one of life's more delightfully bizarre visions.

Everyone had their narrow specialised area and everyone respected the other's first claims. If it was a difficult Lil' Son Jackson Imperial or Gold Star that turned up, Bill Pearson got first refusal. Obscure 45's out of Louisiana were offered to Johnny Jackson ahead of everyone else. Ken Martin would have first pick of the R&B vocal groups, although there was little competition for them in Britain at that time. If a clean copy of Jimmy Rogers' 'That's Alright' ever turned up, everyone knew it would go to Dave Williams (it never did.) Rare downhome 45's generally went to Chris Bentley and, despite hungry looks, if an early and much-desired Chicago or Detroit record surfaced, it was offered to the Elder Statesman of the group, Mike Rowe.

Sometimes, however, something could just sneak by. On one such occasion, Mike displayed a mild interest in a Big Bill Columbia, pulled from a large pile of similar discs:

'How much?' he asked. I gave him a very reasonable price.

'Er... anyone else want this before I buy it?'

'A Big Bill Columbia? No thanks.'

'Okay. Paul, play this for me would you?'

I dropped the needle onto 'Midnight Steppers', a fabulous boogie shuffle with a knockout piano solo from Josh Altheimer. People stood aghast at the missed opportunity while Mike celebrated by executing a perfect boogie woogie dance in the middle of the room.

'None of you ugly bastards knew about this one, didya?' he said. He was dead right.

Foreign visitors turned up regularly. From Paris, Vienna, Bonn, Rome, Chicago, New York, San Francisco, Melbourne and Tokyo. I opened the door in answer to the bell one Saturday morning to be caught like a defrocked vicar, snared by a paparazzo in the glare of a professional flashgun. Kyu Toshido from Tokyo had arrived, unannounced. In the ensuing two hours, he bought slightly fewer records than he took photographs.

Herve Moreau came from Paris with an English vocabulary limited to 'Hello', 'Yes please', 'No thank you', 'Is bathroom empty?' and his two most useful phrases, 'Fine' and 'Not Fine'. Working through a stack of 45's at the turntable for him, he would indicate his enthusiasm, or lack of it, by the emphasis he placed on one of these two phrases:

John Brim on Chess: 'FINE!'
Detroit Junior on Tip Top: 'Ah – not fine.'
Guitar Nubbit on Bluestown: 'Ooooooooooh... FINE!!'
Ann Peebles on Hi: 'Hmm... fine...'
Smokey Hogg on Crown: 'Merde alors! *NOT* fine!!!' etc.

We also had thoroughly immature fun at the expense of another Frenchman when Bill Greensmith and I had already had perhaps one too many teabags. As he came in, I introduced him to Bill; 'This is Patrick Jacquet.' Turning to my fresh guest I said, theatrically, 'May I take your jacket, Patrick?' to which he innocently replied: 'Ah! My name, it is Patrick Jacquet, not Jacquet Patrick.' Behind me I heard a sudden squawk and a thud. Bill had fallen off his chair, helpless with laughter.

Phone calls erupted at any time of the day or night from overseas customers who couldn't figure the time zones. At two in the morning someone would call from Japan or New Zealand to order something. I generally took it in my stride, but occasionally it got to me, especially if I was being interrupted in concluding some other, unrelated endeavour. A call came in at 1:30 am from an agitated Japanese customer who had just got *SD* and was phoning to snatch the apparently rare soul 45 I had ignorantly listed for sale at a pound – something local soul man Adrian Croasdale had driven over to pick up the moment he spotted it. By this time I'd had a dozen requests for what appeared to be a seventy quid record.

'Hello! Is here ichiban soulman from Nippon! You have item 5347 please?'

'No, it's gone.'

'Has gone? Shit! This very expensive phone call.'

'I know.'

'Why you not have it anymore?'

'Because it's bloody gone and it's almost two in the bloody morning.'

'I DEMAND RECORD!!!'

'Sod off!'

'I am ichiban soul man! MUST have record!'

'Well, you can't. Serves you right for bombing Pearl Harbor in the ichiban place. Now, piss off.'

It was, of course, international diplomacy of that quality that made Britain so globally admired.

Every issue of *SD* generated a phone call from a man who sat on an otherwise uninhabited island off the Australian coast, monitoring things in the ether on behalf of his government. He set his own schedule and had an unmetered phone. 'G'day mate, I need a few records.' I reached for my cigarettes. This would take at least 40 minutes. He loved to tell gags at Australian Government expense: 'Here, got a good joke for yez. This blind geezer with his guide dog, he's down town see, and he goes into a department store, picks up the dog by the tail, lifts it over his head and starts whirling it about, full three 'undred and sixty. Manager runs up and says: "Oi, what the bloody 'ell d'ya think you're doing?" Bloke sez: "Don't mind me, mate, I'm just havin' a look round." Hehehehe. 'ere, you got the new *Magpie Piano Blues* album in yet?'

Magpie was one of several labels run by Bruce Bastin, under the Interstate banner. The Magpie 4400 series was dedicated to piano blues of the pre-war period, all drawn from the collection of Francis Wilford-Smith, also known as the cartoonist 'Smilby', of *Playboy* and *Esquire* fame. Francis was of my father's generation but, unlike many of his contemporaries, he had seen deeply into the blues immediately.

As a young naval officer he'd wound up in wartime New York and actually witnessed Ammons, Lewis and Johnson for himself at Café Society. It set him upon a lifetime journey – he was obtaining new Lightnin' Hopkins 78's by 1952 – and he was buying records from me almost as soon as I started. He was quick to invite me down to Sussex, where he then lived, at Bodle Street Green, in the wonderfully named Trumpets Farm, with his wife Pam, a pair of enthusiastic and very large dogs, an incredible book collection and a stunning horde of 78's.

People who don't know him tend to think of him as just a piano blues collector. Nothing could be further from the truth. His tastes are more catholic than many, and his collecting habits reflect that. I was astonished to be confronted with things like the Rube Lacy, a Willie Brown and a Bob Campbell nestling quietly next to a clutch of superb post-war gospel. I was also immediately captivated by his extraordinary range of enthusiasms and interests. He's the only man I know who thought it worthwhile to rescue a year's-worth of the front page of the *Sun* newspaper and have the results bound as a book.

On that first day we met, he gave my son Matthew two things that, almost thirty years later, he has not forgotten. The first was the taste of milk fresh from a cow that he took Matthew to visit. The second was more precious. Invited to cross the old farmhouse via a dark and narrow passage, Matthew, then no more than four, said he was afraid of it.

'Why are you afraid of the dark?' asked Francis.

'Because I can't see who's in it,' he very sensibly replied.

'WELL! If you can't see them, then they can't see you, can they?'

With the fear suddenly removed, Matthew marched off down his long dark tunnel without trepidation.

My – admittedly meagre – career as a radio personality began by accident in 1981. Stuart Colman ran a Sunday morning programme on Radio London called *Echoes*, essentially a rock'n'roll show, but wide enough to encompass R&B, blues, country and Cajun. Dana Gillespie was due to appear one morning and I'd made arrangements to meet her at the studio to deliver a pile of records she had ordered. Good excuse, huh? I arrived a little early, met Stuart, explained that the box was for Dana and was, without warning, invited by him to sit in on the show. I had never been in a radio studio before, and was very nervous, but with gentle coaching from Stuart I managed to get through the show without hyperventilating, barfing into the mike or involuntarily shouting 'ARSE!' on air. As a result, Stuart invited me back for a solo flight.

This is where several independently-developing little woolly strings began to knit into one odd sock.

The first was Bob Laughton. Bob was one of the two principal post-war gospel discographers in the UK, but his interest was much more in the music than the records, and he had amassed a superb collection that, now safely committed to tape, he wanted to turn into cash in order to buy the computer that would produce the discography. I wanted to sell his records for him but warned him that I didn't think here was much of a market out there. He agreed, but the records were so good, and being the instant custodian of so many in one heap, I became an immediate convert. In fact, I just blew a fuse and went into a Gospel Fritz. I asked Bob to write a 'Buyer's

Guide to Gospel', outlining principal groups and labels, which I published in the same issue that I began offering chunks of his collection. Sneaky, non?

Then Stuart's offer of a show came along, and I offered him a gospel special (opportunist, eh?), to which he agreed. It went down very well, but *especially* well in an odd corner of Kent where a spotty youth called Alasdair Blaazer happened to hear the show at the very edge of its range. He too went gospel nuts. More of him later, after his metamorphosis into both Big Joe Louis and one of the world's leading blues and gospel experts.

And so, Bob got enough money to buy his computer, ultimately resulting in the publication of *Gospel Records 1943-69*, and I went out hunting down more gospel 78's to hear and sell. It added a dimension that would underpin the magazine *Blues & Rhythm*. But more of that later.

According to Linda – and she was probably right – I lived on the phone. If I wasn't making calls, I was getting them, often answering with smartarse-morethanone-liners before I had established who was on the other end: 'Good morning. Gus & Russ, truss adjusters. Trusses adjusted without fuss. You can reach us by a number 42 bus. Let us adjust YOUR truss. Trust us.'

'Hello Sailor...' (people *loved* saying that) '...it's Richard Noblett.'

I answered one bright Monday at 10:00 am by saying, in snappy government official fashion: 'Ministry of Certain Things, good morning.'

'Oh? What things would they be?'

'Official government lingerie in men's sizes, vintage issues of *Fiesta*, ripe soft fruit and subsequent frantic masturbation at taxpayers' expense. Recycled Prophylactic Department, Nigel Arsebender speaking.'

'Ah, interesting. It's the Tax Office at Hendon here, sir. Now, about your return for the last financial year...'

Perhaps the tax people had similarly interesting dealings with a fellow named 'Doc' Cox, a BBC sound engineer who suddenly became well-known when he surfaced on Esther Rantzen's TV show, *That's Life*, as a humorous investigative reporter. His alter ego, 'Ivor Biggun', appeared fronting a London pub band called (depending on the gig) Ivor's Jivers or the Red-Nosed Burglars (har!). Because he was a trained recording engineer, his records were superbly-produced chunks of ribaldry including songs like 'Gums And Plums', 'Hide The Sausage' and 'I Can Be the Hot Dog And You Can Be the Bun', inspired – I imagine – by Bo Carter, but taking the innuendo completely out of its closet. Against all odds, he had a No. 22 hit record in 1978 with 'The Winker's Song (Misprint)', that the BBC just couldn't play, followed three years later by the less successful 'Bras On 45 (Family Version)', which they could play, but didn't.

Doc was a genuine blues fan and he turned up at the house regularly to buy stuff, tell jokes, drink tea and say things like: 'Well, I'd best be getting back to Mrs. Biggun.' He sent me a promo of his *More Filth... Dirt Cheap* album with a handwritten note that said: '*Stock this and make me a star!*' I did, and it sold well enough for me to realise a lot more clearly just who – and what – my customers really were. As for Ivor, he's still out there after all these years, gigging, recording and generally being filthy. He has a website, if you're interested, and perhaps you should be.

Running *SD* completely solo took about 90 hours a week. In truth, it probably didn't need that much attention, but my workaholism shielded me from facing the fact that my marriage to Linda had become an arrangement rather than a relationship. I sat in the back room working, occasionally vacated it to go in search of more stock, and generated the money. She ran the house, choosing that over going back out onto the job market, and we both shared in Matthew's upbringing. In all those years I never cooked a meal, washed a dish, made a bed or laundered a garment. I did undertake taxi duty, making the daily school and weekly grocery runs, but I was becoming increasingly autocratic.

SD was published about three times a year, sometimes four (it depended on what else was going on), and its preparation in the pre-computer era took a considerable effort. Everything was typed up – very badly – on an ancient Micro-Elite professional machine, which is where some of the flights of fancy took off from. Rather than start a page again, I simply incorporated the many errors into the magazine by extemporising or accepting them. People sometimes think I did it on purpose. I didn't. I was a self-taught typist and a bad student. Then, with typing finished, I assembled the whole thing by cut-and-paste for offset litho printing. In the meantime, I would crank out address labels and stick them on envelopes ready for mailing as soon as the latest issue came back from the printers.

I took the orders, wrote the invoices, packed the parcels, trundled them to the post office, tracked the stock control and the cash flow, did the banking, kept a day book and receipts to send to Dad every month, and generally tackled whatever had to be done. Apart from the accounts, I had no help from anyone – nor did I want it. My ego roll was getting larger and larger. I was so cocky that, when friends in Boston sent me an invitation to their summer R&B collectors' weekend barbecue swap meet as a joke, I jumped on a plane and turned up in their back yard unannounced. When I got back ten days later, Linda was understandably livid. I had also ingested a greater variety of recreational drugs in a week and a half than I have ever experienced before or since. How about *that* for daftbugger behaviour?

It's time, I suppose, to own up to the thinking behind my fake Robert Johnson photo. The whole idea arose from a conversation Glen Stapleton and I had one evening about the photo that everyone knew existed but no-one had seen. Steve LaVere had it, apparently, and we'd heard that he was holding out either for the best deal or for some long-range plan of his own. We further heard that there was another, different photo that Mike Stewart said he had seen, but again, it was being withheld from the public gaze.

Glen said something like: 'If you could find a picture that looked

THAT photograph.
Will the real Robert Johnson please stand up?

sufficiently genuine and you TOLD people it was Robert Johnson, they'd believe you.'

'Yes, then the hoarders of the *real* photos would have to prove that it wasn't,' I said, grabbing the ball he had just tossed me.

Then I remembered the photo Bill had found in Arkansas in 1979. It portrayed a young, good-looking, sharply-dressed black man standing outside a house; it was clearly a 1930's photo, and with a little cropping to hide the riding breeches he was wearing and the horse whip (a sort of riding crop) he carried, we had our Robert. I cooked up a story about a collector finding Robert's brother, interviewing him and being presented with the photo at interview's end. I wove this plot into a fake interview. Mike Rowe supplied me with a photo of, I think, Milton Sparks' uncle, to serve as R.J.'s brother, and I published the whole thing in *Sailor's Delight* No.9.

Reaction was overwhelming. People bought into it big time. Interestingly, however, some people sussed it right away. Tony Russell held grave doubts and said the interview read like it had been translated from Swedish by a Dane. Piers Harker at Collett's not only realised it was fake but also guessed why. Francis Wilford-Smith saw through it immediately, and was at first annoyed by my irresponsible behaviour until I told him the reason for doing it was to flush out the real pictures. Then, he just cracked up and said: 'I hope it works.' It didn't, but apparently it caused some consternation in the budding Robert Johnson industry.

The video collection was growing and I was spending more and more time quietly running custom-made bootleg tapes for people. I was also becoming more interested in the whole subject of blues and gospel on film and video. In consequence, Glen Stapleton and I produced a three-part series for *SD* called 'TV Guide', which attempted to identify and codify what had been shown on British TV since the 1950's. It was a useful exercise and formed the basis of something that would come back and bite me in the bum years later. But it was also time to go back out and get more records. Again I offered Bill Greensmith the deal: 'All expenses paid, and this time it's California for two weeks. Yes?'

'Yes, mate,' he replied, 'you book the tickets and I'll put the kettle on.'

We headed for San Francisco in October 1981 and had a detailed, low-humidity view of the Bay as we circled it. Bill said: 'Do you know, I believe I can see Andy Williams' heart from here.'

We went and saw Frank Scott at Down Home Music immediately, falling asleep on him in a Chinese restaurant, and then falling further asleep in his house. The next day, I bought all his spare 78's including a Robert Johnson and several Walter Rolands.

We went to see Chris Strachwitz and I rifled through his extraordinary stock room full of duplicate 78's. I'd never seen the Juke Boy Bonner Irma 78 before. I came away with a dozen mint copies. He also had a huge pile of vintage gospel and just about every blues record on Gotham and Gold Star. The exchange of dollars for shellac made us both very happy; a perfect win-win situation.

We took off for Los Angeles with an already severely-loaded car, so we went down Highway 17 – the desert route – rather than the spectacular, but slower and more dangerous coastal Highway 1. We would be in LA for a week, so we found a hotel and booked in. '*For Nicer People*' it proclaimed on a banner across the parking lot entrance. 'We'll soon change THAT!' laughed Bill, preparing to bounce off yet another bed.

We went and saw the Stolper brothers, Darryl and Jeff, who lived opposite each other in Pacific Palisades. Both had things they wanted to sell, but then Jeff let something out of the bag that apparently he shouldn't have. Bob Hite had died suddenly the previous week and his widow was selling things off piecemeal. Would we like her phone number? Ha! Does the Archbishop of Canterbury skate naked through ponds full of Rowntree's jelly at midnight? She lived up in Topanga Canyon, high above downtown LA and, curiously, as we met her at an agreed spot – a country grocery store that could have been transplanted from Arkansas – it began pouring with rain.

In a wooded cabin shielded by deep groves of trees, with water teeming down the window panes, we were shown two high alcoves divided by a fireplace, shelved to the top and filled with 78's. On the right-hand side was the post-war section, on the left was the pre-war. Bill took the right, I the left, trusting him to pull good stuff. I started shuffling through heavy green cardboard sleeves to discover the most heart-stopping array of blues records I'd ever encountered. The prices, arrived at by local deejay and collector Barret Hansen, were fair but not stupid. I couldn't possibly buy them all, I simply didn't have enough money, and Mrs. Hite wanted to sell for cash – she wouldn't consider a commission deal. So, I just bought what I could. The John Byrd Paramount, a Tommy Johnson Victor, a William Moore, an Ishman Bracey, some Gus Cannon, a Henry Townsend, a bunch of buff Bluebirds, a handful of sunburst Deccas... and Bill was pulling things like an Elmore James Fire 78,

Early morning , Long Beach, 1981 – the end of a very long night in a garage.

Aristocrats, Old Swing Masters, Chances, Vee-Jays. We paid up and left.

Outside, in the car, we just looked at each other and, in unison, said '*FUUUUUCK!!!*' We had a way with words. That night, I made a few phone calls to other US collectors. One was on a plane from Chicago the next morning. Others took up to two days to arrive.

It got better. We knew that John Harmer, who had been in partnership with Frank Scott in a record store called J&F Southern Record Sales, had a lot of stuff and we'd heard he needed money. We drove out to Long Beach and, unannounced, pounded on his door one early evening.

'Hallo John, we were just passing, thought we'd drop in.'

John did need money and did have a garage full of records. He also had a job as a night circulation manager for the *Orange County Screech & Gazebo Spotter* or something, so I nailed a quick commission deal together. He led us to the garage and, as he went to work, so did we. We could let ourselves out when we'd done. It was about 9:00 pm.

Around 3.00 am, something like 70 percent of the way through, tired but hugely stoked, we encountered the umpteenth black widow spider as it scuttled out of its disturbed hiding place and across our path. 'Ah, BOLLOCKS!' shouted Bill in frustration and, picking up the first thing he laid his hands on, smashed it into a gooey mess on the cement floor. When we looked at what he had used, we realised that God was probably laughing. It was a copy of the Buster Benton 45 on Ronn, 'Spider In My Stew'!

By about 6:00 am we had the car loaded to bursting-point. 'Do you want another box of mint Willie Love Trumpets, mate?' asked Bill.

'No, we've got enough.'

We found John's hidden collection of porno magazines, left them in the tumble dryer for his wife to discover (yes, John, that was us!), closed the garage door behind us and trundled very slowly back up to the place for Nicer People. We celebrated by going to see Pee Wee Crayton perform at a marina clubhouse. He was bloody good, too.

We returned from California with more great records than anyone in Britain had seen for a long time. The Sunday following the arrival of the air freight was more frantic and jammed than it had ever been, the Juke Boy Bonner Irmas all vanishing the moment they were offered. People stared at the Paramounts, Victors and Bluebirds, inhaled deeply and then said: 'How much?' The answer was not anything like as much as they cost now. But that was then. A clean Ishman Bracey for fifty quid in 1980 was a fair deal. Should I have hung on to it for years as an investment? No! Sell it at the market price *now*. People criticise Sam Phillips for flogging Elvis off to the Nipper men for thirty-five grand, but it was a good deal then and the money helped launch Carl Perkins' career, among others. Besides, who then knew? The lad, rock'n'roll itself, might have bombed within twelve months.

Life continued in the back room at what I had called 'Ora-Nelle Villas'. Visitors came and went, including the 'sixth' Rolling Stone, Ian Stewart, buying for himself and his lads. Records came and went with them. Videos got run. The phone rang constantly. Then, on an August weekday lunchtime, interrupting our sandwiches and cookies, the phone rang, as usual. I was on the way from the living room to the kitchen when it happened, getting forks for the gateau. I segued into the back room and picked up the phone.

It was my mother, and she sounded a little... distracted.

'Hi,' I said.

'Er, I've got bad news,' she replied, as if she were talking from some other planet.

My father had suddenly died of a massive heart attack. No warning, just dead on the floor in Sussex at age 60. Mum had seen it happen, but it was so quick there was nothing to do but try and say goodbye. I was on the road inside of two hours, my head full of all the stuff I wanted to say to a man who had just gone forever. I stayed for two weeks dealing with the 1001 details you have to tackle when someone dies. Things would never be quite the same again. For two years I found it impossible to listen to Django Reinhardt, and there is still hardly a day when I don't think about my father.

A few days after I got back from Sussex, two blokes turned up unannounced at the door. They were VAT inspectors, and they wanted to get all over me because they didn't believe my sales tax returns, which were always claiming monies back, rather than paying them. This was essentially because I did so much VAT-free export business. However, they decided I was attempting – heaven forfend – to cheat them, so they told me they would sit and watch me do business until they were satisfied. They had the authority to do so, they reminded me, and a lot more besides, including impounding the car and the stock, freezing my bank account and calling upon evil goblins to nibble at my balls while I was tied to a gum tree.

They stowed themselves on chairs in the back room for close to a week and observed, with mounting incredulity, as overseas mail poured through the door, the phone rang revealing men talking in funny accents and people just turned up.

'Hi! I'm Werner Simon from Vienna! Man, I thought I was ugly! Who are these pricks?'

Vatman and Robin saw me create invoice after invoice for customers in Oslo, Paris, Berlin, New York and Reykjavik. I played them records and made them tea. I talked their arses off, and they eventually agreed I wasn't cheating the Government. I presented the younger of the two, a rock fan, with an Otis Rush Flyright LP on the final day. 'This could be construed as bribery,' said Mr. Kenneth James Willingham, Inspections Officer of the Hendon & Finchley VAT office, cautiously. 'I won't tell anyone,' I assured him.

I had an idea brewing for another daft-sod *SD* front cover. I always had some kind of joke on the front, often built around a photo that took my fancy, but I decided I wanted to do a Xmas-in-July issue and had an image in my head of what it should look like. The headline would read 'Juke Box Lil Gang in Santa Rooftop Heist Shock', and would feature sexy women armed with guns holding up Santa for his sack full of rare and desirable blues LPs.

Mike Rowe agreed to be Santa, and Wendy Stagg of Nola Records agreed to be a gang member. I decided I would play the part of Juke Box Lil. I approached my cousin Julie, who dabbled in make-up and costume for a local amateur theatrical group, and asked her if she could turn a sow's ear into a silk purse. When she'd finished laughing she said yes. We would use the flat roof and chimneys that sat above Cilla Huggins' large and airy St. John's Wood apartment to take the photos. So, on a Sunday morning, I drove over to Julie's house and, two hours later, emerged looking like Widow Twanky dressed as a streetwalker. I now had to drive about 12 miles from Watford to St. John's Wood. 'You're not going out dressed like *that*,' I heard myself say. But I did.

Everyone who wanted a good laugh presented themselves for this event. Cilla hosted it, Bill took the photos, Mike and Wendy completed the trio of actors and a variety of other collectors, husbands, wives, friends, and general Sunday layabouts also turned up. We ascended via a step ladder to the roof. As I did so a battery of cameras took upskirt photos amid howls of laughter. We posed on the roof while Bill took serious pictures and a dozen other cameras unseriously recorded the event, the beer and surrealism getting to us all. For one photo Mike laid down and Wendy put a 4-inch stiletto heel upon his chest.

'You can press a little harder if you like,' he said hopefully.

Me, Mike Rowe and Wendy Stagg on Cilla Huggins' rooftop.
Furthermore, I drove home dressed like that.

We were helpless with laughter. Amid all this we noticed that, on a rooftop across the street, people were observing us through binoculars. Sweating some in his Santa outfit, his hand round the waist of Wendy, dressed in a PVC basque and fishnets, carrying a bullwhip, Mike Rowe said: 'Who are THOSE weirdos?' With the photo shoot finished, we went back down to Cilla's flat for refreshment: tea, cigarettes, sherbet lemons, Lucozade... This was the afternoon that we re-composed Bob Kerr's 'Knees Up Eva Braun'. I don't know why any more, and I don't know who started it, but the upshot was a song I later finished and published in *SD* in answer to a letter from a German who complained that Nazis were no fun and that my making jokes about Hitler merely perpetuated old myths about the Teutonic lack of humour, inconsiderate behaviour in Poland and an unwillingness on the part of the British to forget about the inconveniences of the Blitz and the Doodlebugs:

> *Knees up Eva Braun, knees up Eva Braun,*
> *Into the bunker you must go*
> *With your Nazi daddy-o.*
> *If I catch you bending, then that's just my good luck..*

Oh, bring me the toe-rag who burned the Reichstag,
He don't give a... monkeys.

Oi vay, what a Nazi song,
Hitler's rotten dong
Wasn't very long.
Oi vay, what a Nazi song
And what a nasty singer too!

We ended the day with several of us, including me still in full drag, going out for a meal at an Indian restaurant. Later that same evening, apparently, Mike Rowe, sitting watching the late night TV news, turned to Barbara, and said: 'Did we REALLY go out for a meal with Paul dressed as a woman?'

Visitors continued to arrive. One of the most engaging was the Frenchman Michel Chaigne. I first met him as he was clambering out of a taxi at my front door on a hot day. He came into the house in a dishevelled state, his shirt untucked and his tie askew. In the backroom, as he talked at high speed about Bumble Bee Slim, he totally and quite naturally re-arranged his clothes. I'd known him for less than five minutes yet already knew the brand of underwear he wore.

His enthusiasms were huge, especially for obscure piano boogies. While listening, he would pepper his remarks with a barrage of Gallic phrases accompanied by complex hand gestures. I once showed him a video of 'Boogie Woogie Dream', featuring Albert Ammons and Pete Johnson, which he had not seen before. He got so excited that he couldn't stay in the same room with the footage, and he ran up and down the hallway shouting 'FEUCK ME DEAD!!!' and waving his arms about in front of him as if they had been suddenly dunked in boiling tea. Matthew clearly remembers the incident even today.

Because I tended to get a lot of 1960's soul records, I also attracted that peculiar but delightful breed, the Soul Collector. I had always loved soul, but had never been able to keep up with the rapidly changing flavours-du-jour inside the soul market, and I had no desire to pull Wigan all-nighters in order to bone up. I therefore simply accepted that I might not be getting the best price for everything, and tended to sell to the few who probably ensured they remained few by not telling any other bugger about me.

However, they all had good stories to tell, and my favourite is this one: Phil Obviouslynameless lived in a converted west London Edwardian house on a street with tight-as-a-duck's-arse parking. He and his flatmates regularly partook of marijuana, and so cosy was the relationship with the dealer that the stuff simply turned up on a Friday night and was handed over to whoever opened the door. It often got left on the hall table as a result, awaiting a late evening division between its customers. One evening, a young rozzer rang the doorbell looking for the owner of a double-parked Triumph Herald. His sharp eye lead his enquiring mind to the plastic bag on the table behind the increasingly nervous Phil.

'Er, do you mind telling me what the contents of that bag might be, sir?'

Snookered, Phil replied: 'Oh, all right, I own up, it's a bag of grass.'

'Now come along sir, let's not play games. We both know it's drugs.'

Paul Jones, once of Manfred Mann, then an Ak-Tore, and subsequently lead singer with the Blues Band and also a blues deejay on Capitol Radio and Radio Two, turned up regularly for his dose of harmonica records. A perfect gentleman, he impressed Linda deeply. 'Why can't they ALL be like him?' she remarked. 'HE doesn't foul the toilet.'

I appeared on his show once with Mike Rowe, which gave me the opportunity to play Luther Huff's '1951 Blues' when asked to produce my favourite record. That it was Mike Rowe who had first exposed me to Luther Huff via the *Memphis On Down* LP was not lost on him or me, although perhaps it glided past Paul.

In 1982, I got a call from a Midwest collector; he was very excited and very anxious. He'd found that a major collection ('I mean MAJOR fuckin' collection, man') could be accessed because the owner was in dire straits and needed money very badly, and right now. He himself didn't have enough cash, but if I could supply the money, he would lead me to this glittering stash, kick in what he could afford and take a slice of the collection for his input. He principally wanted the pre-war stuff he didn't have and said I could take all the post-war and any pre-war he didn't want. There were Charley Pattons and Tommy Johnsons and Garfield Akers he *reeaalllly* needed and... was I interested?

'Who is it?' I asked.

'Tell me you've got the money and I'll tell you.'

'How much?'

'Fifteen grand. Cash.'

'Okay, I can do that. Now, who the hell are we talking about?'

'Henry Vestine.'

A week later I flew into Atlanta for a long weekend that turned out to be Deeply Interesting, in the way that Butlin's was a Deeply Interesting camp. My companion had flown down from the Midwest to meet me at an agreed hotel in Atlanta. I hired a station wagon at the airport, went directly to a Peaches Records outlet for the right kind of free cardboard boxes, and then found him that night in the bar. I had brought him a little gift: the D.A. Hunt Sun 78. The next morning, we began the three-hour drive to South Carolina and the little one-hearse town that Henry now lived in. His house was a large three-storey Victorian on the outskirts, but he wasn't living there; his wife had chucked him out, and we had an address for him in town. We stopped a police car and asked for directions. The officer, a dead ringer for Rod Steiger in *In The Heat Of The Night* said: 'Now, you boys really don't want to go there.'

Me with what was left of Henry Vestine (taken shortly before the mayhem ensued).

We assured him we did. He had us follow him and, as we literally crossed the railroad tracks and entered an area festooned with chain link, he stopped, got out, gave us final directions and drove off the way he'd come.

We found Henry's house, a single-storey wood-frame with a dirt yard, and knocked on the door. There were sounds of scuffling and panic from inside. Eventually Henry opened the door and peered at us from behind the screen. He'd changed some since I last saw him in 1970. His teeth were mostly missing, his stomach had developed a dunlap (as in 'mah belly *dun lapped* ovah mah belt'), his hair was gone on the crown and thin on top, and his arm was full of track marks. He'd also fried his brain. 'C'mon in,' he gurgled.

We entered directly in to the living room, the way you do in houses like this, to be immediately greeted by several empty Jack Daniels bottles strewn across the floor, a chainsaw parked up behind the couch and a Saturday Night Special revolver on the coffee table. We sat down, gingerly. The other occupants of the house came to view us. A Vietnamese guy who acted skittish, like we might be the INS or something, a young teenage pregnancy case, and a cream-suited guy who looked like a sawn-off double for Travolta, still waiting for a call from the *Saturday Night Fever* producers. Except this was Saturday lunchtime and several years too late.

Henry disappeared for a leak, and Travolta vanished also, reappearing almost immediately with a small leather attaché case. He took a seat opposite me and put the case on the table.

'You the guy come alla way from England fer Henry's rekerds?'

Yes I was. He opened the case, withdrew a Colt .45 automatic and an ammunition clip.

'You WILL give Henry a fair deal, right?' he continued, loading the clip into the gun and cocking it. From somewhere inside I heard myself saying: 'If you shoot me now, I won't be able to sign these nice new travellers' cheques.'

He looked at me with a studied Elvis sneer. I lit two cigarettes without realising it and smoked them both. Henry returned, told Travolta to stow it and said: 'Okay, let's go!'

'Where?'

'To my house... er, my *wife's* house. Thasswheertheyallare. I'll drive!'

'You go with him,' said my companion. 'I'll follow in your car.'

So, I climbed into the dying Mustang parked in the yard while Henry attempted to start what was left of it. It finally coughed itself awake, he slammed it into gear and roared off onto the highway, cutting up an enraged tractor driver as he did so. Waving at him, he laughed: 'I know that ole boy.' We got to the one traffic light in the middle of town and it turned red on us. The engine died and Henry attempted to restart it. Time and again. Then I noticed that the paint on the hood was starting to bubble and pointed it out to him in my usual phlegmatic fashion: 'THEPAINTONTHEBLOODYHOOD'S BUBBLINGYOUFOOLIT'SGOINGTOBLOWANYMINUTEANDWE'REALL GOINGTO DIEAAAARGH!!'

'Man, that's fuckin' psychedelic,' he replied.

'PSYCHEDELICBEBUGGEREDGETOUTHEBLEEDINGMOTORBEFORE WEBOTHFRYYOUMADTWERPYEEAAAAAHHHHH!' I think I said.

We exited and got behind the car just before the gas in the engine ignited and blew the hood off, buckling it as it broke the windshield we had just been sitting behind.

'Ohmanwhatabummerman. Lostm'wheelsmanshitman.'

'Look, never mind all that old bollocks,' said my adrenalin, merely using me as a mouthpiece, 'let's just get it off the road.'

We pushed it into an empty lot and opened the back door of the station wagon for Henry to fall into. When we reached the house, the records were all neatly stacked in his collection room. We gave him his agreed price and he said, theatrically: 'Take 'em ALL,' waving his arms in despair.

'We'll take what we need,' I replied, aware I was paraphrasing a line from *Vanishing Point*.

That night in the hotel my companion and I split the loot. He got a very nice taste of the gig for his input: all the Pattons, fifteen of them, both the Garfield Akers ('Ha! Gaaaaarfield-fuckin'-Aaaaakers! Ha!'), a brace of Ishmans, the Roberts and the Tommys, and much more ('Ha! Uncle-fuckin'-Skipper on Decca! Ha!'), but I got what I wanted: thousands of great 78's and 45's including some that no-one in Britain had ever seen.

They arrived via airfreight a few days later, and it was a day or two before I got to the John Lee Hooker and Lightnin' Hopkins 78's. As I began checking them for condition, small packets of white powder started to fall from the bottom inside corners of the sleeves. Within minutes I had a stash of heroin on the table worth probably more than the records! I called Linda in and showed her what the British customs had unaccountably failed to spot – thank God, or I would still be sitting in the Scrubs now (do you honestly think they'd have believed me?). She said: 'Flush it all down the toilet NOW, and don't say a word to anyone.' It was one of the few times I did what she asked of me. Meanwhile, back in the Piedmont, Henry, at some point, must have suddenly realised where he had hidden his stuff. 'Ohmanwhatabummerman lostm'stashman.'

Bill Greensmith had meanwhile become increasingly involved in researching the life and works of Ike Turner. The more he looked into it, the more absorbing it became. A picture emerged of Ike as one of the key figures of post-war American music; he was certainly a lot more than just half of Ike & Tina. From his talent scout days in the Delta for the Bihari brothers, through his Sam Phillips recordings, on up to his time at Cobra in Chicago, and his long spell in St. Louis, Ike had been at the forefront of developing R&B. Many pundits argue that Jackie Brenston's 'Rocket 88' is the first rock'n'roll record, and if you accept that, it makes Ike's Kings of Rhythm the first rock'n'roll band. His influence on blues, R&B and rock is huge, and largely under-appreciated.

It was because of his commitment to Ike Turner's story that Bill's life changed forever. On a trip to St. Louis, he met Stella Holloway, the daughter of Red Holloway, who'd been with Ike in the Kings of Rhythm. They met at a restaurant to talk about Red and what Stella remembered of the old days and, to cut a long story down to size, fell in love with each other pretty much straight away. Stella visited Bill in England, where I first met her, and, to slice up another tale neatly, Bill moved to St. Louis where he and Stella still live happily. So, when it came time to go back to the States in 1983 on another record buying trip, Bill wasn't available because he was already there.

You might pause and ask: 'Why did you always want a companion on those trips anyhow?' (Well, *go on then...*) The reasons were simple: two people can split the driving and navigating, the heavy lifting that is always involved, watch each other's back if things start looking dodgy – which they sometimes can – and, as an old guru of mine once remarked, 'enjoy the dimension of sharing'.

The new Sundance Kidder to my Butch Posturing was a fellow called Keith Briggs.

The first time I met Keith, he was being rained on big time, which he later said was not unusual for him. He'd been buying records from me for a while and had made an arrangement to visit from Lincolnshire – not the county of his birth, but of his choice. He was an Essex man originally, but had escaped that fate. I opened the door and he stood there, rain pouring down his face from the well-spring atop his head: 'My name is Briggs, but we all have our cross to bear,' he said. He was early and I was having lunch.

'I'll come back later then.'

'No you bloody won't. You'll come in and have some lunch.'

We liked each other immediately and he always visited when he was in London. He managed a leisure centre in Lincoln, and whenever I called him his secretary would answer the phone and ask who I was; 'The Reverend J.M. Gates,' I'd reply. Or 'Leonard Chess'. 'Hello Sailor,' he would say, laconically, when I was put through. When it became clear that I could usefully revisit California again, I offered Keith the same deal that I had struck with Bill. He agreed because, as he said, 'I know an Otis Rush Cobra 45 from a hole in the ground, and a hole in the ground from any arsehole who might want to put me in one.' It would turn out to seriously deepen our relationship.

My plan was to retrace the steps I had taken before. Chris Strachwitz still had stuff, and there were a few others in the Bay Area to check out as well. Then it would be Los Angeles again, the Stolpers and others who knew I was coming. Keith turned out to be an excellent choice: he was a big lad and very fit. On our first morning, he turned up for breakfast in belt AND braces, making a very English statement that no bugger in the Bay Area understood. We went and saw Chris at Arhoolie, then peddled off with a trunk full of goodies to see Henry Mariano, king of the bootleg 45's.

Henry had an inner sanctum in his house, a specially-constructed windowless room dead centre of the building, in which he kept his stock of 45's. He'd been in the business for years, selling both originals and reproductions. I bought a lot from Henry, who laid records in front of me grouped by price: the large $5 pile first, followed by a slightly smaller $10 group, chased by a yet smaller clutch of $15 items, hounded by a handful of $25 goodies, and then finally just a very few at $50. I bought most of them. Later Keith said: 'You know, SOMEWHERE in that room there was a box with one record in it at $200!'

We also went over to Oakland to connect with a hapless twit whose name I no longer recall, but who had somehow got his hands on a huge pile of R&B 78's that he was having difficulty shifting. I bought him out as a Butterbeans & Suzie couple in the next apartment went at it hammer and tongs with each other while Keith just stood there appreciating the sheer bizarreness of the situation.

We went to see the cutely-named Rip Lay, who was getting out of the record business and into the baseball card game; I guess there weren't enough nutters for him among the record collectors. Satisfied with the Bay Area haul, we hit the road. We would do Highway 1 properly.

Highway 1, the road that clings to the coastline for much of the Bay Area-to-Los Angeles journey, is spectacular beyond adequate description. So, ignore the rest of this paragraph. It twists and turns and careens around impossible curves, at times leading you to believe you are driving straight out to sea; at others, directly into a rock face. The sun bounces starburst graphics off the Pacific waters that constantly pace you; the colours of the sky, sea, rock and vegetation overwhelm your senses with their pooled beauty. It's a generally under-used route, so you often feel that it's just you and the road alone. We barrelled down it slowly, taking in not only the staggering sights offered to us, but also mindful that any lack of concentration could have us over the edge like one-legged lemmings at an arse-kicking party. We marvelled at the views, tempering it all with a non-stop string of rotten jokes, another practice we both enjoyed.

In Los Angeles, we availed ourselves of a very kind offer from a customer of mine, Dan Pseudonym, who said: 'if you're staying in LA, you're staying with me.' He lived in a very plush neighbourhood, and his home was impossible to find without help, so he met us downtown and we followed him out. The house was a splendid affair, large and airy, with a jacuzzi in the back yard and a conversation pit filled with 'interesting people', whom we immediately joined.

The Daiquiris and the Margaritas flowed like Sanatogen (look it up). So did the marijuana and the cocaine. People came and went constantly, our host vanishing for a few moments at a time to see and deal with them. Keith and I looked at each other and exchanged coded eyebrow messages in Cockney Rhyming Slang. This bloke, clearly, was a dealer. Later that night he owned up to it and said that if we were uncomfortable he would get us a hotel. Taking a line directly from Marlon Brando in *The Godfather*, and moulding it to the moment, Keith spoke for both of us by saying: 'It makes no difference to us how a man makes a living.' We agreed to stay.

Dan's house was designed so that you could see in through his study window from the winding, tree-shaded path that lead to the double front doors. Keith and I were standing in there chatting with him on the second evening, without realising that we could be clearly seen from the path. The doorbell rang, and Dan's wife went to respond to it. We heard a sudden, loud crash and a commotion, then turned to be confronted by a clearly nervous man appearing at the office door, down on one knee and pointing a very large pistol at us with both hands.

'DAN, YOU OK MAN? WHO TH' FUCK ARE THESE GUYS?'

'NONONONO MAN, THESE GUYS ARE COOL, PUT TH' FUCKIN' GUN AWAY!'

As Mr. Inconspicuous – a partner in Dan's business - slowly lowered the hammer back down, that same odd feeling I'd had at Henry Vestine's house revisited me. Later, while we were changing underwear, Keith said: 'Odd way to make a living, innit?' I think he was talking about me as much as them.

In the days that followed, we sampled Los Angeles very deeply. We bought many more records, made quick and often very firm friends, and saw a giant figure of a golfer, advertising the course he stood atop the entrance of, burning down in the night. We agreed that this, as much as anything else, was why we had come to LA. We were told by a very mellow fellow in a restaurant that 'the only crime in California...' (toke) '...is being uncool'. Keith gave me one his looks. Later that week, walking a block somewhere in the city, we passed a vacant lot being shielded by chain link that advertised itself as 'Long Fence'. When it ended, Keith simply said, without cracking a smile: 'I've seen longer.' We met Mary Katherine Aldin, the blues deejay of station KPFK, as well as a regular music columnist, writer and blues expert, who invited me onto her radio show to play a few of the goodies that I'd picked up along the way. We went and saw the Stolpers again, as well as the guys at Rhino Records, who, surprisingly, had a great stash of 78's.

As a result of that sixteen days spent together, Keith and I became much deeper friends. Later, my life took me away from England, but we emailed each other and occasionally picked up a phone – hang the expense – and talked from Prague or Toulouse or Washington, or wherever I happened to be at the time. His closing remark for each conversation, chanted mantra-like with a grin I could see, was simply: 'Keep your arse out of the fire.'

Los Angeles began to appear to me like The Place To Be. I wanted, in my heart, to relocate there. Dan said if that was my desire, he would help. I took my stock back to England and started to think about a move. Three months later, trailed by a hail of abuse from Linda and her family, I went back to LA to get things set up.

The bottom line is that it didn't work. I stayed six weeks, met and talked with everyone, sat in on more radio shows, saw Percy Mayfield, Jimmy Witherspoon, Lee Dorsey, Johnny Adams, Screamin' Jay Hawkins, Joel Sonnier and the Roy Milton Orchestra for entertainment, but could clearly see that my plans were not going to fly for a variety of reasons. Dan offered me an extraordinary deal. He wanted to slide out from under the position he held and offered it to me, schlock, sock and barrel. All I had to do was simply take over and he would vanish quietly with his money. But I looked at his nervous cash-only lifestyle, his constantly-loaded handgun and especially at the hard-looking geezers who supplied him with his stock and, also recalling the Study Incident, said: 'No thanks.'

Rather than sink slowly, I made the painful but obvious decision to abandon Plan A and go back to London. When I arrived, I was met by an incandescent Linda and told, rightly, that she had had enough of all this and was filing for divorce. She wanted custody of Matthew, the house, alimony, and a car. I managed to pull one last *SD* together while all this was going on and then, as far as I could see, it would all be over. Maybe I could get that job at Woolworth's?

Chapter Eight

1984-86: DID YOU FLY HERE IN YOUR OWN PLANE?

In January 1984, things looked bleaker than I could ever remember. Then, in quick succession, so much happened that I seem to recall it all occurring to the tune of 'The Devil's Gallop'.

My mother had moved up from the coast following my father's death and was living back in Mill Hill in a large house just a mile or so from Ora-Nelle Villas. Knowing the situation, and being my mother, she offered me a place to stay, and I gratefully moved in. Then, with the fate of *SD* hanging in the balance, I got a phone call from Mark Sinclair Harris. Mark had been running a magazine called *Pickin' The Blues* for two years. It was a modest affair, but it arrived regularly every month and kept punters up to date with new release information, reviews and news about live gigs.

The early 1980's were a time of immense activity in the international blues record market, but with *Blues Unlimited* then only being published as an occasional, there was no magazine devoted to keeping up with it all. There was, of course, the excellent Red Lick Records, but a mail order catalogue couldn't be expected to review every last album in detail. As *Pickin' The Blues* grew, Mark expanded it to include discographies and artist histories. I had always supported his efforts because I believed he was doing a very necessary job and doing it well. Now, however, he had reached an impasse at about the same time I had. He was going to have to wind down *PTB* and refund outstanding subscriptions. Once again, an impulse blindsided me and I heard myself say: 'Don't do that, I'll take over.' When we both recovered from this surprise, he agreed, and the phoenix that rose from *PTB*'s fag ash was *Blues & Rhythm* – the name suggested to me by Dave Clarke.

I connected with a local collector, Mike Quinlan, whose wife Maureen was both a knowledgeable fan and a professional computer typesetter. We sat down at their kitchen table and worked out a partnership deal. Maureen and I would be active co-editors and the three of us would be partners, with Mike as the sleeper who input the bulk of the seed money, funnelled from his landscape gardening business. I talked to everyone I could think of, and we structured a team that would launch the new magazine: Ray Templeton agreed to be reviews editor; Sue Witherden, Glen Stapleton's ex-partner with whom I'd kept in touch, would be our photographer; Mary Katherine Aldin would contribute US news; reviewers were drawn from the ranks of the combined *PTB* and *SD* team. Articles came in from all manner of people including Paul Oliver.

Sailor's Delight ceased publication, and all existing subscribers to both magazines were offered equivalent issues of the new one, without any price increase, or the option of a refund. One lone nerk demanded his money back. I sent it to him in cash with the word 'BULLSHIT' rubber-stamped in red across both sides of each banknote.

We launched the first issue in July 1984 with a party at the Dublin Castle in Camden Town. Everyone we wanted to turn up did so:

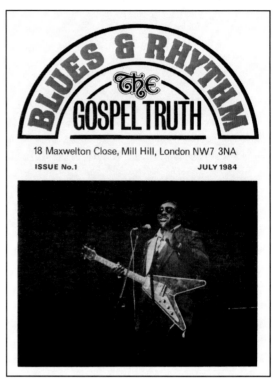

18 Maxwelton Close, Mill Hill, London NW7 3NA

ISSUE No.1   JULY 1984

Blues & Rhythm, inaugural issue.

Eddie C. Campbell, Dana Gillespie and a pick-up band including Sam Mitchell played the magazine in, all the record company people were there, as were the *Blues Unlimited* team, several overseas visitors, and most of the British writers, reviewers and collectors. Maybe the free food and bar tab helped some, but the general atmosphere was one of openness and good spirited celebration.

Meanwhile, I had been approached by Barry Martin of Making Waves to join his team. Barry – nowadays with the Hamsters – was a very tall, loud, self-assured, intelligent and funny man who had started his career as guitarist for a rock band, the Kursaal Flyers, then moved into the distribution business in order to continue eating, but still played regularly ('I'm leaving early tonight lads, gotta teach Stevie Marriott 'ow to fuckin' rock'n'roll').

Making Waves was an aggressive, independent record distributor that I had been using, in conjunction with Robin Gosden and Simon Napier's Swift Record Distributors, ever since they got going in 1981. Now successfully expanding and recently moved to new premises at Alie Street in East London, Barry wanted to add a 'direct mail order' wing to the empire, and offered me the job of setting it up. I liked Barry and the idea, the money was very good and so I said yes.

By August 1984, I was co-editor of a new magazine and director of the newly established Rapid Records, the mail order department of Making

THE COMPANY THAT TAKES THE WAX OUT OF YOUR EARS
AND PUTS IT ON THE TURNTABLE

The friendly RAPID team - ready to serve your needs.

Waves. I saw Matthew regularly, I still had the video bootlegging business and I still ran occasional private auctions. In a celebration my father would have understood, I bought Bill Greensmith's beautiful 1972 Rover 3500 that had sat in Wimbledon since he left; he needed to sell because he couldn't ship it to St. Louis. I loaded it with cassette tapes and jasmine-scented wooden balls and called it, with a studied lack of originality, 'The Bluesmobile'. It was the '80's, what else can I say?

I put in five days a week at Making Waves. We all worked extremely hard, and the atmosphere was very Self-Indulgent Rock'n'Roll Good Time Or Die. I willingly jumped in with both feet. At 35, I was the oldest member of the team, but I became more rock'n'roll than anyone. I blossomed (or, more accurately perhaps, burst like a ripe zit) into a Hawaiian-shirted, Filofax-toting, highlight-hairstyled Indie Muzicbiz Person, part of the team seen drinking Tequila Slammers and Grolsch chasers immediately after work.

Then, in my other life, I was Mr. Blues & Rhythm, out many evenings catching live gigs at Dingwalls, the Dublin Castle, or the 100 Club, ostensibly as the B&R live gig reviewer, but actually more interested in drinking, talking shop and bollocks, posing and being seen. (I'm glad I didn't waste my energies on anything shallow.) This was a time when the Big Town Playboys, Diz & The Doormen, Dana Gillespie, Ron Kavana and others were all playing round London regularly; we saw visitors including Albert King, Johnny Copeland, Albert Collins and Robert Cray, as well as Los Lobos, the Blasters and Joe 'King' Carrasco. I knew everybody, and my name was always on the door. I guested on radio shows, worked constantly, and was on another, bigger, ego roll, but you couldn't have told me that at the time. Two short planks can be very durable.

In 1984, Robert Cray was a new name to me. He played Dingwalls in Camden Town and I went without knowing anything about him, but he was

175

very good. He had fresh, new tunes that still sat within a blues framework and supported mature lyrics about love, infidelity and heartbreak that perfectly fit the urbanely self-aware mood of the yuppie era. His guitar style was his and his alone. The moment you heard a Cray solo you knew it was Cray. I wrote enthusiastically about him as Demon issued his first two Hightone albums, which were revelations as far as I was concerned. I saw him as the new path for the blues: one that would take us through the rest of the '80's and beyond on a fresh and glorious curve. A quarter of a century later I still think he's good, but the new path got somewhat overrun by half-assed wannabes. Mike Rowe once said to me, in about 1992: 'We've come a long way in the last twenty-five years – mostly in the wrong direction.' The more venerable and curmudgeonly an old git I become, the more I tend to agree.

Johnny Copeland, too, was a superb bluesman to see live. His hard, taut solos embroidered beautifully constructed tunes that meshed with well thought-out lyrical themes. Again, it was Demon records that pushed his music into the British market. At Making Waves we distributed all this and much more. I had instant access to everyone and everything at Ace, Charly, Demon, Interstate, Red Lightnin' and all the import labels. I talked to people from a *Blues & Rhythm* platform with my Making Waves hat on and vice versa. Our visitors included the Batman & Robin team of Billy Bragg and Andy Kershaw buying their way through the shelves, Joe Boyd and Nick Perls, whose labels we distributed, and Martin Carthy looking, as always, for the obscure and unusual music that helped feed his creativity. I felt myself to be at the centre of the universe I wanted to inhabit.

Life began to alter because a woman in Scotland died without warning. She was the mother of our export specialist at Making Waves and, understandably, he went home immediately he got the news, leaving a gap that Barry asked me to cover. We were in the middle of holding down a booth at a London trade show; there was no-one else to bridge the gap. Would I...? Yes, of course. In the late afternoon of the final day, I staggered onto the tube at King's Cross carrying a ton of samples and looking for a seat. There was only one, and an immaculately manicured hand was resting on it. I coughed a little and the owner moved the hand to let me sit down. We started to talk. She looked like a brown-haired Barbie Doll and, although I didn't know it at the time, I had just met my second wife. Barbie was from California.

'Which part?' I asked.

'San Francisco.'

'Oh, sure, I know it well.'

She looked unimpressed by this easy line.

'In fact, I have friends in San Mateo, El Cerrito, Oakland and Berkeley,' I continued.

'Oh, you really DO know the Bay Area? I thought you were just bullshitting me.'

'Now, do I look like the kind of lad who'd do that?'

She was in London visiting family. We became a couple within a week. The seed packet of change had just been opened.

Maureen and Mike dropped out of *Blues & Rhythm* after little more than a year. They had their own reasons and I didn't argue with them, but I needed to restructure in order to continue. The man who helped me do that, and bailed out the magazine in the process, was the present editor, Tony Burke. Tony was a trade union leader in the print industry and the nemesis of Eddie Shah, if anyone remembers the Wapping battles. Through his connections, we could get the magazine typeset professionally without a problem. I was still the editor, but Tony was the right-hand man without whom I could not have continued.

In the meantime, Making Waves appeared to be going like an old slapper in a sausage factory. The sales team, headed by Californian ex-pat Scott Lund, were a hyper-hard working bunch committed to quality music and naturally at odds with the MIGS – Men In Grey Suits – who represented the mainstream industry and who hated us with as much passion as we despised them. They called us 'Musos'. We wore the label proudly, and continue to do so.

Our promotional guy was Spike Hyde, possessed by one of the most extraordinary minds I've ever encountered. He was laser-sharp and very funny. When someone injured her knee by colliding with a desk he simply said: 'I've got some haemorrhoid ointment you can use; it won't help the pain but it'll take your mind off it.' With Sue Witherden I accompanied him to see people like the unique John Otway, author of 'Really Free' and the only man I'd ever seen dance on a ceiling without support. Okay, I can hear you asking: if you're tall enough, and the ceiling is low enough, and you stack enough milk crates on the stage, and you can execute a decent handstand...

It may have been that gig at which Sue deflated an ego more successfully, more pointedly and more effectively than any I've ever seen pricked. Leaning up against the bar was a freelance writer, attending the gig on behalf of the *New Musical Express*. He was talking to us about this and that, all centred around him, and he actually said: 'Well, now I've reached forty, I really feel I have a book in me.' I was about to reply: 'Who inserted it?' when Sue bested me by saying, simply: 'Oh, the male meno*prose*, eh?' The laughter spread quickly round the bar, and I have never seen an ego implode quite so fast.

As well as distribution, Waves had its own labels, Spindrift and Making Waves. The catalogue was an eclectic selection of new rock, blues, country and folk. We had constant sellers in Dave Swarbrick, Adrian Legge and Chris Hillman, and experimented with leased material from a variety of sources. We issued a Sammy Myers blues album and a Jessie Dixon gospel album, we recorded a live Big Town Playboys gig for their first LP, and Andy Frain, in charge of A&R, had Napoleonic plans for the future. This included some vast errors like David Knopfler and the Electric Bluebirds, where you could hear the sound of money going down the drain even if you left the building. But we were all on our ego rolls. And that's the trouble with ego rolls. You get a good one, and an hour later you're hungry for more. What really did the label in, however, was not failure quite so much as near-success.

Waves was the sole UK distributor for Rhino Records of Los Angeles – not what they later became, a serious and high-quality reissue company. At that time, they still had both feet planted firmly in the roots of LA weirdness: Barnes & Barnes, Wild Man Fischer, the Temple City Kazoo Orchestra, Circus Royale and Rhino Royale.

Big Daddy was one of their weirdnesses, a studio band, made up of consummate session musicians who cut an album of current rock and pop songs in the style of a 1950's rock'n'roll band. The spoof liner notes to their album told the story of their touring Laos in 1959 on a USO gig, being captured by the communist forces and held captive, but allowed to continue playing as an example of Western Decadence, until 1984, when they were rescued by an elite CIA squad. Brought back to the USA by the government under the strictest secrecy, they were not permitted to see or hear anything until they had been thoroughly debriefed. They were, however, furnished with fresh sheet music. They had, the notes reported, missed the Beach Boys, the Beatles, Flower Power, progressive rock; everything, in fact since the summer of 1959. So, they simply and naturally played the new songs they way they knew best. 'Ebony And Ivory' became a Little Richard rocker; Prince's 'Purple Rain' sounded like Bo Diddley; Van Halen's 'Jump' came out as an Eddie Cochran carbon copy; the stalking 'Every Move You Make' was now a doo-wop ballad; and Springsteen's 'Dancing In The Dark' sounded just like Pat Boone.

It was very funny stuff and very well done. We issued the album and it started to get a reaction. So well did it go, in fact, that the band reformed, got togged up in the right gear, and came over to do a promotional tour. They were fabulous live, and people loved the whole schtick. We released 'Dancing In The Dark' as a 45, and to our astonishment it started to climb the charts. We invested heavily in a video that was shown once on *Top Of The Pops*. It got as high as No.18 on the national charts before our inexperience caused its downfall. We didn't have the promotional balloons and T-shirts. The deejays didn't get the 45 delivered on a nice cake with icing that said: 'Here's a gift for you.' More to the point, we weren't organised enough to press sufficient quantities to meet the demand we had NOW. By the time we got the stock, ten days later, the moment had passed. We'd spent thousands promoting it and it had stiffed because we couldn't follow through.

We got stuck with several hundredweight of a 45 no-one wanted except, some months later and at a vast discount, the Norwegians. We shipped them off to Oslo along with our collective arse, and it left damage that was irreparable. I went into the accounts department one day looking for someone, to find it emptied by lunchtime needs. I noticed, lying on the desk,

Sorting Robert Shoenfeld's MAJOR fuckin' collection, 1985.

final demands for large amounts from British Telecom, the electric company and, most worrying of all, the tax men – both Inland Revenue and VAT.

Nevertheless, we kept going brightly. I said nothing about what I'd seen and no-one said anything to me, although the talk of 're-financing' that occasionally intruded upon a staff meeting rang a nasty bell for me. I still hoped that we could survive, but dumb stuff kept happening. Elvis Costello's *Blood And Chocolate* LP was supposed to be a blockbuster, and the day it was released we were all in the shipping department boxing them up for Our Price outlets across the country. Six weeks later, the dog-eared unsolds started to drift back. You couldn't move in the office for tatty piles of Elvis Costello.

And coming back also was all the stuff we had put into Our Price and scores of indie stores on a sale or return basis. Ace, Charly, Demon, Yazoo, Flying Fish, Rounder, Arhoolie... they turned up like walking wounded from the Somme. We didn't have onward sale or return agreements with many of these companies, so we were stuck with stiffed albums in shop-soiled condition. Rapid Records got out its Del Boy trading hat and, using the returned stock, I launched a series of cheap-and-cheerful mail order sales aimed directly at people on my mailing list. It helped some, but not enough. We all started looking around for something else to shore up the business, and I suggested that Rapid go into the rare 78 market. There was a major collection ('I mean MAJOR fuckin' collection, man') up for grabs. It would cost a few bob, but I could turn it around and we could make a profit for the company.

Interested? Barry and Clive Davidson, the company's owner, thought about it for a week and then said yes. In the meantime, we were preparing a new trade catalogue, rethinking the old printed-and-bound system that had the disadvantage of being out of date almost as soon as it was published. We produced individual hole-punched sheets divided into categories and loaded them into hardback ring binders – the advantage being that update sheets could be produced regularly and the shops could put them straight into the ring binder. It was a huge job, but we did it and I put it together, including all the jokey illustrations and gags. It was like creating another *Sailor's Delight* as far as I was concerned.

Both the catalogue and the deal to buy the 78's were ready on 17 December 1985, the night of the Ace-Charly-Demon Christmas holiday party. Barbie and I attended this, and the following morning, feeling at the top of my game, I flew to St. Louis to buy Robert Schoenfeld's blues collection. The middle man for this splendid deal was Bill Greensmith.

Bill met me at the airport following a bizarre interview with La Migra. I was stopped and asked to open my suitcase. Inside they found what looked, for all the world, like a handgun wrapped in heavy plastic. It was a specialist SME tone arm for Bill's turntable. Then they asked me to open a package that contained several dozen bags of PG Tips teabags Bill had also requested. They didn't like the look of this either, and began debagging the tea searching for something with a little more edge to it.

'Did you fly here in your own plane?' one of them asked me at one point.

Did I what? They took my passport and disappeared for an hour. When they came back, having decided that I was not a threat to national security, merely a nutter who travelled with tone arms and teabags, they let me go without a word of apology. Thanks, lads.

I spent a few days with Bill and Stella, always talking, laughing, reminiscing and planning, bought the collection, rummaged through it on Bill's living room floor, gave him his shellac finder's fee, drank tea, listened to music, did a little shopping and came home on Christmas Eve.

As 1986 groaned into life I was still sculpturing an impressive ego. I had gathered an I'm-An-Indie-Musicbiz-Person wardrobe about me that included white leather shoes, cream suits, hand-painted silk waistcoats, pastel ascots and exotic pre-war jewellery. I looked like a right prat most days. But then so did a lot of us. Peter Shertser of Red Lightnin' Records often turned up at gigs in Generic Outlandish and together we looked like the Capo di Tutti Pimps Brothers.

Pete was fun. Manic as they come, talking nineteen to the dozen, smoking and drinking everything, he was always involved in some bizarre legal wrangle or disaster. 'Cor, you wouldn't fuckin' BELIEVE what 'appened this week mate...' would be the regular opening line of any conversation that then involved tales of severe arguments, stitch-ups, lawsuits, court appearances, crazed and urgent journeys in the Mercedes, and unannounced visits to premises with iron bars.

Blues & Rhythm goes A4.

I spent a lot of time and energy selling the 78's and 45's that had come back from St. Louis. Some got auctioned, but many got sold directly to visiting collectors. One was a closet rock'n'roll fan who actually *enjoyed* his job as a legal conveyancer: 'I find it very satisfying work,' he said, in a scoutmaster-on-acid voice. He was dressed for the part, terminally single, very dedicated to obtaining a collection as good as Breathless Dan O'Coffey's and prepared to spend serious money to do it. He wasn't spending any on wine, women and wardrobe, that's for sure. Barry took one look at his haircut and toothbrush moustache and called him 'Hitler's nephew', but he couldn't argue with the several hundred quid in fresh banknotes that were being counted out on the desk prior to dozens of 45's slipping quietly into good-quality nylon tote bags for the journey back to Surrey.

With Tony Burke's help, we turned *Blues & Rhythm* from an A5 pocket-sized fanzine into an A4 size newsstand magazine. It looked more professional, its subscription base was growing steadily and I was having success putting it into the London shops. I spent every fourth Saturday doing this, generally meeting Barbie somewhere in Camden after I'd finished.

But there were issues that needed addressing. Barbie wanted to go back to California; she was homesick and missed her daughter. After much discussion ('I'M FUCKIN' LEAVING AND YOU CAN COME OR NOT. IT'S YOUR GODDAM CHOICE BUSTER, BUT IF YOU LOVE ME...'), I elected to go with her and so, in August 1986 we got married, I handed *Blues & Rhythm* over to Tony Burke, quit Making Waves, sold the video collection, made a gift of the Rover to my gobsmacked hairdresser, said *au revoir* to my family, and in September we left for San Francisco.

181

Chapter Nine

1986-98: WHO *NEEDS* A PARROT?

San Francisco is, of course, a delightful place, and perhaps the most European of all American cities. We found somewhere to live, downtown by Opera Plaza, in the Barbara Apartments, a charismatic old brownstone building that had been mentioned in a Dashiel Hammet novel more than forty years earlier. I made the rounds of friends and acquaintances, learning from Frank Scott in the process that Making Waves had gone down the tubes amid great acrimony shortly after I left.

I began setting up a new record-trading magazine, modelled on *Sailor's Delight*, to be called *Old Sailor's Almanac*. It lasted for three issues, kept us alive for almost a year, but was not the success I had hoped for. However, in the meantime, other veg were coming to the boil.

My interest in early ethnic recordings had begun in London when I acquired Chris Strachwitz's sod-busting reissue albums on Folk Lyric. I absorbed his pioneering anthologies of Hawaiian, Irish, Polish, Greek, Ukrainian and especially Tex-Mex and Norteño with great relish (£1.95 a jar, from the ethnic section at Sainsbury's). Within weeks of arriving in San Francisco, I met Sherwin Dunner, who, as well as possessing great blues, hillbilly and jazz 78's, had one of the best and most fascinating collections of early ethnic records I had never encountered. What he played me, from rare Norteño through hot Irish to raw East European immigrant bands, quickly expanded my horizons and left me with a taste for more. It was like being let into a fresh field and handed a brand new shovel.

Then, on a bright spring day in 1987, I was wandering through the record bins at the Purple Heart Thrift Store, an echoing old barn in downtown San Francisco run by a bunch of hard-arsed Vietnam Veterans. I began to find an increasingly engrossing selection of 78's on familiar and unfamiliar labels by artists I'd never heard of, in a language I wasn't sure I could identify. It was neither Spanish nor transliterated Greek, but the labels said '*Acc. Guitarra e Viola*' and they looked authentic. At 25 cents each, I took a very small chance and bought all 27 of them, clearly survivors from a single, now-abandoned source.

When I got home and began to play them, the sound I encountered filled me with a strange mixture of emotions. Although I had never heard this music before, it carried a sense of déjà-vu; it reminded me, perhaps, of something from a past life. It seemed like a bowlful of echoes from every imaginable source, it excited and intrigued my imagination more than anything had done since those 1963 encounters with the blues, and it sounded like another planet's version of it. What I had found, or perhaps what had found me, was the Portuguese fado.

I went to the then huge and ancient San Francisco Public Library where, amid the stacks at the back, I found dozens of books about Portugal, many more than fifty years old. One, especially, held interest: *Portugal, A Book of Folkways*. It included a superbly-written capsule history of Portuguese folklore and the fado by Rodney Gallop, an English diplomat posted to Lisbon in the early 1930's. It had last been checked out three months before I was born. By the time I had finished absorbing this and dozens of other works, I realised that the records I had found represented an uncannily accurate portrait of the different styles I was reading about – almost as if I was meant to discover this perfect fado starter kit. The 78's offered me fados from Lisbon, Coimbra, Porto and Rio by both men and women well known, like Amalia Rodrigues; legendary, like Alfredo Marceneiro and Antonio Menano; and completely obscure, like Carlos Leal. There was nothing for it. I *had* to go to Portugal.

Barbie, her entire 0-sized wardrobe, emergency back-up nail repair kit and I arrived at Lisbon airport on 4 November 1987. We had put our California life on hold; subleased our apartment; stowed some of our stuff and brought some with us. Who knew? We might stay forever. It was that loose.

We stayed seven weeks. During that time we walked every inch of Lisbon that we could, spoke to everyone about the fado, from street lottery salesmen to the Minister of Culture, haunted the vast and ancient store of Valentim de Carvalo, the biggest record business in Portugal, wading through their amazing archive of 78's and sheet music, interviewed Amalia Rodrigues' manager, and spent every night in fado houses listening, talking to people, observing, photographing and making sonically challenged field recordings.

By the time we were ready to leave, I felt I knew the fado much better, but the job of chasing it to a conclusion would last a few years yet. We didn't stay in Lisbon partly because Barbie again felt a need to return home ('LISTEN BUSTER, LET ME EXPLAIN SOMETHING...'), but also because I knew we couldn't get anything clucking before the money ran out. Chickens were rare in Lisbon.

We trekked back through Paris and London visiting relatives, and arrived in California in early January to find our apartment trashed, the sub-leaser gone, and rent due. There was also the matter of this illegal king-size waterbed that he had left behind.

Question: How do you empty a large water bed in a small apartment?

Answer: VERY carefully.

It took a whole day.

San Francisco in 1988 was a community under siege. The Gay Capitol of America was being decimated by AIDS, and the joke 'Your face or mine?' was no longer funny. The gay life continued, because it was deeply woven into the San Francisco infrastructure, but it was in depression and every morning the obituary columns of the *San Francisco Chronicle* would be filled with the names and brightly handsome, hopeful photos of choreographers, artists, dancers and writers who had succumbed. We weren't just losing members of the gay community, we were losing the *arts* community as well. You really cannot live in San Francisco successfully and still be homophobic, although some people tried ('IT'S GOD'S WRATH UPON THE WICKED!' someone once yelled at me when the subject came up. 'MAY THEIR ABUSED ASSES ALL BURN IN HELL!!') Our landlord was gay. Everyone except Barbie at the designer lighting company she worked for was gay. Our grocer was, if not gay, perhaps occasionally festive.

One of the people who was decidedly *not* gay, however, was Jeff Richardson. Jeff co-owned Jack's Record Cellar, a collectors' record store that sat on the corner of Scott and Page streets, a block up from Fillmore Street going towards the park, on the very edge of the old Haight-Ashbury district that hosted the hippie revolution of the 1960's. The Haight had never really got over it, either. The house that Jefferson Airplane had once occupied still stood, the head shops still operated, peddling every last thing you needed for extended drug culture involvement except the stuff itself. Hippies old and wannabe-new hung out on the street, on stoops, in old hand-painted VW vans, and called each other 'man' regardless of sex. People who looked like Zippy The Pinhead read comics by R. Crumb.

In amongst all this quietly ongoing mayhem stood Jack's, sandwiched between the hippies and the small African-American area known as 'The Fillmore'. Jack's had been founded in the late 1940's by a fellow called - surprise! - Jack, as a jazz record store. He almost immediately left to join a circus and was never heard from again, but the name never changed. The place was run for years by a guy called Norm, a colourful fellow who would throw you out if you dared asked for a discount, kept a loaded pistol under the counter and used it on more than one occasion. In the late 1970's Norm died, and the shop simply closed its doors for a few years, stock, furniture, catalogues and all. Jeff and his business partner Wade Wright negotiated its purchase and re-opened it as a collectors' record shop. In fact, the *classic* collectors' record shop.

Both men had connections to the San Francisco blues-rock band, the Flaming Groovies. Wade's brother was the drummer, and Jeff had been the band's manager. They also employed the ex-lead singer and guitarist, Roy Loney, to run the store. It was, the day I first stepped through the door, the most welcoming place I'd encountered in years. It simply said: 'You're home now. Come in and relax.'

The building itself was Victorian, and the shop was wooden

throughout: floors, walls, browser boxes, counter, stairs, shelves, high ceilings and a small mezzanine – on which a struggling Chris Strachwitz had slept in the late 1950's – ensured a perfect ambient sound. It was a giant wooden loudspeaker. To stand in the store and listen to Uncle Dave Macon or Kokomo Arnold or Janis Martin or Charlie Parker was to hear American music as it should be heard: warmly, openly, delivered in full, rich sound waves. I very much wanted to be a part of this and, by great good fortune, in early 1988, an opportunity arose.

Back from Europe and knowing that *Old Sailor's Almanac* was a mortuary-bound mallard, I approached Jeff and asked if he needed any help from a likely lad. He did; Roy Loney had other commitments and could now only work half a week in the store, and Jeff's position as representative for City Hall, the local indie record distributors, had been complicated by the emergence of the CD. He needed someone three days a week in the store and someone else to occasionally help him on the road, taking stock and writing inventory. I went to work the following week in both capacities.

Through Jeff I learned an enormous amount. His knowledge of and enthusiasms for American music were staggering, and he shared it all willingly, almost evangelically. He introduced me to Western swing, playing me dozens of examples of pioneering recordings; Bob Dunn's first electric guitar solo; Moon Mullican's premier, uncredited, piano break; and titles by bands I'd never heard of which swung like crazy. He believed that 1930's Western swing was where rock'n'roll had really started, by merging elements of blues, jazz and hillbilly into a new format using the cutting edge technology of amplification. Arguably, the first rock'n'roll record was cut in 1934 when Western swing emerged. Jeff ran two small indie labels, Western and Rambler, that issued the best of it. He shared my interest in Norteño, but was ahead of my game. He was as keen a Washboard Sam fan as he was an enthusiast for Charlie Feathers. He kept up with contemporary country music and showed me how far it had managed to drag itself from the Jim Reeves days. I learned more from Jeff by just listening than from anyone I'd ever encountered.

Jeff could also be an irritable old sod, frustrated and appalled by the way American life was going; I often got the full 'mankind is doomed' speech on the way out to a Tower Records outlet. He saw his mission, I think, as attempting to stem the tide of yuppie-based shallowness by riding the Jack's Record Cellar warhorse into battle.

'I'm a fuckin'... *GLADIATOR*, man. I'm out here every day fighting,' he once told me in the car, punching the air with his fist to ram the point home and injuring his knuckles on the sun visor. Jeff also introduced me to real Mexican food; he was familiar with a network of mom-and-pop pits south of the Mission district, where we would go and eat cheaply and well following a day's inventory-writing. He always treated me to these refried beanfeasts and I've never yet encountered better Mexican food anywhere. Then again I've never yet been to Mexico, unless you count a mad day in Tijuana.

Jeff Richardson and me behind the counter at Jack's Record Cellar, 1987.

Writing inventory in the record stores around the Bay Area was a job I found I did well, and Jeff was happy to let me wrestle with CDs, a format he had not yet – and did not wish to – come to terms with. He did the vinyl while I handled what Sherwin Dunner refers to as 'calcified jizz'. I got to know Berkeley, Richmond, Mountain View, San Mateo, San Rafael and downtown San Francisco well. But it was my three days a week in the store that held real meaning.

Jeff gave me a set of keys and let me open up on Thursdays, Fridays and Sundays. The store traded from midday until 7:00 pm. Most days I was on my own until at least 4:00 pm, when Wade, perhaps the most laid-back and altogether unflappable man I've ever known, turned up from having spent his day restoring yet another vintage Rock-Ola or Wurlitzer juke box. Wade was the perfect foil for Jeff. He was almost impossible to irritate, a tall, slow-moving, walrus-moustached man who smiled constantly. I once asked him why he was so mellow and he told me, in a nutshell, that it was gratitude. He'd had another, wholly different life before this one, and what there was now was so very much better than what there had been, that he had to be grateful. He never elaborated, leaving me to my imagination.

My duties were simple: make coffee and keep it topped up, sweep through once a day, keep interesting and relevant music playing, water the plants, answer the phone, sort the mail, tidy the browser bins and serve the customers. You call this a job? It seemed like heaven to me, albeit as humbly-paid as the business could afford. The shop held large quantities of vinyl albums in wooden browser bins, organised into sub-categories. Not just 'Jazz', but 'Classic Jazz', 'Chicago', 'Dixieland Revival', 'Early Bop' and

'Mainstream'. Blues was divided into 'Mississippi', 'Chicago', 'Memphis' and so on. We stocked a large selection of what Jeff called 'real' country music, from Charlie Poole up through his beloved Western swing, on past Hank Williams to Highway 101. But if you wanted Charlie Pride or Jim Reeves, you might just as well check the grocery store across the street. We also carried bluegrass, rockabilly, R&B, rock'n'roll, Hawaiian, Cajun and zydeco, 1960's US garage bands, and early British Invasion. We didn't stock Frank Sinatra or Dean Martin, John Denver or – especially – Barry Manilow, but we took a vicious delight in carrying original, bad taste 'sleazy listening' albums by the likes of Martin Denny and cheesy Las Vegas lounge acts, especially Buddy Greco. 'My man Buddy,' Jeff would laugh as he played a live-in-Vegas rarity. Perfect. I couldn't have done better myself.

In addition to albums, Henry Mariano's bootleg 45's and a wide selection of oldies on re-pressed singles, we had thousands of 78's sitting in boxes on shelves stretched across two of the four walls, under the album browsers, on the mezzanine and in the basement. Some of the better ones had been sorted onto shelves behind the counter and serious collectors could ask to look. They'd find Carter Family Bluebirds, early white jazz, original bebop, a Hank Williams MGM, some decent R&B and always a few surprises ('Holy SHIT! A Muddy Aristocrat... Er, how much?').

I began an in-depth excavation of the rest of the 78's to see if we could add to the goodies pile. It was like junk shopping in your own home. Neither Jeff nor Wade had had the time for this exercise, but in spare moments I would grab boxes and sift them. I found mint Cajun records on Goldband, overlooked rock'n'roll, early ethnic stuff on Columbia, Victor and Vocalion, a few stray African 78's, some very early ragtime, and records of local interest.

Our customers were mostly people we knew well. Occasionally someone would drift in, ask for the latest Bette Midler and drift out again confused when we told them we didn't have it, wouldn't order it and didn't care anyway. Friday evenings could be busy, exciting times. Jeff would come back from City Hall with all the latest releases on Ace, Charly, Relic and other relevant labels for shop stock. People browsed, records played constantly, the shop's considerable discographical library was consulted, coffee was slurped by anyone who fancied a cup while the huge rubber plant shaded a superb Wurlitzer 1015 bubble-tube juke box and two wicker chairs in the window where people lounged, talked, smoked and listened.

Regulars in the store included Roger Collins, the blues singer whose wonderful 'Foxy Girls In Oakland' 45 Roger kept pressed up himself. We sold several copies a month; a delightful man. Also Little Caesar, an early R&B artist, still sharply dressed no matter what time of day he appeared, and always ready to talk about music and the old days. But to me the most interesting character was an older black guy whose name I never knew. He had lived in Chicago in the 1930's and 1940's, and had been a regular in the South Side blues clubs. He'd seen Memphis Minnie, Big Bill, Jazz Gillum,

Sonny Boy, and told me interesting stuff, like how they had been using saxophones and clarinets in the clubs long before Lester Melrose allowed them appear to on record. Jazz Gillum was duetting with alto sax players on stage in about 1938, and blowing directly through the microphone, he said. Memphis Minnie had an electric guitar around the same time. It was about being HEARD above the hubbub.

On a beautiful, clear, summer day, an old hippie wandered in with a vast birdcage containing a parrot that was apparently in training for death; or at least sleeping very soundly. Images of alternate *Monty Python* sketches skedaddled through my head and I attempted not to laugh.

'Hey, man, do you, like, need a parrot, man?' he enquired. 'He's free.'

Like, who *NEEDS* a parrot? I mean apart from the obvious Parliamentary backbenchers, that is.

I thanked him and politely refused. He looked around at the records, the wooden browsers, and also at the remarkable collection of original rock posters that had simply been up on the walls for years. Psychedelic art announcing Jefferson Airplane at the Fillmore East, Quicksilver Messenger Service at Candlestick Park and the Doors at the Great American Music Hall.

'Wowmanlikecool. Do you have the records too?'

'Yes, sure, we stock psychedelia. This is San Francisco.'

'Er, have you got Jefferson Airplane's 'White Bird', man?'

'You mean It's A Beautiful Day, yes?'

'If I gave you a quarter, would you play it for me?'

'No need for money, I'll play it for you anyway. Lay down your weary parrot and have a wicker seat.'

And so he did and I played him his request, becoming personal disc jockey for a partially-fried old hippie and the soundly-kipping caged bird he was attempting to part with, listening to a song about a white bird in a gilded cage. When it was over he thanked me, got up and left. It was a very San Francisco moment.

Jeff also pitch-forked me into the tango. He got tickets to see Astor Piazzola at the Great American Music Hall, a wonderful old theatre in downtown San Francisco. Piazzola's music is not easy listening. He was one of the first, and most committed, of the immediate post-war 'new' tango movement in Argentina, a sort of Charlie Parker for Buenos Aires. His music had always been political, and the Argentinean government had consequently taken a dim view of him, so he often performed outside his homeland, and frequently in North America. His style was almost atonal, but not quite. He pulled it back from the edge time and again by basing his extemporisations very firmly in the rich soil of traditional tango. New Guard players, like early beboppers, didn't abandon their roots, they simply re-examined them and saw different things to be drawn from the heritage. Like moving around a prism and harvesting shifting perspectives.

The complexities of his music are beyond any adequate description, but his stage presence was extraordinary. When he himself was not playing the bandoneon, allowing the contra-bass or the violin to take a lengthy solo, he would stand at attention, parade ground style. His music had an almost paramilitary air to it. He himself was a rebel, a fugitive from the system that weaned him. His anger and frustration, translated into his music, fuelled the rich sound pattern the group generated. He died shortly after I saw him and I am both glad I had the opportunity to see him and desolate that I could never repeat the experience. He was one of the most deeply moving musicians I've ever seen. I'd put him in the same emotional league as Son House.

In the Fillmore one day, I heard the sound of an electric guitar playing 'Rollin' And Tumblin' '. Drawn like a mothball to a flaming queen, I tracked down the sound to an older man seated on a low wall. He was playing a semi-acoustic guitar through a portable amp and looked every inch the classic traditional blues singer. I took a seat on the wall opposite and listened. When he finished, I went over and introduced myself, and asked him how long he'd been playing the blues. Fifty years at least, I imagined; perhaps he'd known Joe Callicott or Eli Framer? He told me: 'Last coupla months.'

What!?!? His street name was Chester D, and he'd spent his working life in the shipyards of Oakland, raising a family, putting his kids through college, being Joe Serious. He'd retired earlier that year and was now fulfilling his own fantasy of being a street blues singer. He had bought a guitar, practised some, found he could make chords easily and went straight out on the street. He didn't need the money – he was comfortably off; he just liked what he was doing and it got him out of the house.

I worked at Jack's for close to a year, happy as a sandboy's pig in a daylong clover field. Then, suddenly, pressing family matters in England forced us to uproot and return to deal with them. We stayed for nine months, basing ourselves in Reading. Both Barbie and I found jobs, but we needed to conserve as much money as we could, and so spent autumn, winter and early spring in a rented room. It was dreadful, and we fought often. The few bright spots during that time were more often than not provided by Alan Empson and his family. Alan is my absolute contemporary. He heard the same music at the same time, bought his Pye 45's just like I did, his first album had been *The Blues (Volume 1)*, as mine had happened to be *Volume 2*. He had seen the same gigs as I had – we probably rubbed shoulders and spilled beer on each other without knowing it. He'd listened to Mike Raven on the same evenings as me, and bought his first original American blues records from the same man I had – Mike Rowe. Brothers in arms.

We would go and fill up with the excellent Indian food Alan's wife Angie prepared, and sit, talk and play records all evening. Alan and Angie were the perfect hosts, providing warm bright jewels of comfort in otherwise Dickensian Hard Times.

We got back to San Francisco around Easter 1989, got another apartment and, by great good luck, Jeff and Wade found they could use me again, so I went back to my old life at Jack's Record Cellar. But not for long. Six months after our re-arrival, family issues in England again burst over us and we had to leave once more. This time there was no going back.

Barbie and I scuffled for the next four years; our fortunes severely depleted, our mood soured by events and arguing constantly. I remember it only as the worst time of my life. We moved out of London after a few months to Sheerness in Kent, and I became a cab driver. It seemed like a good idea at the time. Sometimes, in the middle of the night, waiting my turn at the rank, listening to Jazz FM at the edge of its range and hearing Tony Russell play a blues record, I wondered how we had managed to slip this far.

We sat in Sheerness for fifteen long months,

San Francisco, c.1986.
Look, it was the fashion in those days!

subsisting and squabbling in a rented top-floor two-room apartment, trying to live on a minicab driver's wages. We might be there yet, had we not been rescued by Gill Cook. Gill had come to London in the early 1950's, on her own, when that was not the thing for a young woman to do. She had fallen directly into the then fast-expanding world of folk music and wound up working, for the longest time, in Collett's, the left-wing book and record shop. She WAS the folk record department; everyone knew her and everyone liked her. When I first met Nigel Gallop, Rodney's son, hers was a name that surfaced almost immediately. For years she quietly did what she was good at: sell folk and blues records to people who wanted them. I had known her since the *Sailor's Delight* days (Collett's stocked it, thanks, I think, to Gill) and I had always known her as the warmest and most generous of people.

But Collett's had closed and Gill was now working at the Mechanical Copyright Protection Society, in the National Discography section. Her job was to process in-depth recording information to the computer databank,. to enable royalties to be correctly collected and moved onwards to their rightful recipients. It was a huge operation, and National Discography had a policy of hiring specialists to do the data processing, because they knew that was what was needed. As well as Gill, Alasdair Blaazer, Mike Rowe and a host of others worked there. Through Gill's efforts, I was offered a job. We moved back to London within a week. It felt very good to get out of the taxi.

At National Discography, I sat at a desk facing Alasdair with Mike Rowe to my right. Alasdair had come a very long way since I first met him back in 1982. Now a key member of the discographical team at MCPS, specialising in blues and gospel, he lived with an increasingly large and enviable record collection, and was building a successful career as 'Big Joe Louis', a Blues singer, guitarist and bandleader and who, in my humble opinion, ranks alongside the late Jo-Ann Kelly and Cyril Davies as one of the three best British Blues musicians of all time. I spent my days inputting data that I understood well, talking to Al and Mike, with Gill next door.

There were others too: Alex Ash, a jazz specialist and a black Londoner whose accent left African-Americans baffled on his frequent US trips; and Hans Fried, an old folk warrior who had worked in the record department at Collett's for years and was a deeper mine of arcane information than almost anyone else I ever encountered. He would often be so wrapped in thought that he was unaware of a greeting or a request or an offer of coffee. He spent his life in hyperfocus.

Barbie and I lived just up the street in rented rooms. I was happy to be at MCPS. It was also the seed pod for a new and quite different floral path to dance down.

Because I wasn't just some oik off the street, but an oik disguised as a representative of MCPS, I could call up record companies with requests for information. That was how I came to be calling the EMI Archives. On behalf of MCPS, I trekked out to Hayes, in Middlesex, to see Ruth Edge, the head archivist, about an MCPS matter.

When I got there, I realised that the place was a huge depository for anything and everything connected with The Gramophone Company and EMI, going back to 1898. I asked her if she had any material on Portugal or the fado and was shown incredible catalogues from the 1920's to the 1950's filled with exactly the kind of information I lusted after. Could I make copies please? Yes, I could. I came away in a state of delirium.

By the time I had absorbed all this and meshed it with what I already had, I had enough information about the fado to be confident of writing something salient; I offered an article called 'Chasing The Fado' to Ian Anderson at *Folk Roots* and he accepted it. It was published in February 1992, but by that time I had left MCPS because their financial restructuring was based upon last in, first out. So, I was now Bert Unemployed-Git of Streatham. Oh, lovely. To call Barbie unhappy would have been a stretch of the truth. She was alternately enraged and depressed, shouting or sleeping. Again I wondered how we'd fallen so far. And in the darkest moment, another small light switch was thrown.

During my time at MCPS, I had gone to the EMI archives regularly, digging deeper and deeper into not only old Portuguese files but everything else as well. I couldn't avoid it, it all surrounded me. Even though I was now on the dole, I still went once a month, to spend a day searching the archives and photocopying as much as I could afford.

The EMI Archives, before they moved them at the end of the Twentieth Century, were a vast, old, settled and dusty repository that looked like an abandoned library, but were, in fact, very well organised. The Gramophone Company and, after the 1931 merger, EMI, had always been involved in recording and manufacturing music for the rest of the world.

In the early days, when most countries had neither recording nor pressing facilities of their own, the Gramophone Company was one of the companies that did it for them. An engineer would visit, for example, Lisbon, liaise with their appointed local agent, and make recordings that were then taken back to Hayes for mastering and pressing onto 78 rpm discs in specially allocated series.

Thus, the Parlophone series prefixed 'ML-' was specifically for Portuguese recordings aimed at the Portuguese market. The finished product would be shipped back to the agent for sale. All the correspondence, copies of catalogues and other printed ephemera was archived at Hayes and, in 1992, close to ninety years'-worth of material had accumulated, largely untouched. As I wandered through shelves filled with leather-bound catalogues of Indian records from the 1920's and rounded a corner to discover a drawer filled with original 1930's company reports about the record industry in Greece sitting next to a file of 1940's West African promotional flyers, I began to realise just what depth of history had been fossilised here. It was, in fact, the biggest and most important archive of early ethnic recording data in the world. And it was largely untapped.

I began, at first just out of interest, to photocopy a wide selection of material. Visiting regularly, I compiled files on not just Portugal but also Spain, Brazil, Argentina, West, East, North and South Africa, Italy and Sardinia, Greece and Crete, the Caribbean, France and her colonies (especially Madagascar), Turkey, Albania and India.

Other stuff surfaced: the *Voice of Victor*, the US Victor company house magazine of the 1920's and '30's, was there, as was the same era's *Talking Machine World*, which to my delight listed new releases, month by month, on labels like Victor, Vocalion and Columbia. This is how I discovered, for instance, that Garfield Akers' 'Cottonfield Blues' was actually released in January 1930. Discographies concentrate on recording dates, rather than release dates, and sometimes the gaps can be longer than one imagines. It's an under-researched area that deserves greater attention. The Garfield Akers is so rare because it was issued directly into the teeth of the Depression.

One day Ruth mentioned to me that they also held copies of all the records the Gramophone Company and EMI had ever pressed. One mint copy from each pressing had immediately been archived, right from day one. Not only that, but under an agreement that had lasted for years, they held mint copies of just about every US Victor pressing as well. They were all sitting quietly in waxed brown sleeves on metal shelves in a cool vault. She took me to see them. Row upon row of eight-foot high metal shelves, containing thousands of mint original 78's. I wanted to move in, camp bed under my arm, and stay for a year or two.

We talked some more, I looked at the log books that were the Rosetta Stones for this huge archive and realised that it contained thousands of examples of the world's folk music from the first half of the Twentieth Century.

'This stuff ought to be reissued,' I remarked to Ruth, dribbling ever so slightly.

'So do it,' she said, or something like that.

'What?'

'We'd lease some material for a fee to anyone who wanted to use it. Not English-language recordings, but just about anything else.'

'You mean I could select a bunch of fados and you'd lease them to me?'

'Yes.'

I began hyperventilating. I thought about all this and wondered how it might be possible to achieve my new fantasy of reissuing prime early ethnic recordings. I didn't have the infrastructure for it: I couldn't re-master, Cedarise, or press CDs, produce cover artwork, slap them together into jewel cases and get them distributed. But I knew someone who could! I called Bruce Bastin and explained what was on offer.

'Come on down and let's talk,' he said.

It turned out that early ethnic music was exactly the path Bruce wanted his record company to take next, and he already had a foot on it; his problem being where to get prime stuff. EMI was the obvious answer. The deal we nailed together was a simple one. I would hold the principal contract with EMI for leasing, and Bruce's company, Interstate, would be my only client. Interstate would meet Ruth's remastering fees, Bruce would select the material, in conjunction with advice from experts, and draw all the discographical information from me, as I was the mole with instant access to the system. I would go in and do the first-stage mastering at EMI, delivering the tapes directly to him. Bruce would manufacture and distribute, and pay me agreed-upon fees for the work I would do. Simple.

We began with fados and early West African recordings. I did the remastering in EMI's archive, using their equipment to transfer onto digital audio-tape. I'd never remastered a 78 before, but the learning curve was one I wanted to take and I had superb equipment and unplayed source material to work with. Then, I would pull all the relevant discographical material and original photos together and deliver the package to Bruce.

Sometimes I wrote the notes, sometimes others did. We produced a fabulous series of Greek rebetika, under the guidance of Charlie Howard, the leading expert, who sat in Greece drooling over what I was finding in Hayes. Bruce and I worked well together, and he was, despite wearing an uncalled-for reputation as 'difficult', a generous, easygoing and honest man to do business with. Bruce wasn't difficult, he simply would not suffer fools and told them so immediately. It saved a lot of time. At a gathering somewhere, he was listening to a critic drone on about what, in the critic's view, was wrong with a new book on African music by a friend of Bruce's, Viet Erlmann. Having had enough, Bruce simply said: 'When's your book due, then?' It stopped the bore dead in his tracks.

The bulk of Bruce's early Cuban CDs came directly out of EMI. We found some astonishing other stuff, and projects like the Sardinian and Albanian CDs emerged simply because I stumbled upon the raw material while looking for other things. The EMI project ran actively for several years. Much of what was issued was still in catalogue as the Twenty-First Century turned, and those involved in it are still talking to each other today. I'd call that a success.

Meanwhile, a further outcropping of being at the open end of this new information fire-hose was that I had enough material to write fleshy, fax'n'info packed articles about various aspects of early ethnic recording histories. I went back to Ian Anderson at *Folk Roots* and basically said: 'Oi, mush, want erudite articles on a wide selection of vintage ethnic recordings then?' He said yes, and for the rest of the 1990's I wrote about the recording history of India, Africa, Spain, Italy, Brazil, Argentina, the Caribbean, Greece, the Ottoman Empire and elsewhere. Ian started to send me relevant CDs to review, and I found I had clambered onto the *Folk Roots* platform, where I remain to this day – not a bad place to be at all. Ian's decision to say yes to a series of articles that was then regarded as arcane was perhaps courageous, and his part in establishing a forum for ongoing research into early ethnic music was crucial. It also helped me transform myself from Bert Unemployed-Git into Jim Freelance-Git. But first, there was a trauma to undergo.

Barbie and I had reached a point where we could hardly speak without abusing each other and it was getting steadily worse. In September 1993 we split – suddenly, acrimoniously, loudly – in Streatham High Road, just a few yards from Dave Carey's old shop. It was over. My mother, being my mother, said: 'Come here until you find your feet again.' And so, at age 44, I went home to Mum.

The *Folk Roots* articles generated patches of interest. From the one I wrote about Egypt grew my involvement with EMI-Dubai's reissue programme in which, working at Abbey Road studios, I put together CDs of early material by Omme Kolsom and Mohammed Abdel Wahab. I took advantage of a government scheme that assisted people to turn self-employed. It didn't pay any more than the dole – in fact slightly less – and it only lasted for six months (by which time you were supposed to be on your own feet), but it made me feel a lot better about myself. It was a fresh start and I knew the paths I wanted to take. I was going to freelance my way back into the music business! I had the work for Bruce and Ian, and I supplemented it by starting a very modest company called 'Ethnic Shellac' to buy and sell records.

Almost immediately a handsome collection of blues and hillbilly 78's came my way on commission, and it took a year to sell them at auction. I supplemented this by junking around London and began to find, to my astonishment, that I could turn up great ethnic 78's just by digging in odd places like classical music stores, charity shops, old libraries, and general secondhand record shops. In one, I encountered close to 200 Greek rebetika 78's, thrown out the day before by a family who didn't understand or care anymore. I taught myself some very basic Greek to evaluate what I had bought.

By mid-1994 I was divorced from Barbie, selling rare records again, fostering a growing reputation as Mr. Early Ethnic and writing my first book – the snappily titled *Ethnic And Vernacular Music On Record 1898-1960: A Resource And Guide*. Fortunate young sod, but this time, at least, with an enormous sense of gratitude; to Bruce, to Ruth, to Ian, but most of all to my mother. I really must stop all this sodding about and get serious.

Bruce was always on the lookout for records to buy, and had told me that if I ever found anything, at any time, I should call him. I was a regular visitor to the London record swap meets that erupted several times a year. They were splendid affairs, where tens of thousands of records and hundreds of gnarled, obsessive and looney collectors would gather and discuss important matters like who was the first bass player to be recorded by the Western Electric process, or the meaning of the gap in the numbering system at Gallotone, or whose turn it was to get the cheese sandwiches in.

If you wanted to conduct an in-depth study of eccentricity, then a record fair was a superb place to start. I played my part, flitting from stall to stall in a pre-war three-piece tweed suit asking for old foreign language stuff. Most of it was junk, but I could generally come away with a few interesting things. One day I asked that question of a huge man called William Breslin, whose principal interest was acoustic operatic recordings;

'Foreign language? Come and have a quiet beer with me, would you?'

It turned out that, not only could he supply foreign language records, he could supply *thousands* of them and, moreover, the bulk of them would be Portuguese.

'How can you be sure?' I asked.

'Because they're in Portugal,' he replied.

Breslin had been working for more than two years from a huge stock of 78's in the northern Portuguese city of Porto. It wasn't a collection of anything, so much as a collection of everything. The owner had principally been an enthusiast of phonographs and gramophones themselves, and bought the shellac 'software' only to demonstrate the metal and wooden hardware.

He had died, and his family, fed up to the rear molars with all this nonsense, had immediately sold the machines, but then got stuck with the records. Two whole garages full. Somehow, Breslin had found out about them and asked to go look. What he found dazzled him; the very first Carusos on original, light blue Zonophone pressings; and every other rare operatic record imaginable. It was like finding a run of 13000 series

Bruce in the Flyright office: 'Fado CDs? Sure.'

Paramounts! He also found mountains of jazz and rock'n'roll, all of which he could easily shift, but he was having a problem with the leftovers, which turned out to include just about every fado 78 ever pressed from 1904 to 1963. He'd made a commitment to the family to get rid of everything, and was delighted to find someone – anyone – with an interest in the Portuguese material. There was also, he told me, other stuff: Cuban, Brazilian, other Latin-American, some Spanish... I called Bruce.

The upshot was that, several weeks later, Bruce, his wife Diane, and I were crossing the Bay of Biscay on a ferry to spend whatever time it took to sort and pack the two garages full of 78's that Bruce had agreed to buy. We motored from Bilbão to Porto, stayed ten days, took about half of what was there, and had them shipped back to Bexhill by road transport.

What we had pulled, principally, was a vast archive of fados that included all I knew about from the EMI catalogues and the very much more I knew nothing about until we found them. There were series we knew nothing of on labels we knew; there were labels we'd heard of but had never seen before; there were labels we'd never heard of at all, and there were *dozens* of them. In one experience that Bruce called 'frightening', he found a paper Paramount record sleeve advertising Charley Patton, Bullet Williams and Blind Blake, but unfortunately no record to slip inside of it. In the ensuing months, Bruce gave me access to all the fado 78's, and, working directly from them, meshing the information with that I'd found at EMI, I compiled a discography of 78 rpm fado recordings, and created a tape archive for reference.

This huge boost to the fado research led me to think about tackling a proper, in-depth history of the subject. There had not been anything in English since Rodney Gallop's writing in 1936. I had become friends with his son Nigel, a delightful fellow who had inherited his father's interest in folk music and had also kept all his papers, to which he graciously gave me full access. I started to look for someone who might be foolish enough to publish a book like this, and connected with an organisation dedicated to cultural exchange between Britain and Portugal, called Portugal 600 (so named because the two countries had not found any excuse to go to war with one another for 600 years). Incredibly, they got me a grant from the Gulbenkian Foundation to write the book, found a publisher called Ashgate and also came up with enough petty cash to send me to Lisbon on a research trip for a week ('Ah, Mr. Vernon. Take this bag of money, go to Portugal with it, *and don't come back until you've spent it all!'*). Amazed by these events, I sat down and began to write my second book. Snappy title? *A History Of The Portuguese Fado.*

In July 1994 I was invited to a reception at the US Embassy in Grosvenor Square, for a 'Celebration of the American South', taking place at the South Bank Arts Centre. I arrived directly from EMI Archives and found, among others, Chris Strachwitz, Flaco Jiminez, Paul and Valerie Oliver, Tony Russell, Anne Savoy, Cilla Huggins, Mark Sinclair Harris and a lady called Judy Rolph Ebner, an American diplomat posted to the Embassy. She and I began to talk, but were overtaken by events that pulled us both away. A week or so later we went for a drink to continue the conversation that had been so rudely interrupted. That was in 1994. Today the conversations continue. I finally stopped sodding about.

Throughout 1995 and into 1996, I became involved in a project for Channel 4 Television, a three-part documentary tracing the history of African-American gospel music. Gospel and snooker expert Viv Broughton, whom I had known since the *Blues & Rhythm* days, had got the project off the ground and, in gathering his research team, remembered me as Mr. Bootleg Video. He called and asked if I'd like to be the archive film-finder for the project. There'd be money in it, a chance to look at all that wonderful footage and my name in lights as the end credits of each episode rolled. Did I say yes? Does Jeremy Paxman's stretch-skateboard chauffeur report for duty each midnight?

At the end of the project, I had amassed a huge amount of footage and made many new contacts inside the film and TV industry. The archive and information I'd assembled led me to realise that there was enough material for a book: a filmography of blues, R&B and gospel. It would be fairly large and could be quite complex. I went back to Ashgate, and saw my editor Rachel Lynch. She listened and said yes. Working with other blues film experts like Australians Gary Le Gallant and Mike Kredinac, Americans Chris Stoval Brown and Len Rosenberg, Austrian Kurt Hriczucsah, Brits Howard Rye, Chris Smith and Tony Russell, and many another generous collectors, the compilation began.

Discographical research is almost always international, and the spirit of cooperation is almost always genuine and enthusiastic. I think discographers should have a crack at running the world. Any time someone gets out of order and starts threatening his neighbour, we won't send in the troops, we'll send in the Matrix Number Reciters, squads of them, who will immediately deploy throughout the area and begin chanting detailed recording information on desperately obscure sessions to the warring factions and *bore* them into negotiations. Anyone who tries anything will be taken to a small windowless cell where a trained discographer will recite Gennett matrix numbers at them until they plead for mercy.

In the meantime, I was still working with Bruce, writing for Ian and selling records, but something else loomed. Judy and I had been dating since 1994, and she had introduced me to her family the following year on a trip home. Her children, Adam and Lia, liked me as much as I liked them and now I virtually lived with them. Then one night, she got a call from Washington to tell her that her next post was to be Prague, in the Czech Republic – but first via Washington for a year to learn the language.

Both previously married, and both now very cautious, we had not really broached the subject of what would happen when it was time for her to move on, but now we had to. We did the obvious, right thing and tied the knot at Westminster Town Hall the day before some geezer from Oasis did the same, only he got a lot more press coverage.

We invited our friends, Francis and Pam, Bruce and Diane, Nigel Gallup and his wife Bertita, Mike Rowe ('Of course I'll be there Paul – I ALWAYS come to your weddings'), and our mothers, mine from Mill Hill, Judy's from Delaware. Judy's wonderful Uncle Sam (no, really) flew over via a military refuelling flight to be with us. Matthew was our best man and my new grandson Cornelius was guest of honour. Never, in my view, had a woman looked more beautiful than Judy on the day we did this. Two months later, we set off for a year in Washington DC.

Leaving London with our travelling circus of kids and animals in June 1997, we moved to northern Virginia. We bought a house there, partly because the kids and I fell in love with the lightning bugs in the adjacent fields. If you've never seen lightning bugs, let me assure you there are simply magical. Judy went into intensive language training – Czech is a complex language – and I finished compiling the even more snappily-titled *African-American Blues, Rhythm & Blues, Gospel, Cajun and Zydeco On Film & Video, 1926-1997*. I wanted to call it *Not A Dry Eye In The One-And-Nines*, but Ashgate is an academic publishing house.

During that year I was also handed something on a plate, that others might have killed for: American citizenship. Under an obscure and narrowly-used rule, foreign-born spouses of American military and government officials being posted overseas for three or more years could be granted what was termed 'Expeditious Naturalization', which essentially meant citizenship immediately, rather than waiting for five years on an alien registration or a green card. It made sense for the government to have government spouses be Americans – the irony being that you had to be leaving the country in order to qualify. I was sworn in two days after my birthday, which was one day after America's birthday and thirteen before Judy's. It makes July a very special month.

When, just a few days before we left for the Czech Republic, I was presented with my diplomatic passport, the lad from north-west London looked at it and could only think how fortunate a young sod he was – and also how very far from Cricklewood.

Chapter Ten

1998-2002: PRAGUE AND ALL THAT JAZZ

In August 1998, we arrived in Prague. Judy went to work almost immediately, and I began thinking about what I might be able to do to remain useful. The Embassy had a policy of trying to find work for spouses wherever possible, but nothing was guaranteed. I presented myself to the right department for inspection and assessment ('Turn your head to the right and cough...'). I'd been told by some folks in the Foreign Service Institute in DC, with whom I'd worked on a seminar, that I'd be a good Community Liaison Officer. The current one was leaving, and they thought I'd be suitable for the job. Being a CLO means you look after the interests of Americans and their families while they are posted abroad by doing a thousand small things. You are the party planner, outings organiser, librarian, local information conduit, newsletter editor, morale officer, agony aunt – it's a bit like being a Butlin's redcoat posted to the front line.

Ludicrously, as we two painfully white boys paddled in the Ambassador's regal marble swimming pool on one of our first days at post, the officer who supervised the CLO position tried to talk me into a more 'manly' job – repairing things, or something else butch. (If only he knew that the tool kit in our house belongs to my wife!) No, I insisted, I really wanted to be the *CLO*. I think it was at that point he gave up on me, but he did let me apply and the hiring committee chose me.

Of the 186 CLO's posted worldwide, only four, at that time, were men. It had traditionally been viewed as a job 'to keep the wife happy', but, as attitudes and demographics altered, more and more women were officers and more and more men were spouses. In the four years I spent as CLO in Prague I encountered not a single example of reverse gender prejudice. Other CLO's emailed enthusiastic welcomes and offered sound advice based on experience. Incoming spouses didn't bat an eye at a six-foot tall, bearded, hairy old geezer greeting them at the airport with a bunch of flowers and saying: 'Welcome to Prague! I'm your CLO.'

Any CLO I ever met agreed warmly that the job is very much what you make it. You work on your own, out of an allocated office, with great autonomy, and essentially, with very little training.

You are expected to minimise wack-evacs (the ironic term for Foreign

Service officers or family members who wig out at post and have to be sent home on psychiatric med-evac). How a CLO approaches this task depends a great deal on where the job is, how big the community, and daily stresses (Are people being mugged on the street? Insurrections? Shootings?). If you're riding to work daily in bullet-proof vehicles from a guarded compound to an armed camp of an embassy, then it's a very different game of old balls from tubing in to Grosvenor Square from your Hampstead apartment. Prague was safe – except from adultery, several staffers who had the reputation as the 'good time had by all', and a few other pecadillos, but then an embassy is a village, and everyone knows its secrets. But on the streets, we didn't have to fear Kalashnikov pot-shots or landmines – just extremely adept pickpockets, who being Czech, were finely skilled artistes at their craft. And all around us was Prague's great architecture, classical music everywhere, the world's best beer and the wonderful Czech people.

The Czech Republic, then under the presidency of the charismatic Vaclav Havel, a man with greater integrity than any politician I've ever known, had only been flexing its newly freed muscles for a little over a decade when we arrived.

The First Republic of Czechoslovakia, established in 1918 and placed under 'protection' by the Nazis in 1938, had been, for those two brief decades, a wondrous place, filled with genius, success, architectural innovation (Cubist and the best Secessionist architecture only survive in Prague), music, literature, film and art. In its prime, about 1935, it had been the eighth most vibrant economy in the world. It boasted manufacturing, mining, financial trading, Parisian style, and a creative capacity that made other countries jealous. The Czechs invented plastic explosives and the contact lens (though thankfully no-one ever thought of combining the two); designed the Bren gun, a staple weapon of the British army for years; and also manufactured the Tatra, the first car with three headlights – never mind the Tucker or the Austin Atlantic – so well engineered, ahead of its time and flat-out popular that, in 1940, a memorandum had to be issued from Gestapo headquarters discouraging their officers from buying it because it was not German.

Czechoslovakia suffered Nazism from 1938 until 1945, bravely attempted to re-establish the Republic between then and early 1948, but was outmanoeuvred by communists allied to Moscow, who took power in February 1948.

The first twenty years of Czech communism were not Moscow hard-line in flavour, but closer to the Swedish socialist experiment. Post-war Czechoslovakia traded freely with the West – especially Austria – exported wonderful glassware, released Beatles and Beach Boys records in the 1960's, took jazz to their hearts as they always had done, and generally created a pleasant, family-oriented and virtually crime-free country. Only after Alexander Dubček attempted, in the 'Prague Spring' of 1968, to introduce further changes that alarmed the New Tsars in the Kremlin, did the tanks arrive.

Many of the soldiers who motored in from Russia were ignorant rabble who had been told that the Third World War had begun and that they were invading Paris. Parts of Prague can look enough like Paris to easily convince an uneducated brainwashee who has only seen a few selected photos.

The Russian soldiers were generally underfed, and there's an interesting tale of two of them breaking into the terraced orchard gardens of the American Embassy to help themselves to a few apples and being challenged by US Marines with the clear, hammer-cocked message that that's American fruit you're stealing and would you please put it back or we'll shoot the shit out of you.

When the Iron Curtain came down for the final call, Czechoslovakia, in a typically non-violent Czech way, used brainpower and the legal system to stage the 'Velvet Revolution'. They turned themselves quickly and effectively from a communist state into a free democracy without the loss of a single life.

Havel, the heroic dissident who had been arrested so often under communism that he carried a razor and a toothbrush with him at all times, led the country to freedom and then oversaw the peaceful divorce between the Czech and Slovak Republics. The Czechs thought it ill-advised; the Slovaks insisted. The Czechs said: 'Okay, but you have noticed that we have all the infrastructure and you have mostly farms?' The Slovaks nevertheless continued to insist, and it took them years to catch up to the Czechs.

By the time we arrived, changes had been enormous but patchy. Some things, like the availability of goods, had altered radically; others, like the state phone company, hardly at all. You could now get just about anything in the shops, and older folk found it confusing that there were 20 different soaps to choose from instead of just the one. And, in a country where the economy had been so stable that the price of a plastic bucket was moulded into the product itself, the sudden influx of a free-market economy confused some as much as it delighted others. There were a few old hard-liners left who suffered from what might be termed 'Communist Nostalgia', but in general the Czechs were happy to be out from under the Kremlin's shadow. It was, in short, a land in a state of flux, and one that was generally enjoying the experience. The old communist-era joke, 'We pretend to work and they pretend to pay us', was receding quickly.

The Czechs themselves are delightful people: open, warm, friendly and often devastatingly honest. There is a certain benign sense of anarchy in them that translates into non-threatening behavioural patterns. An anecdote: I witnessed a motorist pull up to a 'Road Closed' sign beyond which the road was clearly navigable, get out, pull the barrier away, drive past, get back out, put the barrier back and drive up the street – all of this witnessed by a policeman lounging on a wall having a quiet smoke. Hey, he wasn't causing a problem, and if he fell into the big hole just around the bend, well...

Prague architecture is a wonderful layer cake of styles that have survived because history decided to twist the city's fate in specific ways. The Germans didn't fight to get in – that bloody old fool Chamberlain handed Czechoslovakia to them on a plate – and because, in 1945, the struggle to keep it was given up pretty quickly, the infrastructure was largely undamaged by war. People don't bomb the crap out of a city they've already taken, and because there was no war machine in Prague, the Allies left it pretty much alone (except for a few random bombings when Allied night bombers mistook it for Dresden, but then everyone makes mistakes). Certainly, Prague had suffered nothing like the fate of Warsaw.

When it became clear that it was all over for Hitler's lads, the Praguers rose up, armed with their secret caches of weapons and fought them on the streets, convinced that Patton's army would be there from Plzen at any minute. Unfortunately for the brave Czechs, Patton, to his incandescent fury, had been given orders to stop at Plzen so that the Russians could liberate Prague for political reasons. Even more unfortunately, the Russians took their sweet disorganised time getting there. The Czechs fought ferociously for several days before the Russians turned up, and the loss of life was as significant as the heroism and commitment to freedom. Let no-one ever tell you that the Czechs are a bunch of wimps. Walk down the major thoroughfares that saw street battles, and you'll find the plaques dedicated to men and women who lost their lives fighting the Nazis on home turf. From the airmen who flew to England in 1940 to join the RAF, to the resistance fighters who assassinated Reinhardt Heidrich, Czechs displayed a courage that might have occasionally been matched, but was not often bested.

For forty years they hid their Bohemian lights under a bushel, playing a waiting game. When they knew they were free, the culture emerged as deeply and purely Czech as the moment it was forced underground. And if, as a result of reading all this, you come away with the sense that I think the world of the Czech people, then I've done my job.

Despite the misgivings of my new boss, I began work as the CLO in September, in an office overlooking a cobbled courtyard in the Sixteenth Century palace that is the US Embassy in Prague. Three months after we arrived, we got a new ambassador, John Shattuck. He and his wife, Ellen, and daughter Susannah, arrived just in time for Christmas and the traditional parties at his new official residence, a huge and wobbly old pile of brick and sandstone with an extraordinary history.

The Ambassador's Residence is a separate building from the Embassy, and in another part of town. It was built between 1929 and 1934 for Otto Petček, a Jewish entrepreneur who owned vast mining interests in Slovakia and was an important financier during the First Republic. Some credit him with single-handedly keeping the country financially afloat during the Depression.

Constructed in neo-classical style, but incorporating every latest technological innovation then available, it was, by the time it was finished, one of the most impressive residences in Europe. Its huge 'winter garden', with vast electrically-operated glass doors that drop into the floor, turning the inside into an outside, overlook a dance floor-sized patio and a massive tree-trimmed lawn leading to tennis courts and the previously mentioned marble swimming pool, which looks as though Jean Harlow might step out of it at any minute.

It was built with its own cinema, proto-jacuzzi, gymnasium, zinc-lined rooms for fur coat storage, an Olympic-sized heated indoor swimming pool, again of marble; bloody great kitchens, huge bedrooms, opulent bathrooms, a music room, dining room, ante-rooms and a reception area that could hold an orchestra. The Petček family lived there from 1934 to 1938.

When the Nazis arrived, the Petčeks could clearly see the writing on the wall and quietly packed 12 railway cars full of their stuff, withdrew their funds, told people they were going on a week-long hunting trip and left the country forever, abandoning the house. The Nazis took it over, using it as a base of operations for the duration, and Hitler had dinner there on his one visit to Prague. Alone in the dining room once, I stood on the spot where he had sat and sang 'Knees Up Eva Braun'.

When the Russian army arrived in 1945, they commandeered the residence for some months and left it in a mess. Eventually, war restitution restored the house to the ownership of the Petčeks. But it had too many bad memories and echoes, and they sold it to the American government in 1951 for use as the US Ambassador's residence.

Because the Nazis had fled so suddenly, not even taking time to loot, and the Russians left rather speedily as well, many original furnishings remain. The elderly mother of an Embassy staffer had spent time in the house as a child, as her uncle was the *major domo*. She remembers saying goodbye to the Petčeks as they left for their 'hunting trip', and remembers Mrs. Petček keeping her jewellery in a lovely old desk that still sits in one of the reception rooms.

So, by the time I got to know it, the Residence had been through Jewish, Nazi, Communist and American diplomatic hands. Its history would make a good mini-series, with Brad Pitt as Otto Petček, Kenneth Brannagh as Reinhardt Heidrich, Ralph Fiennes as any stray Hungarian who might need a cameo, Dom DeLuis as the Russian army, Dick Van Dyke as the first US Ambassador and, for my old time's sake, Mary Tyler Moore as his wife.

Ambassador John Shattuck turned out to be a genuine and knowledgable blues and jazz enthusiast, and had a story to tell of finding himself in a Chicago club directly between Junior Wells' handgun and the guy he was pointing it at. That he survived to recount the tale was not only immense relief for him, but also an interesting omen for his Prague days. He was the first of a fresh selection of woolly strings that would knit together into another wonderful odd sock.

Gene Deitch, Petrin, July 2007.

For Christmas after our arrival, Judy bought me a book called *For The Love Of Prague*, the story of how an American man, an animator, had been sent by to Prague 'for two weeks' in 1959 to oversee the animation of the post-Hanna-Barbera *Tom & Jerry* cartoons. His two weeks kept getting extended, he fell in love with a Czech woman and stayed throughout the communist period. He'd been in Prague for more than forty years, quietly making children's cartoon films.

The man's name was Gene Deitch. Of course! Gene not only directed *Tom & Jerry* cartoons but was, more importantly, the creator of Tom Terrific, Crabby Appleton and... The Cat. 'The Cat' was a cartoon published in the jazz collectors' magazine, *Record Changer*, in the 1940's, and was a superbly acidic and very funny view of the foibles of record collectors that remains as true today as when it was drawn. Which is comforting, in a way.

I remembered that I'd heard some years before that he had 'disappeared into Poland', and no one was quite sure what had happened to him. He was in Prague was what had happened. From his book, I figured out roughly where he lived, which turned out to be about a block and a half from the Embassy. So, on a misty November lunchtime, I was poking around in that area, and spied his name on a door buzzer of an apartment building. A hurried-looking man with a mouthful of toast and a briefcase under his arm came out the door. From the photos in the book, I knew it was him, so, again using the deductive powers that make me a world-class discographer, I said: 'Are you Gene Deitch?'

'Uh-huh,' the toast said, warily.

'I'm a fan of yours.'

'Oh-oh,' said the toast, expecting another *Tom & Jerry* nerd (they exist, and are generally about as welcome as an excited Trekky in a funeral parlour).

'Especially "The Cat",' I continued.

He brightened: 'The Cat? You don't look old enough.'

'I'm a historian. Plus I *live right*.'

In mentioning 'The Cat' I'd hit the right button – the one closest to his heart. We began talking about music, and both wanting to continue the conversation, arranged to have lunch.

A few days later, we met at J.J. Murphy's, Prague's best Irish bar, for beef stew and Guinness. We swapped stories to get the measure of one another. He told me he'd grown up in Hollywood, seen Leadbelly play in 1948 ('Loudest voice I EVER heard') and had moved to Detroit in 1951 to take a job at the Jam Handy animation company.

'Detroit in 1951? That must have been interesting,' I said, harbouring fantasies of his L.C. Green and Baby Boy Warren collection.

'Yes,' he continued, 'we'd have jazz parties at the house, local collectors would gather, sometimes we'd have musicians over. One of the guys who came over and played was a blues singer called John Lee Hooker.'

'In 1951, eh? Shame you weren't able to record him, huh?' I said, taking a long draught of Guinness.

'Oh, but I did,' replied Gene.

The Guinness froze in my mouth. I seem to remember the oxygen in the room suddenly going on strike. I was aware that my eyes were bulging. I managed to say something like: 'Do... you... still... have the recordings?'

'Sure,' he replied, with the nonchalance of someone who'd been asked if a bus was due, 'in my basement'.

My heart sank. I knew Prague basements. Little more than damp caverns, I imagined what they could do to audio-tapes left unattended for more than forty years.

Happily, this basement proved to be the exception: the tapes were clean and unscathed. The following day, I was sitting in Gene's apartment listening to John Lee Hooker performing in 1951. He was in great form. Gene had recorded him well using what was then a top-of-the-line professional tape recorder, and the atmosphere was relaxed.

I realised with mounting awe that what I was hearing predated any known live recordings of John Lee by almost a decade. I said to Gene, wiping the foam that had gathered at my mouth's corners: 'This stuff should be on CD.'

'Yeah, but who'd issue it?'

'I know a man,' I replied.

Later that day, I called Bruce Bastin: 'Got a little story to tell you,'

I said, 'and you're going to like the ending of it.'

About six weeks later, copies of the Flyright CD, *The Unknown John Lee Hooker* arrived in Prague. To say Gene and I were excited would be to woefully understate. The Czech media picked up on the story as a local-interest item, and Gene was interviewed by the daily papers and on radio.

The news reached the ears of John Shattuck, who asked me to come and see him in his office. The CLO doesn't often get into the Ambassador's office; this was a big deal. He asked me to tell him the story, and when I'd finished and he'd listened to samples from the CD, he took me completely by surprise by saying: 'Of course, we'll have to have a launch party for this at the residence. I'd like to invite the record company people too. Can you set it up?' Can I? Do smuggled wine gums light up the eyes of deprived British ex-pats?

I came directly out of this event to meet Judy in the Embassy cafeteria for lunch. She was sitting at a table with someone I didn't know: a tall, poised, black woman called Lacey O'Neal, an officer from Washington DC in Prague on official State Department business. Judy introduced me, and I sat down to join in the conversation, mentioning to Judy, with pride and astonishment in equal measures, what had just occurred.

'John Lee Hooker?' said Lacey. 'I *love* John Lee Hooker. Muddy Waters was my uncle.' Huh? I went off into a diatribe about how much I loved Muddy, how I'd been listening to him since 1963, how I'd seen him in London over the years, and how he was, in my far-from-unique view, one of the most important musicians of the Twentieth Century. Lacey sat looking at me in amazement, a forkful of garlic mashed potatoes halfway to her mouth.

'But you're *English*,' she said. 'How do you know so much about Muddy?' I gave her a thumbnail history of blues appreciation in Britain. She'd never realised before that her uncle meant that much worldwide. She knew he was well-known in America, but to Lacey, he was a favourite uncle more than a famous musician – and with good reason. It turned out that Muddy, as well as being the womaniser and autocrat that some biographies have been keen to point out, was also a quietly generous man. He put Lacey through college, paid for every last expense – and she wasn't the only family member he helped out. Lacey told us that Muddy was determined that his family would not have to struggle the way he did.

She loved him not just for his no-strings generosity, but also because, she said, he was 'a joker'. He would do anything for a laugh – she cited the photographic session for *After The Rain* as a good example – and, although he was serious about his music and his life, he didn't take the world seriously. She painted a portrait of a warm, generous and funny human being who she thought the world of.

When I told her that he was the founder of the Chicago Blues style, that without him there would be no Chicago Blues as we know it, nor, come to that, much post-1950's rock, she was genuinely amazed. I made copies of Muddy performances on video for her to take home. On her last day, she hugged me and said: 'I had to come all the way to the Czech Republic and meet a Brit to find out about my own back yard.'

We had our reception for the John Lee release at the Residence. Bruce turned up, with his tiara at the ready, to accept the Ferrero Rocher from the heaped silver platter, and found that an Embassy reception is really just a bunch of people constantly grazing off canapés as they move past on trays and quietly chugging as much alcohol as they can before some other bugger gets it. Nevertheless, he was gobsmacked at being there.

The Ambassador invited both Gene and myself to speak about the events that had lead to this evening and, as I took the podium, I looked around me in sheer amazement. I was in an ex-communist country, at a house where Hitler had once sat down to dinner, sharing, with an animator I'd admired for years and an old friend I'd known for a third of a century, an ambassadorial reception for the music of a blues singer I'd been listening to since I was a spotty twerp in a daft school uniform. Isn't life wonderfully odd sometimes?

While he was in town, I took Bruce to Buštěhrad (pronounced Bush-tee-hrad), the vast, straggling open-air market that sits hard by the airport, just outside the city limits. It's a real market: a rough, loud, dirty, smoky, downhome, tough-and-rumble mêlée operated on the grand Czech principle of benign anarchy. People sell out of the front trunks of dying Škodas, off carpets laid across the dirt, from battle-scarred trestle tables and, at the bottom end, straight out of their pockets. People are speaking Czech, German, Russian, English – you name it. You can, if you're feeling brave, get a fried chicken or cheese sandwich, or a traditional plate of hot sausage, mustard and bread, which you rinse down with bottled beer.

You can find just about anything from cheap jewellery and gaudy lingerie to relics of the First Republic, bric-à-brac and vast quantities of militaria. If you ever, on a quiet night, wondered what happened to all those steel helmets the Wehrmacht left behind when the Russians arrived, the answer is they are still at the market, stacked like jawless skulls in great heaps. You want an old bazooka? No problem. Commando knives? How many? Dodgy-looking geezers in faux combat suits stood about checking boxes full of shell cases, bullets, ammunition clips, holsters, and the firearms that the police said were most assuredly illegal but were nevertheless sitting out openly for sale.

I saw a Spandau machine gun resting on a carpet along with a Luger. 'Is safe: no firing-pin, no ammunition,' said the vendor cheerfully. Three carpets down, I found the firing pins and ammunition for both. Bruce happily absorbed all this, coming away with a genuine Gramophone Company enamel advertising sign. I showed him what, in my opinion, was the most fascinating and appalling aspect of the market: the dead guns.

Using metal detectors, people had been digging up the rusted skeletons of WWII firearms: an American Colt .45 automatic, a German MP40 machine pistol, a Russian sub-machine gun. Any wood integral to the weapons had long since passed, and often the surviving metal was so rusted and fused that only a vague shape of the weapon remained, dung-brown with a hard-fuzzy surface of flaking rust.

Yet these relics also contained something else: frozen emotions. Fear, panic and pain were attached to each piece. Some had been dropped in death, others perhaps abandoned at the approach of an impossibly overwhelming force. They had lain in the mud and been ground under by events, resting quietly in their makeshift graves until they were dug up by market-driven technology and displayed, like circus freaks, on low brick walls and carpets for sale at haggled prices. They had all the fascination of a major train wreck. I never bought one and I still can't be sure if I regret that or not. It would be like living with a ghost.

Ellen Shattuck, the Ambassador's wife, had been a successful journalist for much of her career. Her new temporary job as Ambassador's Wife was one she took upon herself with great and serious enthusiasm, and she was, in real terms, a partner in ambassadorial duties. But she was also an old-school radical, a child of the 1960's, of campus uprisings, underground newsletters and folk concerts, a true *democrat* in the old sense of the term, a delightful, nonsense-free, spirited person with a quick intelligence.

During the 1970's she had been an investigative, whistle-blowing reporter in what she called the 'Washington Trenches'. One of her companions in those days was a woman called Nadine Cohodas, who had graduated to the status of successful author, publishing *Strom Thurmond and the Politics of Southern Change*, and other socio-political blockbusters.

Nadine had now turned her attention to music history, and had written a book about Chess Records and the Chess brothers called *Spinning Blues Into Gold*. Knowing my interests, Ellen came to my office and explained that, at her own expense, she was going to fly Nadine over to Prague and hold a private launch party for her and the book at the Residence. She asked me if I would like to help organise it, and gave me a copy of the book to read.

Knowing nothing of Nadine's track record for accuracy, I took it home fearing that it might be politically-correct nonsense, but found, instead, one of the most even-handed, well-researched and beautifully-written music histories I had ever encountered. Ellen asked me to make opening remarks at the reception, and then to introduce Nadine to the assembled Rocher-quaffing tiara mob.

I stood in front of the guests and, for the second time in just a few months, caught sight of myself and was simply blown away by the bizarre notion of introducing a subject so close to my own heart in such strange circumstances. I had carefully prepared notes to read from, I had rehearsed them to Judy *ad infinitum* and had timed them. I stood on the podium, looked around me, and the fifteen year old lad from Cricklewood inside me suddenly began to laugh. I threw the notes away and spoke off the cuff. There had been no need for notes or rehearsal. I was talking about *Chess Records!*

Visitors came and went. Francis and Pam, Keith Briggs and Paul Swinton, Alasdair Blaazer and his wife Sarah, Chris and Sheila Smith and Alan Empson and his family. Francis and Pam we took out on a road trip, in perfect weather, to Mělnik (pronounced 'mu-YELL-nick'), a grand old castle high up on a hill north of Prague. It had an attached restaurant terrace commanding a truly sublime view of the deep, verdant gorge through which the river ran. Francis sat in the sun, drinking wine and atmosphere in equal parts and said, simply: 'This is *perfect.*'

Two of Alan Empson's three lads, Matthew and Nick – Dan didn't come – had grown some since I last saw them, and the father had taught the sons well. Matthew had developed a taste for the blues and when, I was showing Alan some video footage at the house, Matt came through the door and said: 'Oh, Otis Spann, eh?' Alan looked at me with pride. 'Did I raise him right or what?' he smiled.

Judy plays a baby grand piano that we schlep around the world with us. It sat in the corner of the lounge, at an angle. Matt said, quietly, as we all sat talking, drinking beer and sodas: 'Do you mind if I play something?'

'No, go ahead,' she replied, leaving for the kitchen to get drinks. He shifted the stool and commenced playing superb boogie piano. Our mouths fell open. Judy flew back in from the kitchen, amazed at the sounds coming from her piano.

Not only was Matthew playing technically well, he was playing *emotionally* well. He has real understanding of the genre and, unlike many Ammons wannabes, knows that you don't have to play flat-out. So many people make the mistake of believing that the faster you can play, the better boogie you produce. Matt understands that the right tempo, coupled with a sense of swing, means more than pace. If there is anything approaching justice left in this world, he will become a successful and popular musician.

Sometime during early 2001, I got an email from a company called The Blues in New York. They had seen my blues and gospel filmography and wondered if I would consider the position of vintage film researcher for a series on the blues that Martin Scorcese was producing. They would pay money and send me copies of any and all footage they managed to procure from the various archives that the name 'Scorcese' would open doors to. I thought about it for 1·5 seconds and said 'Yes'. The job lasted about eighteen months, on and off, and became my contribution to the seven films – each created by a different director, including Wim Wenders and Clint Eastwood – that appeared on PBS and in French and other cinemas in 2003, and still rattle around on cable TV. Easiest gig I ever had: I'd already put 27 years of prior research into it.

Gene Deitch and I now lunched together at least once a week, cackling about our John Lee Hooker escapades, talking about jazz, blues, animation, Czech history, anything and everything. Bruce had asked me to ask Gene if he had any other aural surprises up his sleeve, and he had: Gene and Pete Seeger had known each other as young men sharing political and social views, and, during the very bleak and nasty McCarthy era, Gene had assisted Pete in constructing a log house deep in the woods that Pete felt he might have to retreat into if Senator McCarthy's madness did not abate. In 1964, Pete turned up in Prague, a courageous manoeuvre considering the Cold War and his reputation, but a very Pete Seeger thing to have done. He appeared in concert and on the radio, and Gene recorded him. There was enough for a double CD and, with direct assistance from Pete, it was issued and promptly sank without trace. Oh well.

Life at the Embassy continued. We attended the Marine parties, on the lawn in summer, in their cellar bar in winter. The community always turned out in strength for a Marine party, not just because they knew it would be good, but because the sense of gratitude for what the Marines do is genuine. Every US Embassy has a detachment of US Marines responsible for interior security. How many depends on the size of the Embassy. Their duties are to ensure that no-one who isn't supposed to be there is there, and that security violations are kept to a minimum. They are, in short, the front line between the Embassy staff and the madman with the bomb or the gun. Most years some Marines die in this line of duty.

Prague was regarded as a safe post, but then, so were Nairobi and Dar-es-Salaam until their horrible bombings, and our Marines took their duties as seriously as those posted to Tirana or Kabul. Every US Embassy in the world is a target, whether for terrorists or random nutters, and it was the Marines' job to protect us.

Every morning, as Judy and I arrived for work, she would get out of the car in the street to enter while I waited for a local Czech embassy guard to search our car for bombs that might have been attached to it in the night. It was routine and you get used to it, just like you get used to the fact that the Marines are armed with automatic pistols and combat shotguns. As I waited my turn, and as Judy was about to open it, the door to the Embassy crashed open and a man flew out, in full horizontal position about four feet off the ground, hit the barrier at the road's edge and flipped over, landing on his back. He stood up, turned round, yelled: 'Thank you very much,' checked his mobile phones, and strode off with only his dignity damaged.

What had happened inside to cause this striking piece of early morning street theatre was this foolish American's insistence that he would not go through the X-ray machine, would not check his mobile phones with the local guards and that, when it was pointed out to him that the Marines would therefore ask him to leave, he stupidly replied: 'They will have to kill me first.' Nanoseconds later he was leaving the building. Marine Corporal J.C. Hawks had simply picked him up by his collar and belt and thrown him through a door that one of the Czech guards had opened in expectation of the event.

I had, for some time, wanted to do something for and about Django Reinhardt. I'd been quietly putting information into files for years, from the National Sound Archive, EMI and elsewhere. I had a notion of creating an integrated bio-discography, and thought I probably had enough material for it. Rachel Lynch at Ashgate listened with her usual insightful patience and, again, said yes.

I began to compile a detailed and comprehensive discography as the ground upon which everything else could be built. I would lace into it all known Django information in chronological order, decorate it with contextual history, create cross-referenced files for tune titles, musicians, bibliography, filmography and record releases. It would be the most satisfyingly anal-retentive work I had yet produced, and one of the major tools I used for research was the Internet. The Google search engine offers, on average, 30,000-plus hits for Django, and I looked at all of them in a twelve-month period (I really must get out more, but then when I do the police keep bringing me back).

One hit was a home page from some young fellow in Iowa who was talking about his personal Grand European Tour the previous summer. He had been to Prague. He said: 'There's this great place in Prague called Jazzova, filled with cool old jazz magazines from the 1930's with people like Django Reinhardt in them.' What!?!? I looked, and found that Jazzova was a booking agency for local jazz musicians, operating out of the Waldsteinska Palace, just about a quarter of a mile from the Embassy (Prague, formerly capital of the Austro-Hungarian Empire, is chock-a-block with palaces – you get used to it), roughly the same distance as Gene but in another direction.

I went down there and introduced myself to Karel Srpksa, who ran the operation. I was shown into his office but didn't need to ask about the jazz magazines. They were all around me, sitting on shelves in bound volumes, a roomful. Karel, with the ethic of the Melly generation, poured me a slivovic plum brandy and invited me to help myself. While he busied himself with his tasks and serenaded us both with an Ishman Bracey CD, I went to work.

Within an hour, I understood that what he had here was exactly what

I had been looking for, but couldn't have hoped or expected to find. Every issue of *Jazz Hot, Melody Maker, Swing Music, Down Beat* and *The Gramophone*, as well as magazines I'd only heard about like *Hot News, Swing, Hot Club de Belge, Ballroom And Band*, and also, incredibly, *Jazz Tango*, the legendary Parisian magazine from the 1930's that nobody else had anything like a full run of. He had a complete set!

What this meant was that I could trace Django's career, from his emergence to his death, directly from the best of all sources: *Jazz Tango* and *Jazz Hot*.

This extraordinary library had been compiled by Emmanuel Ugge, the Hungarian-born president of the Hot Gramo-Club of Prague in the 1930's and 1940's. The archive he created had survived Nazism and Communism and had wound up with Karel because he cared about it and the surviving Ugge family didn't. Karel was willing to loan me anything and everything for copying purposes, and in a mad, sweaty weekend I hauled a van full of bound volumes away, photocopied 1,500 pages and hauled them all back again.

The book, *Django Reinhardt: A Contextual Biography 1910-1953* (snappy or wot?) is about twice the size and depth it would have been, had not a guy in the US created a home page and the custodian of printed jazz history been so completely and utterly generous. And I had to be in Prague to find it! It was – just like John Lee Hooker – nowhere else. Bruce said to me, not long after I had mailed copies of *Jazz Tango* to him: 'Er... you gonna stay long enough to find the missing film of Elmore James?'

On the afternoon of 11 September 2001, a relatively new American officer put her head round my door and said: 'Do you know where there's a TV I can watch CNN on?'

'Yeah, either the Political Office or the Consular area. Why?'

'Because apparently a plane just crashed into the World Trade Center,' she replied, and left to follow the news.

Deeply engrossed in work, I imagined there had been some horrible accident involving a light aircraft. This sort of thing had happened before – the Empire State Building in the 1940's for instance. But curiosity got the better of me, and I phoned Judy, who was writing a speech for the Ambassador to give the next day. I told her about the crash and that I was going to the Consular section to check it out on TV. Did she want to join me?

'Not now,' she said, 'I have to finish this speech.'

So, I went to see for myself. When I arrived in Consular, people were just standing, mute, horrified. It wasn't, of course, a light aircraft at all, but a fully-loaded jetliner, and the unedited footage that streamed into the Embassy was holding us in fascinated horror. But we still thought it was some terrible accident until the second plane hit. Then we knew full well it was no accident. Events had suddenly gone beyond a belief that we wanted to accept, and people groaned, cried, screamed and held each other. The news that the Pentagon too had been attacked confirmed that we were under somebody's siege, but we knew not who or why, or when it would end.

The security officers in the Embassy instructed an immediate lockdown. For all we knew, it could be us next, we had no idea. There were rumours that the White House had been attacked, then those were denied. Perhaps other embassies had been attacked and the news had not yet been reported. Adrenalin flooded the building. The Marines suddenly were everywhere in full combat gear, fully armed. The gates were shut, huge chains were padlocked about them, and we waited for what seemed the longest of all times. Our son, then nineteen, called via cell phone from his university in the USA, reaching out to his mother as people do in awful tragedies.

Within hours, messages of sympathy and bunches of flowers appeared outside the Embassy gates. By the following morning, the bank of flowers was two feet long and three feet wide; within another 24 hours it stretched over fifty feet up and down the road outside the Embassy, and had become a deep and complex collection of tributes: flowers, wreaths, hundreds of lit and potted candles, handwritten messages, teddy bears, a fireman's helmet on which someone had carefully lettered in English '*Good bye, good boys*'; photographs of people, and of the awful recent events; messages of sorrow and of anger, of sympathy and of revenge. A steady stream of solemn Czechs paraded up the street, carrying flowers and candles. The candle store at the foot of the street sold out; the flower stall around the corner did as well. American tourists seemed drawn to the Embassy – one man, seeing a postcard of the World Trade Center with a lit candle, suddenly broke down sobbing into the arms of his wife and daughter. Later, in a bizarre twist, the wind would blow the candle flame onto the post card, igniting it, and we watched in horror as the World Trade Center disappeared yet again in front of our eyes. People stood in the street and looked at each detail, sobbing, holding one another, walking slowly from message to message. This impromptu tidal wave of sympathy was mostly Czech in origin.

In the following days, we hosted memorial services inside the gates and outside on the street. Old and venerable Czech RAF fighter pilots, some in their WWII uniforms, some in wheelchairs, came with their wives to deliver a huge wreath that the Ambassador came out to accept. The Czech pilots also brought a message of support and a warning: they had fought terrorism in the 1940's, and now we all must fight it again.

These proud old warriors stood to attention as a Czech army corporal played the Last Post. Overwhelmed by emotion, I went and talked with them, thanking them not only for their efforts on this day but for those sixty years before. They still looked and dressed like ex-RAF pilots, with handlebar moustaches and stiff upper lips. They had fought for freedom, returned to their Czech lands and been jailed by the communists for, of all things, treason, often spending years locked away because the rigid doctrines of propaganda could find no room for them in their stupid plans. They struck me as the most courageous group of men and women I was ever likely to encounter. And, if you are sufficiently interested in their story, the Anglo-Czech film, *Dark Blue World*, is the one you should see.

In those first few days of shock and grief, we thought that the tragedy had at least the silver lining of unity about it. Everyone felt the pain. One message, in Czech, hand-painted in blood red, said simply: *'We are all Americans now.'* The mood, of course, did not last, and the world fell to bickering over tactics in the ensuing years. The sad lesson I draw from this is: enjoy the fruit immediately, whatever its origin or flavour, for it will surely rot before long.

Four years quickly passed, experiencing all this and much more: hosting the Wynton Marsalis Orchestra at the Residence and watching it turn into an impromptu jam session; learning about Czech jazz history, from the pianist Joe Turner's 1938 visit through the Graeme Bell Band's post-war triumphs to the purism of Pavel Klika's 1970's revivalism; listening to the somewhat bizarre sounds of local bands singing the blues in Czech; spending time talking about and listening to music with Ed Zawadski, an American who had lived in Prague for years and worked at the Embassy, but whose real life was as the Czech Republic's top rock session guitarist. (Ed had an amazing ear. Upon hearing Gene's John Lee Hooker recordings, he immediately informed me that Hooker had been playing a cracked guitar. Gene later, remembering, confirmed that this had been so.) And once, in a perfect moment, standing in the courtyard, with Alfreder McQueen, Vince Skalicky, the Czech-Australian motor pool boss, and Andela Kunstova, a Czech employee, all listening to Ray Charles on someone's car stereo system.

Suddenly, it was time to go. We packed up and left, leaving – as Judy said – a piece of our hearts behind, but taking a chunk of Prague in our hearts with us. Fair trade. There are times in your life when you look back and say: 'That was a great period,' but if you are very lucky and stay aware, just occasionally you can say: 'THIS, NOW, is a great time.' That was Prague for us. Fortunate sods!

We got back to Virginia knowing that our next post would be Toulouse, France, and that Judy had been selected as the officer-in-charge, La Grande Fromage. Or American Consul, if we are being pedantic. We spent a year back at our house while Judy polished up her already good French by spending five days a week with a good French polisher. She spoke student 'tu' French, but she needed to learn very, very 'vous' diplo-speak – especially important as we were to arrive in spring 2003 at a *very* tense time in US-French relations.

I finished the Django book and went to work in the State Department with a wonderful group of people committed to worldwide refugee issues. I was introduced by my boss, Nancy Iris, to her husband Tom Costello, an

Irishman with vast enthusiasms for music and movies and history and literature and much more, a talk-the-hind-legs-off-a-donkey-and-back-on-again joke factory of a man who had come to the US at age eighteen in 1960, witnessed much that I too had witnessed and is, without doubt, one of the most colourful people I've ever encountered.

The four of us, Tom and Nancy, Judy and I, sat in a restaurant while Nancy and Judy talked of the theatre and dance they both loved, and Tom and I swapped tales of musicians we'd seen and of our lives in the Old Countries. We shared parallel experiences growing up in England and Ireland. At one point I said to him: 'You know, the life that you and I knew as lads has completely gone.'

His simple but emphatic reply 'Oh, *yes!*' was filled with such empathy and understanding of a shared bygone era that, also hearing Bill Greensmith's encouragement in my head, I resolved then and there to write this book. But we are not *quite* finished yet.

Chapter Eleven

2003-07: I OFFER YOU THIS

We arrived in Toulouse, France, on the last day of May 2003, straight into the teeth of the hottest summer on record, with temperatures reaching as high as 107 degrees Fahrenheit and more than 15,000 woefully unprepared French people actually dying as a result. We stayed for a steaming, breathless, dehydrating three months in an ancient, beautiful and un-airconditioned apartment in the heart of the city. Between midday and 4:00 pm, all you could really do was lie down and keep hydrated. We were fortunate enough to have purchased the last two fans from a local store, but all they did was blow the hot air around. Our refrigerator, unable to keep up, barely cooled its contents. We began shopping daily and eating out a lot.

However, outside our third-floor window in the bearable early morning, life in Place St. Georges offered matinal rituals clearly established decades, even centuries, before. I got into the habit of taking my coffee to the window to watch the morning swooping and screeching of the swallows, local dogs walking their owners, sweepers and cleaners removing last night's excesses from the cobblestones, and yawning waiters unchaining and setting up neat regiments of tables and chairs at the sidewalk cafes that surrounded the square on three sides. Then, right on time, the dreadlocked street person arrived, and with his toothbrush, toothpaste, soap and face flannel, dutifully abluted in the ancient public water fountain below my window.

On one such morning, a truck arrived with a crew of workers who unloaded what looked like a giant Meccano set. I watched, puzzled, as they methodically assembled a round platform, topping it with a metal structure. In the late afternoon, they began cloaking the metal structure in its outer trappings, added a striped roof and horses, and by evening there stood a giant and wonderfully traditional children's roundabout. We spent the summer watching parents watch their children recreate the memories of generations.

And the *music!* The city erected a small bandstand in the square, and bands would arrive some nights and play French chanson and folk music. One evening, a horde of folk dancers turned up and began doing 'traditional French dances' that Judy recognized as identical to the Appalachian square dancing she'd learned as a child. We still remember one tiny man who looked for all the world like a miniature Bruce Bastin in sandals and an aloha shirt, lightly and perfectly dancing every reel, every step, swinging whichever partner fell into his arms, totally immersed in the sheer joy of dancing.

And one evening, for reasons we didn't understand, what appeared to be a re-creation of Carnival came exuberantly drumming and rattling down our street, with scanty, brilliant costumes of feathers and sequins and drumbeats that compelled us to spontaneously join the conga line of festivities snaking down the side streets. All of this musical activity made it very hard to sleep, but it was fun. We ended up moving our bed into the dining room so Judy could get enough sleep to go to work in the mornings.

We spent early evenings and weekends exploring La Ville Rose, or 'the Pink City', so called because of the tint of the locally-made brick, discovering street names in French and Occitan, an ancient language of the region. We learned the skill of sharing sidewalks meant for a few people with a few thousand. Toulouse is ancient and well worth seeing, but because it isn't on the way to anywhere from anywhere, it isn't infested with tourists at any season. The Canal du Midi runs through it, an ancient waterway that Thomas Jefferson traversed while recuperating after he foolishly broke his arm doing tricks on horseback to impress a French girl far too young for him. It is said to be the inspiration for the C&O canal that still runs through Georgetown in Washington, DC.

In August, just as the heat wave broke, we moved to our 'permanent' air-conditioned house in Cornebarrieu, a small village 18 kilometres out of town. We were supposed to be there for four years, but, as one of Paul McCartney's chums once famously remarked, 'life is what happens when you're making other plans'. I had been experiencing increasing glaucoma and cataracts in both eyes for about three years, and had had an operation on my left eye (the worst affected) to insert a synthetic lens while we were in Virginia. Unfortunately, the damn fool egomaniac arsehole bastard shithead wanker who performed the operation – I bear him no grudge – tore the back of the lens capsule in my eye while doing so, but didn't own up. He sent me off to France with a purportedly clean bill of health, but actually bestowing upon me a ticking optical time bomb. On the morning of 3 November 2003, I awoke to a curiously beautiful sight in my left eye, like a spectacular California sunset. It took a coffee-brewing length of time for me to figure out something was wrong. I came back to the bedroom where Judy was preparing for her day and said: 'Uh, I need your full attention. I think there's a problem with my eye.' A mad dash to the local hospital confirmed that my retina was detaching.

To précis a long and painful saga, I had several operations over the next few months – in London, Paris, and finally in the US – none of which were successful, and I lost my left eye. But, because life is never tidy one way or the other, there were still things to enjoy despite the handicap. I had wonderful fun during my eye-patch period when little children would loudly point me out to their mortified parents: 'Regarde Maman – un PIRATE!'

Toulousians see themselves as, and indeed are, a very different breed from Parisians, and they view the North with deep suspicion. The Midi-Pyrenees is a splendidly laid-back place to be, filled with delightful towns and villages connected by refreshingly beautiful country roads. We spent whole weekends exploring the topography by car.

From spring to mid-autumn, we charted our explorations by the locations of '*vide-greniers*' (literally, 'empty attics'), essentially village-wide garage sales, where displayed on tables and in booths was all the old tat that people had hung onto until the day when they said 'enough already' and brought it out for sale. We bought everything from old videos to picture records to enormous, ancient wooden oxen yokes (don't ask) to Judy's favourite find, a circa-1903 Parisian dressmaker's dummy with an impossibly small waist and the pigeon-breasted form of ladies of 100-plus years ago.

Since Judy is as keen on historic costume as I am on ethnic music, I had no objection to the purchase. Of course, I was elected to carry the dummy back to our car through the one, long street of the mountain village in which we purchased her, Judy trailing behind like an acolyte in a religious procession. I soon attracted an amused following of locals making friendly, but clearly ribald comments. I may not have understood the dialect, but I understood the sentiment – blokes are blokes, everywhere – and played along, holding the curvaceous dummy even higher aloft by the pole of her wooden stand. Some of the locals danced behind us. We named her Lucille, and at subsequent *vide-greniers*, Judy bought her a Victorian linen camisole and pantaloons, leather gloves, a white linen parasol, an ostrich feather, and a pair of lace-up boots (although Lucille had no legs) so that she could be properly dressed. Our daughter Lia and her friend Katie declared her 'gross' and 'scary', and Lucille was exiled to a spare room for the duration of our stay in France.

The city of Toulouse has decent record shops, including a very good FNAC that I haunted regularly; superb restaurants with outdoor terraces for leisurely dining in all but the coldest months, and air-conditioned cinemas nestled amongst the superb, sometimes downright stunning architecture that enhances the experience of moving from Point A to Point B. Street life was a constant delight, with cafés crowding the pavements and sheltering their clients with giant umbrellas. To eat out under a canopy on a warm, clear night in Toulouse is an experience worth its expense. The Midi-Pyrenees region is the home of foie gras, Roquefort cheese and Armagnac. Eating it all was a tough job, but somebody had to do it. Our doctor was appalled at our cholesterol when we returned to the US. But then American doctors are appalled at all sorts of things.

Robert Crumb, cartoonist, record collector, musician and perfect gentleman, lived in the same area, though somewhat further east. We had shared our enthusiasm for early ethnic music for some years, exchanging information and views with each other. Now, with both of us in France, we spoke more often. He is a lovely human being and expressed genuine concern about my health, as well as cheering me up no end by getting down to the grit of ethnic shellac detail with me. Talking to him was another series of bright spots in a time of medical turmoil for which I will always be grateful.

However, after sixteen months we finally had to admit defeat and return to the US to have my deteriorating other eye operated on, this time in Baltimore, Maryland, sixty miles away from our house in Virginia. Judy and I made many worried trips there for surgery and follow-up, and if I was well enough after being poked in the eye with a high-tech version of a sharp stick, Judy would show me highlights of a city she already knew to cheer me. I came to love Baltimore, especially the restored colonial port of Fells Point, where we had many a post-consultation consolation lunch.

Having experienced legal blindness in the months immediately before that final operation, I now have a much finer appreciation of the varying degrees of sight loss, *some* insight into what it means to be blind, and an immense gratitude for the one decent peeper I have left. A VERY Fortunate Young Sod. Well, okay, now that my doctor has begun prefacing all his comments to me with 'for a man your age', maybe not so young, at least in body. How did Sailor Vernon become a 'man my age'? I don't know – it's 10:30 and close to my bedtime.

We spent two years in Virginia while I had my final surgery and Judy undertook a Washington assignment. During that time, Sailor Vernon – sporting the *very* winsome 'pirate' eye patch – went all cyberspacey, and took his wide boy act onto eBay. There was good junking to be had in and around Virginia, and we discovered the wonderful fun of weekly auctions, where absolutely anything could turn up, including much shellac. As in the past, local collectors also gave me things to sell for them. That, and continuing to write for *Folk Roots* kept me off the streets.

Back in London, my mother died peacefully in December 2004, six months past her ninetieth birthday. 'A good innings' as people used to say. Although we had known the end was near, it came much quicker than expected, and I hadn't yet left for England when Matthew called with the news. No matter how much you think you are prepared, you aren't. In no way. I suddenly felt very alone. Both my parents were now gone. Driving out to the airport, I said to Judy with sudden realisation: 'I'm an orphan now, aren't I?' and realised that being an orphan is an emotional, as well as physical, state.

I stayed two weeks in England sorting everything out, with help from Matthew and his wife Lorraine. It was a painful time, but it was also a joyous one, as I had the opportunity to get reacquainted with my latest grandson, Jack. I rescued that which was important – family papers and photos, mostly (although an antique skeleton clock in my carry-on luggage gave airport security a moment's concern) – and bade farewell to a bunch of stuff I had known most of my life. My mother was of the generation that threw nothing away. 'It might come in handy, you know, even if you never use it,' was actually uttered more than once in my childhood home.

Three months later, on 6 March 2005, I got an email from Mary Katherine Aldin titled 'Very Bad News'. It sure was. Keith Briggs had been felled by a heart attack that morning; dead before he hit the floor, apparently. When Judy came home that evening, she knew immediately that something was wrong. She asked: 'What *happened*?'

'I'm in shock,' I replied. 'Keith died this morning.'

'Oh my God,' she said. 'He was one of your best friends'. Yes, he most certainly was. Judy just held me, and I cried.

With my medical problems now behind us, we got the news that we could go 'back out' again, as Foreign Service people say. This time, our posting was to be Madrid. And so, because she is a linguistic sponge, Judy's already good but Latin-American Spanish was massaged into Madrid Spanish by a professional tutor, and in May 2006, we arrived in this most beautiful, under-rated, exquisitely liveable city.

So, we reach a point where the saga, for now, is up to date, but life goes on. I still have projects. Writing stuff for *Folk Roots* is one of them, another is stalking the hallways of the Internet for serious headbanger-bluesophile sites offering the deepest, most arcane blues information imaginable. There's a *lot* out there, and I find more every day, filled with cyber-anorakism. Yeah, I know I'm one of them, and I'm not arguing.

But I offer you this: if you are as hungry for the real blues as I was at age fifteen, simply invest in a copy of *The Penguin Guide to Blues Recordings* by Tony Russell & Chris Smith (about 30 quid new) and subscribe to the online Yahoo Music Juke Box. This will give you two essential tools. The book is very thorough and completely trustworthy. It's also a great read. The Yahoo site contains literally thousands of blues performances that you can log in unlimited folders of your own creation. It includes just about all the pre-war stuff, lots of Chess material, everything on Arhoolie and bags of new blues, for openers. Use the book to find the best albums and log them employing a system of your own creation. The subscription fee is $60 a year, so you can play all this back through your computer for 16 cents a day.

Then, create free accounts on YouTube and the lesser-known but equally valuable French site DailyMotion, and go exploring for the classic filmed performances. They are there. *Then*, Google 'The Blue Highway' and go to 'Links', which is what it says it is, a site filled with access to blues-info websites, doors that lead to other doors that lead on. All of this is web-based, so as long as you back up the web addresses, you won't have lost anything if or when your hard drive fries. And, for under a hundred quid, you can amass a bigger multi-media blues collection than I've ever had in my lifetime until now. Yes, I've done all this, that's how I know. Go sequester yourself in a small dark room with a decent laptop and broadband. I'll see you in a decade when you will emerge, muscles atrophied, spotty and short-sighted, but with a head full of great music. By which time you will be able to obtain, from Wal-Mart, a $10 swipe card that allows access to every single piece of music ever recorded, which you can then slide into the aperture installed in your forehead.

The blues has always been the soundtrack to my life, and, despite many a premature obituary, is still alive and well. However, I find that I am far too busy right now flagging Barry Manilow videos on YouTube as 'inappropriate' to comment further. So, as I sit here turning a lovely shade of Dorian grey, I leave the last wise words on the subject to my old chum Alan Empson: 'What did we want from it? What did it do to us? Why did we want to preach its gospel like missionaries? I have still not really fathomed out what is in the music that moves us so much. Perhaps it is the sheer humanity: the highs and lows, the joy and pain, the true essence of being alive. And when that beat hits you, man, you just *have* to get up and boogie!'

OTHER TITLES FROM MUSIC MENTOR BOOKS

American Rock'n'Roll: The UK Tours 1956-72
Ian Wallis
ISBN-13: 978-0-9519888-6-2 *(pbk, 424 pages)*

The first-ever detailed overview of every visit to these shores by American (and Canadian!) rock'n'rollers. It's all here: over 400 pages of tour itineraries, support acts, show reports, TV appearances and other items of interest. Illustrated with dozens of original tour programmes, ads, ticket stubs and great live shots, many rare or previously unpublished.

Back On The Road Again
Dave Nicolson
ISBN-13: 978-0-9547068-2-1 *(pbk, 216 pages)*

A third book of interviews by Dave Nicolson in the popular *On The Road* series, this time with more of a Sixties flavour: Solomon Burke, Gene Chandler, Bruce Channel, Lowell Fulson, Jet Harris, Gene McDaniels, Scott McKenzie, Gary S. Paxton, Bobby 'Boris' Pickett, Martha Reeves & The Vandellas, Jimmie Rodgers, Gary Troxel (Fleetwoods), Leroy Van Dyke and Junior Walker.

Daynce of the Peckerwoods: The Badlands of Texas Music
Michael H. Price
ISBN-13: 978-0-9547068-5-2 *(pbk, 350 pages)*

From a childhood spent among such key roots-music figures as Bob Wills and Big Joe Turner, and an extended dual career as a musician and journalist, Michael H. Price has forged this frenzied chronicle of life among the denizens of the vanishing borderlands of Texas' indigenous music scene over the past half-century. Contains essays on Billy Briggs, Ornette Coleman, the Light Crust Doughboys, Big Bill Lister, Rudy Ray Moore, Eck Robertson, Ray Sharpe, Robert Shaw, Major Bill Smith, Stevie Ray Vaughan and many more.

Elvis: A Musical Inventory 1939-55
Richard Boussiron
ISBN-13: 978-0-9519888-7-9 *(pbk, 264 pages)*

This 'musical inventory' is the product of over 30 years' original research including interviews with Elvis' teacher, church ministers, work colleagues and fellow musicians. Presented like a discography, it is an extraordinarily detailed listing of the King's earliest musical influences, with full historical details shown for each song. The book also includes — for the first time anywhere — complete details of all the legendary Sun sessions, taken directly from the personal files of Marion Keisker. Quite simply a 'must have' for anyone with an interest in early Elvis.

Elvis & Buddy – Linked Lives
Alan Mann
ISBN-13: 978-0-9519888-5-5 *(pbk, 160 pages)*

The achievements of Elvis Presley and Buddy Holly have been extensively documented, but until now little if anything has been known about the many ways in which their lives were interconnected. The author examines each artist's early years, comparing their backgrounds and influences, chronicling all their meetings and examining the many amazing parallels in their lives, careers and tragic deaths. Over 50 photographs, including many rare/previously unpublished.

Let The Good Times Rock! – A Fan's Notes On Post-War American Roots Music
Bill Millar
ISBN-13: 978-0-9519888-8-6 *(pbk, 362 pages)*

For almost four decades, the name 'Bill Millar' has been synonymous with the very best in British music writing. This fabulous new book collects together 49 of his best pieces — some previously unpublished — in a thematic compilation covering hillbilly, rockabilly, R&B, rock'n'roll, doo-wop, swamp pop and soul. Includes essays on acappella, doo-wop and blue-eyed soul, as well as detailed profiles of some of the most fascinating and influential personalities of each era.

Long Distance Information: Chuck Berry's Recorded Legacy
Fred Rothwell
ISBN-13: 978-0-9519888-2-4 *(pbk, 352 pages)*

The lowdown on every recording Chuck Berry has ever made. Includes an overview of his life and career, his influences, the stories behind his most famous compositions, full session details, listings of all his key US/UK vinyl and CD releases (including track details), TV and film appearances, and much, much more. Over 100 illustrations including label shots, vintage ads and previously unpublished photos.

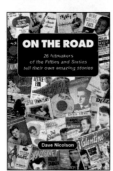

On The Road
Dave Nicolson
ISBN-13: 978-0-9519888-4-8 *(pbk, 256 pages)*

Gary 'US' Bonds, Pat Boone, Freddy Cannon, Crickets Jerry Allison, Sonny Curtis and Joe B. Mauldin, Bo Diddley, Dion, Fats Domino, Duane Eddy, Frankie Ford, Charlie Gracie, Brian Hyland, Marv Johnson, Ben E. King, Brenda Lee, Little Eva, Chris Montez, Johnny Moore (Drifters), Gene Pitney, Johnny Preston, Tommy Roe, Del Shannon, Edwin Starr, Johnny Tillotson and Bobby Vee tell their own fascinating stories. Over 150 illustrations including vintage ads, record sleeves, label shots, sheet music covers, etc.

On The Road Again
Dave Nicolson
ISBN-13: 978-0-9519888-9-3 *(pbk, 206 pages)*

In this second book of interviews with the stars of pop and rock'n'roll, Dave Nicolson delves deeper into the dazzling and often treacherous world of the music industry, with more revealing and highly personal first-hand accounts from 15 pioneering performers who were at the forefront of the Fifties' music revolution: Freddie Bell, Martin Denny, Johnny Farina (Santo & Johnny), the Kalin Twins, Robin Luke, Chas McDevitt, Phil Phillips, Marvin Rainwater, Herb Reed (Platters), Tommy Sands, Joe Terranova (Danny & The Juniors), Mitchell Torok, Marty Wilde and the 'Cool Ghoul' himself, John Zacherle.

Railroadin' Some: Railroads In The Early Blues
Max Haymes
ISBN-13: 978-0-9547068-3-8 *(pbk, 390 pages)*

This groundbreaking book, written by one of the foremost blues historians in the UK, is based on over 30 years research, exploration and absolute passion for early blues music. It is the first ever comprehensive study of the enormous impact of the railroads on 19th and early 20th Century African American society and the many and varied references to this new phenomenon in early blues lyrics. Includes ballin' the jack, smokestack lightning, hot shots, the bottoms, chain gangs, barrelhouses, hobo jungles and much, much more. 118 illustrations.

**Music Mentor books
are available from all good bookshops
or by mail order from:**

**Music Mentor Books
69 Station Road
Upper Poppleton
YORK YO26 6PZ
England**

Telephone: **+44 (0)1904 330308**
Email: **music.mentor@lineone.net**
Website: **http://musicmentor0.tripod.com**